CW00421906

HEGEL AND THE HISTORY OF
POLITICAL PHILOSOPHY

Hegel and the History of Political Philosophy

Gary K. Browning
Professor of Politics
Oxford Brookes University
Oxford

First published in Great Britain 1999 by
MACMILLAN PRESS LTD
Houndmills, Basingstoke, Hampshire RG21 6XS and London
Companies and representatives throughout the world

A catalogue record for this book is available from the British Library.

ISBN 0–333–67085–X

First published in the United States of America 1999 by
ST. MARTIN'S PRESS, INC.,
Scholarly and Reference Division,
175 Fifth Avenue, New York, N.Y. 10010

ISBN 0–312–22023–5

Library of Congress Cataloging-in-Publication Data
Browning, Gary K.
Hegel and the history of political philosophy / Gary K. Browning.
p.   cm.
Some chapters have appeared in several journals and some chapters
have been presented at conferences at different places and times.
Includes bibliographical references and index.
ISBN 0–312–22023–5 (cloth)
1. Hegel, Georg Wilhelm Friedrich, 1770–1831—Contributions in
political science.   2. Political science—History.   I. Title.
JC233.H46B78   1999
320'.01—dc21   98–46225
                                                               CIP

This book is printed on paper suitable for recycling and made from fully managed and
sustained forest sources.

10   9   8   7   6   5   4   3   2   1
08   07   06   05   04   03   02   01   00   99

Printed and bound in Great Britain by
Antony Rowe Ltd, Chippenham, Wiltshire

Contents

Acknowledgements

This book covers a lot of years, conferences and sleepless nights. For the last twenty years or so I have been engaged in thinking about Hegel and the history of political philosophy. This book reflects and refines my thinking on Hegel and a number of political philosophers. The individual chapters in this book draw on a number of articles I have written and conference papers I have delivered over the last ten years. Every topic, however, has been turned to afresh, and all previous writings reconsidered and revised, if not always improved. I have tried to ensure that the essays in this book take account of recent scholarship, harmonise with one another and express my current thinking.

In the processes of reflection, creation and reworking that shaped the essays in this volume, I became highly conscious of many debts incurred and it is a happy circumstance that allows me to acknowledge, if not discharge, them. I am very grateful for the permission I have received from a number of sources to draw upon articles already published. Chapters 1 and 6 draw upon articles that first appeared in *History of Political Thought*: 'Plato and Hegel: Reason, Redemption and Political Theory' (vol. VIII, no. 3, 1987); and *The German Ideology*: 'The Theory of History and the History of Theory' (vol. XIV, no. 3, 1993). Chapter 3 is a revised version of 'Hegel's Plato: The Owl of Minerva and a Fading Political Tradition', which appeared in *Political Studies* (vol. XXXVI, 1988). I have used material from my article 'New Leviathans for Old', *Collingwood Studies*, vol. 2, for Chapter 8 of this book, and *Hobbes Studies* has permitted me to draw upon material from 'Hobbes, Hegel and Modernity' (vol. VIII, 1995), which I co-wrote with Dr Raia Prokhovnik. Chapter 7 is a revised version of 'Infinity in Hegel and Marx: From the Notion to the Notion of Capital', which appeared in *Studies in Marxism* (vol. 5, 1998), which in turn drew upon a conference paper, 'Good and Bad Infinites in Hegel and Marx', which appeared in I. Hampsher-Monk and J. Stanyer (eds), *Contemporary Political Studies*, vol. 2 (Belfast: Political Studies Association of the UK, 1996). Chapter 5 drew inspiration from a conference paper, 'Stirner and the Ghost of Hegel', which was published in G. Stoker and J. Stanyer (eds), *Contemporary Political Studies* (Nottingham: Political Studies Association of the UK, 1997).

I tried out some of the ideas in Chapter 9 in conference papers delivered at Oxford Brookes University and a PSA Conference at the University of York in 1995. I have been living with and worrying about ways of comparing Hegel and Rawls for some time. I have tried out ideas expressed in Chapter 10 in papers delivered at the University of Birmingham and Manchester Metropolitan University. I have also given papers on Plato and Hegel to helpful and critical audiences at the University of Oxford and the Hegel Society of Great Britain.

The biggest debts are owed to people who have helped without being overtly conscious of their role. There are countless academics at conferences and pubs who have said things that have made me think. Bob Stern, Nick Walker, Michael Petry and Howard Williams at Hegel Society of Great Britain conferences have raised issues to which I have tried to respond. Chris Arthur, Ian Fraser, Jo McCarney and Jules Townshend have made me think again about the relationship between Hegel and Marx. Students at Oxford Brookes have emphasised to me that thinking about and teaching political philosophy are worthwhile activities. Raia Prokhovnik has been a persistently thoughtful and critical reader of my work. I would also like to thank Raia, Eleanor and Conal for revealing the value of thinking about values.

GARY K. BROWNING

1 Introduction

This book consists of a set of comparative essays on Hegel and other political thinkers. It draws upon articles and papers written and delivered for a variety of publications and audiences over the last ten years. The essays express the author's preoccupation with Hegel and his political philosophy, and a commitment to the value of a critical interpretation of Hegel's political philosophy. Hegel's political philosophy is linked to a conception of the historical character of the enterprise. While Hegel's substantive political philosophy and his notion of its historicity are interdependent, the Introduction and Conclusion of this book focus upon the claims of his substantive political philosophy and his idea of the history of political philosophy, respectively.

The aim of this Introduction is to explain how the essays reflect a critical engagement with Hegel's own reading of the history of philosophy. Hegel's notion of the history of political philosophy and the Hegelianised conception of the history of political philosophy maintained in the essays of this book are reviewed. The essays, whose lines of argument are also sketched below, are shown to disclaim a telos within intellectual history. They are explained, however, as subscribing to the Hegelian notion that political philosophy is an historical activity. Within this historical perspective, frames of reference and ways of theorising entertained in political philosophies emerge out of a political and intellectual past, and their claims are reviewed and assessed by relating them to past perspectives. The Conclusion of the book takes stock of Hegel's political theory today. It shows how a revisionary Hegelianism, inspired and revised through a dialogue with other positions, discloses the intertwined dilemmas and possibilities of modern politics.

The interpretive agenda of this book is distinctive in its adoption of a comparative, historical perspective. Hegel has attracted a host of commentators, including the subtle and the elegant, but also the one-sided and the strident.[1] The density of Hegel's conceptual style tends to attract commentary that is either painstaking and uncritical in its tracking of the Hegelian path or unremittingly hostile in its denunciation of Hegel from the critical sidelines. The very process of situating Hegel in wider traditions of political philosophy undertaken in this book, however, allows for a critical perspective that is neither a rehearsal of Hegel's own language nor an unmediated subordination of Hegel to the standpoint of the commentator.

An argument running throughout the book is that the identity of Hegel's political thought, along with its merits and limitations, can best be captured by reflecting on its affinities and disparities with other political theories in the Western tradition rather than solely fixing upon his words. Hence to compare the political philosophies of Plato and Hegel is to ask interesting critical questions about Hegel. The process of adopting a framework for comparison invokes an examination of Hegel's own account of the relationship between his political philosophy and Plato's. Appraising Hegel's own reading of Plato, given Hegel's general views on the interdependence of past and present, is to review Hegel's self-conception of his own political philosophy. Likewise, to investigate Hegel in relation to his immediate successors, Marx and Stirner, contributes to a critical reading of Hegel in at least two ways. On the one hand it reveals a recognisably Hegelian style of thinking, underlying distinct theoretical and practical projects, and on the other hand it highlights pointed if polemical critiques of Hegel in the turbulent Hegelian aftermath.[2]

Connecting and disconnecting Hegel to a series of political philosophers invokes Hegel's conception of the history of political philosophy. The idea of locating Hegel on the map of political philosophy assumes an identity to the history of political thought, whose problematic character has been controversially explored by Hegel. The identity underlying the history of political thought can be seen as fragile and mobile; like an opportunist's career, its meaning is stretched and twisted by imaginative leaps inspired by the demands of changing contexts. Alternatively the identity may be conceptualised as reflecting a continuity, maintained by a persisting sense of what politics and its philosophical comprehension entail.

Hegel combines these ways of conceiving the history of political thought, perceiving its continuity as being conditioned by the specificity of successive intellectual and political contexts. His own political philosophy is presented as encompassing and synthesising a tradition. In so doing Hegel recognises the historic character of political philosophy and yet assimilates the conditional validity of past standpoints within the compass of his own philosophical perspective. The process of historical assimilation is taken by Hegel as establishing the suprahistorical, universal status of his own standpoint. The essays in this book interrogating Hegel's reading of historical predecessors, such as

Plato, provide a focused means of assessing Hegel's theory and practice of the history of political thought. Likewise the essays that relate Hegel's political thought to post-Hegelian developments[3] undertake a searching examination of the supposedly suprahistorical credentials of Hegel's thought in the light of alternative standpoints generated in the post-Hegelian history of political philosophy.

The essays in this book acknowledge the continuing value of Hegel's conception and practice of the history of political philosophy. They dissent, however, from the view that all intellectual routes, so to speak, lead to Hegel. Their collective critique of Hegelian absolutism sees Hegel as insufficiently responsive to plural and dissonant voices. This critique, however, does not take post-Hegelian political philosophy to be an uncomplicated emancipation from a supposedly superseded Hegelian standpoint. Hegel's political philosophy is seen as a significant contextual condition for subsequent, distinct and contrasting perspectives on politics, such as those explored by Marx, Collingwood, Rawls and Lyotard. Hegel is not taken to be assimilated without remainder in any or all of these perspectives, for subsequent perspectives are shown to be vulnerable to Hegelian critique. To see the relationship between Hegel and his successors as a living one, in which subsequent thinkers, while absorbing aspects of Hegelianism, can be subjected to a Hegelian critique, is to highlight the continued and contemporary relevance of Hegel as a political philosopher.

HEGEL AS AN HISTORIAN OF POLITICAL PHILOSOPHY

In the *Philosophy of Right* Hegel sets out an account of a rational state in the guise of a philosophical elaboration of the implications of the premises of human conduct. The argument is developed through the conceptual derivation of the specific conditions of a free political community from the general concept of freedom. Notwithstanding the predominantly trans-historical idiom of the account, Hegel's conception of politics is decidedly historical. In a series of famous but controversial epigrams, political philosophy is explained as representing a retrospective elaboration and justification of a form of political life, expressive of an historic political culture. He observes, 'The Owl of Minerva spreads its wings with the falling of the dusk'.[3] Hegel's comments in lecture courses on political philosophy do not consistently rehearse a severe dependence of theory upon prior practice.

Nonetheless political theory is invariably linked by Hegel to contextual political cultures.[4]

Hegel is in effect making two profound claims. The general claim extended on behalf of the state set out in the *Philosophy of Right* is that its political and social practices and institutions are demonstrably and universally rational.[5] The institutions and practices of *The Philosophy of Right* are taken to compose a concrete social world of freedom and derive logically from broad notions of what it means to be human and free. At the same time, however, the rational political community articulated in the *Philosophy of Right* is understood to be the distillation of the principles evident in modern political states, so that political freedom is claimed to be the product of historical development. The synchronic, systematic elaboration of the conditions of a rational political community are comprehended by Hegel as being the outcome of diachronic, historic progress. The course of the historical development of an increasingly rational political culture is narrated in the *Lectures on the Philosophy of History*, and the correlative development of philosophical perspectives on politics is traced in the *Lectures on the History of Philosophy*.

The claims to rational objectivity and the revelation of historical progress maintained in Hegel's account of politics are intertwined, so that their reciprocal justification renders each of the claims more rather than less plausible. Hegel's standpoint is neither an *a priori* rationalism nor an uncritical historicism.[6] The reciprocity of history and philosophy in Hegel's understanding of politics is canvassed at the outset of the *Philosophy of Right*. Hegel observes that without the actual development of political associations there would be no theories of politics. Political reflection is taken as exploring actual traditions of political life. The practices of historical political communities are the objects of reflection. Philosophical reflection, however, is seen as engaging critically with political practice. What is merely given in experience is not to be endorsed. Existing tendencies and developments are clarified and their fit with one another and the general categories of experience reviewed and rendered coherent.

For Hegel, 'What is actual is rational and what is rational is actual'; but he does not equate actuality with the merely existent.[7] Criticism of practice is implied by the criterion of judgment, for the actual is what underlies but is not to be equated with current institutions. Philosophical reflection distils principles either embedded within or suggested by the given empirical world. The relative autonomy of philosophical reflection is exemplified by the differing accounts of the working of constitutional monarchy presented by Hegel in distinct lecture courses on political philosophy.[8]

The dependence of thought upon an object of thought, an actual world of objects and subjects, is the starting point of Hegel's enterprise in reflecting on politics. In *The Philosophy of Right* the foundational concept is the freedom of the will; freedom, for Hegel, is inseparable from any conceptualisation of human beings as either agents or thinkers. Just as *The Logic* reviews categories of thought that register the free character of human conceptualisation, so Hegel's practical philosophy attends to human freedom. The meaning of human freedom by definition is neither fixed nor formulated prior to its expression; it is not to be grasped by the inventiveness of abstract thought, rather by an historically informed perspective.

The study of history, for Hegel, presupposes the freedom of historical actors; history consists in the narrative record of their actions. The distinctiveness of philosophical history, in contrast to the forms of reflective history practised by historians, is that it reflects upon the development of history in relation to its postulate of human freedom. In so doing, the philosophical historian reviews how political cultures have emerged that express the freedom integral to human activity.[9] Hegel's argument in his *Lectures on the Philosophy of History*, assumed and rehearsed in *The Philosophy of Right*, is that modern political culture, when scrutinised in the light of its relationship to the notion of freedom, exhibits a set of institutions and practices that enable all members to express and appreciate their freedom. Just as comprehension of natural phenomena must be undertaken via empirical examination, so freedom, the master category of spiritual thought and action, is only to be known through its actual expression in human history. The content of free human action cannot be known in advance, hence reflection upon the meaning of human freedom must examine its practical expression in historic political cultures.

The form of philosophical speculation, like the substantive content of political culture, is seen by Hegel as developing over time. Thought is as free as human action. Thinking cannot be reduced to a deterministic scheme or structure; its logic, encapsulated by the reflexive understanding of thought maintained in the category of the notion in *The Logic*, is self-determining. For Hegel the character of philosophical reflection is determined historically as philosophers develop patterns of thinking. Hence to engage in political philosophy is to engage in the history of political philosophy. Both the object and process of reflection in political philosophy have an historical character.

The form of philosophical reflection about politics is not a self-contained product, unconcerned with previous philosophical developments. Equally, however, given the reflexive character of philosophy, to engage in the history of political philosophy is also to subject the past thinking of philosophers to critical, philosophical interrogation.[10] An historian unversed in reflexive philosophical practice could not establish a critical comprehension of the history of philosophy. The reading of a past political philosophy presumes a critical, philosophical turn of mind, which in appraising arguments assesses their validity. For Hegel, neither the historical nor the philosophical dimension of this relationship is prioritised. Philosophical reflection presupposes an historical development so that its character and standpoint emerge from the interplay of preceding speculation, but the character of past reflection is only to be appreciated by a philosophical turn of mind that is a product of the past to which it turns.

Hegel's conception of the history of political philosophy is distinct from contemporary conceptions. For instance, notwithstanding Hegel's recognition of the contextual conditionality of political philosophy, his understanding of the history of political philosophy differs from that of contemporary contextualism. The contextualist approach to the history of political thought, as currently practised notably by Skinner and Pocock, originated out of a dissatisfaction with a prevailing scholarly orthodoxy. This orthodoxy tended to read the texts of the classic political thinkers as conveying abstract political ideas, whose significance and generality transcended specific historical contextual features.[11] A distinguished pedigree for this treatment of ideas may be distinguished in Lovejoy's notion that the history of ideas is to be practised by tracing the persistence of general, unit ideas within more complex, dynamic intellectual formulations.[12]

Contextualist historians of political thought, in contrast to a textualist approach, characteristically maintain that political thought takes place in specific contexts defined preeminently by political and ideological factors. Consequently the texts of political thought are to be interpreted by historical scholarship, which establishes the author of the text's standpoint in relation to these contexts.[13] On a Skinnerian reading of the history of political thought, texts of political thought are historically situated so that their arguments draw significantly upon contingent linguistic and ideological practices.[14]

The contextualist idea of the history of political thought focuses upon the conditionality of specific historical contexts, so that conceptions are taken to supersede their provenance merely by maintaining a degree of abstraction that renders their substantive content exiguous.[15] Contextual specificity is thereby seen as running counter to the Hegelian notion of an absolute standpoint, by which perspectives of the past may be assimilated within an historically conditioned but objectively rational conception. For Hegel, philosophy and history are reciprocally determining. Philosophical and historical questions are not to be dissolved into one another. Political philosophy is taken by Hegel to be an historical subject; political theorists are to be comprehended as reflecting against the backdrop of historic political cultures and preceding modes of thought. The contingent contexts of the generation of specific political philosophies, however, do not preclude the aspiration to develop a perspective that demonstrates the objective rationality of a form of political community.

The conception of an historical but absolute understanding of politics renders Hegel's historicism distinct from contextualist historians of political thought. Hegel's sensitivity to the historical conditionality of concepts distances him from classic Enlightenment exponents of the universality of abstract judgements. His concern to maintain the objectivity of philosophical discourse, however, separates him from what Stern has referred to as the new historicism, that is, contemporary philosophers such as Macintyre and Rorty, who tend to collapse judgement into the relative by locating the object of philosophy in contemporary and historical cultures and traditions.[16]

Hegel's notion of the reciprocity of philosophy and history makes his historical treatment of past political philosophers a crucial site for understanding and evaluating his own political philosophy. Political philosophies are comprehended as historical products by Hegel in terms of their form and content. They are seen as modelling the substantive institutions and practices of specific political cultures, and their form of theorising is held to reflect historical assumptions about the nature of philosophical reasoning. Hegel's critical exploration of the history of political philosophy draws upon empirical features of past political cultures and incorporates close textual readings of past theorists. Hegel's notion of the continuity of political philosophy, however, in which the present is taken to emerge from and to supersede the past, means that he reveals much about his own political perspective in highlighting the omissions and limitations of past perspectives.

Hegel's sensitivity to the specificity of historical cultures and intellectual traditions enables him to develop subtle and informed judgements about past political theories. Plato's readiness to override the value of individuality in specifying the practices of an ideal political community, for instance, is explained in terms of its reflection of a holistic political culture. Likewise, Hobbes's realistic, scientific theory of political organisation is taken to spring from a specific cultural context, namely one in which a dominant religious perspective that sets limits upon human intellectual exploration recedes in favour of a renewed confidence in human agency and knowledge.

Hegel's historical evocation of political philosophies enables him to appreciate the ways in which theory depends upon and makes sense of practice. He judiciously refrains from labelling past political ideas as simply false insofar as they disagree with his own ideas. While Plato and Aristotle underplay the notion of human freedom, it is recognised that they identify the irreducibly political human interaction celebrated in the experience of the ancient *polis*. Moreover Hegel's historical sensitivity alerts him to the dangers of anachronistic interpretation whereby an author is condemned for omitting principles developed in subsequent political practice.

Hegel is also instructive in connecting his manner of philosophising to preceding theories. For Hegel, ways of thinking are not to be seen as invented by individuals ruminating on the idiosyncrasies of private experience. Rather, the language of political philosophy is traditional insofar as theorists register their insights and originality by developing and discarding prevailing assumptions. Conceptual innovation is taken to occur amidst a wider continuity of thinking. Again the absolutist claims of Hegel may be seen as sober realism rather than bombastic egoism in the light of his recognition of the connections between past and present theories. The contribution of an individual theorist, from an Hegelian standpoint, is not to be trumpeted as the product of a maverick, mysterious genius who, like a gunslinger in a Hollywood movie, cleanses a town by erasing its past.

The true worth of a theorist, for Hegel, resides in his capacity to assimilate and explain preceding and alternative standpoints. Hegel evidently developed his own political philosophy through critical reflection upon past theoretical perspectives. Greek political culture exercised Hegel; he recognised the unity and sense of integration promoted by the *polis*, but was mindful of its neglect of the troubling presence of individuality. He also accepted Plato's notion of the object-ivity of mind but construed mind in subjective as well as objective terms. Hegel's critique of Plato's philosophical endorsement of Greek political life thereby reveals key features of his own reading of the present. Likewise Hegel's critique of a Hobbesian theoretical reduction of the notion of community to the public conditions requisite for the satisfaction of individual desires informs his own complex, ethical account of a political community.

The interdependence of political philosophy and its history is corroborated in the invocation of historical concepts such as the social contract and the state of nature in contemporary political philosophy.[17] Nonetheless Hegel's claim that the tradition of political philosophy culminates in a single standpoint, namely his own, is decidedly questionable. His reading of this tradition as leading inexorably and directly to his own political philosophy tends to distort his reading of earlier political philosophies so that their richness and diversity are underplayed in the interest of rendering them progenitors of Hegelianism.

Again, Hegel's objectivist, absolutist standpoint does not allow sufficiently for the essential contestability of ethical and political judgements. The closure of Hegel's historical thought signals the closure of his substantive ethics. A more open reading of the past would allow a more open, less dogmatic approach to political philosophy itself. Given the multiplicity of perspectives on politics exhibited in the history of political philosophy, it is unreasonable to presume that a standpoint is to be reached that can reject a plurality of political standpoints.

The essays in this book reflect an Hegelianised conception of the history of political philosophy. In comparing Hegel with a range of predecessors and successors, differences of standpoint are traced to divergences of context. In essays comparing Hegel to his predecessors, Hegel's own framework of historical comparison is reviewed to determine its value as an historical guide and for the light it sheds on his philosophical viewpoint. Examining Hegel on Plato is instructive about Plato, and also about Hegel's historical perspective and his overall political and philosophical perspective.

The essays that relate Hegel to succeeding thinkers necessarily assume a post-Hegelian view of their relationship. Hegel himself observed how philosophy could not predict the future.[18] The standpoint adopted in these essays, however, follows Hegel in assuming that subsequent theory, in reflecting upon practical developments, criticises and aims to supersede preceding theories. Hence the extended reach of the Hegelian tradition is exhibited by the connections that are made between Hegel's thought and a number of subsequent theories. The intellectual continuity that is established testifies to an Hegelian conception of the internality of the relations obtaining between successive theorists. Marx, Stirner and Collingwood, for instance, are seen as framing social and political theories, exemplifying aspects of an Hegelian notion of explanation of society. This identification of Hegelian aspects of their thought runs counter to influential readings of their work.[19]

Even Rawls and Lyotard, who are generally interpreted without reference to Hegel, are shown to subscribe to positions that either share or depart self-consciously from an Hegelian standpoint. And yet Hegel's notion of clear teleological historical progress will be shown to be subverted by the failure of either postmodernism or Rawlsian liberalism to assimilate or supersede Hegelianism without remainder. The subsequent history of political philosophy confirms a truth maintained in Hegelian historicism, namely that the validity and significance of any political theory turns upon its relationship to the history and present situation of the discipline. Political philosophy, however, cannot be comprehended exhaustively in a single synoptic perspective. Experience and reflection upon experience may be taken in a variety of ways and the dialogue between the past and the present exhibited in the history of political philosophy does not express an inexorable logic but is a conversation conducted in a variety of idioms.

HEGEL, PREDECESSORS AND SUCCESSORS

Subsequent chapters relate Hegel to a number of preceding and succeeding political theorists. The opening essays in distinct ways examine the relationship between the political theories of Plato and Hegel. The significance of the relationship between Plato and Hegel is highlighted by Hegel himself. In the *Philosophy of Right, Lectures on the History of Philosophy* and *Lectures on Rechtsphilosophie* Hegel emphasises the pivotal role played by his reading of Plato's political philosophy in the generation of his own political thought.[20]

In 'Plato and Hegel: Reason, Redemption and Political Construction' the distinct ways in which Plato and Hegel construed and elaborated the rationality of a political community is examined. While both theorists are seen as sharing a vision of an integrative, holistic community, the relationship between their designated rational communities and the experiential world is specified in sharply contrasting ways in their political theories. Plato, in contrast to Hegel, is seen as committed to a conception of reason as transcending the imperfections and free interplay between individual agents in unplanned practical life. Hegel, on the other hand, is recognised as perceiving reason to be evident within the imperfections of practice and the freely chosen but seemingly discordant activities of individuals.

Hegel's own reading of Plato is the focus of Chapter 2, 'Hegel's Plato: The Owl of Minerva, Political Philosophy and History'. Hegel's perceptive but partial reading of Plato is acknowledged to capture Plato's espousal of the traditional value of political order above freedom. Hegel's interpretation of Plato's political philosophy, however, is criticised for ignoring the openness, irreducible ambiguity and iconoclastic radicalism that render Plato's political thought too complex and subtle for an univocal explanation. The Hegelian tendency to force Plato's political thought into a rigid interpretive framework, disavowing its openness and radicalism, signals general problems for Hegel's standpoint on history and philosophy. While the present is linked to the past, and a work of contemporary political philosophy is at least implicitly related to and critical of what has gone before, there is no necessary, logical reason why past standpoints are to be taken as assimilated without remainder into present ones. A tradition can abridge and distort as well as comprehend what has gone before. It is plausible, in the light of the ineluctability of Platonic interpretation, that there is no final, comprehensive interpretation of Plato's dialogues.

Hegel is self-consciously a modern political philosopher. His preoccupation with Plato reflects this self-understanding. He sees Plato as heroically maintaining the objectivity of reason in the world by articulating an integrated order of politics reflective of the ancient *polis* at the time of the latter's disintegration. While Hegel is attracted by the ideal of an harmonious, integrated political order whose rationality is objectively demonstrable, he recognises that the condition of modernity admits of no nostalgic escape to a bygone age. His political philosophy represents a reflective engagement with the conditions of the modern world, and his critique of Plato emerges out of his understanding of the superseded limits of the ancient world. Hegel sees modernity as turning upon the emergence of individual freedom, which is absent from the ancient *polis* and Plato's political theory.

Hegel's notions of modernity and the freedom of the modern self inform the third chapter of this volume, 'Hobbes, Hegel and the Modern Self'. In this chapter the acuity of Hegel's concise reading of Hobbes in his *Lectures on Rechtsphilosophie* and *Lectures on the History of Philosophy* is recognised. Hegel's identification of Hobbes as a modern theorist, reflecting the emerging culture of modernity, in respect of his realistic, self-consciously scientific derivation of the logic of political order from the capacities and behavioural propensities of individuals, is confirmed. Likewise Hegel's concentrated criticism of Hobbes's reductive account of individual behaviour is endorsed.

Hegel's reading of Hobbes, though, is developed further so as to highlight the contrasting conceptions of a modern self entertained by Hobbes and Hegel. Hobbes's self-determining but non-developmental notion of the individual is contrasted with Hegel's conception of a self-determining individual who recognises and develops a sense of community in conscientiously maintaining the obligations of membership of a rational state. The self-determining individual for Hegel, unlike Hobbes, is not enclosed within his or her own subjectivity. The contrasting notions of the self maintained by Hobbes and Hegel recur in subsequent political theories and are revisited in the contemporary debate between individualism and communitarianism.[21]

The essays in this volume that relate Hegel to his immediate successors, Stirner and Marx, show how the pattern of Hegel's thinking is exhibited by its affinities with succeeding theorists. Equally, the questionable, polemical critiques of immediate successors, whose critical focus underplays their intellectual debt to Hegel, nonetheless highlight controversial aspects of Hegel's thought. Chapter 5, 'Stirner's Critique of Hegel: *Geist* and the Egoistic Exorcist', exhumes the Hegelian skeleton of Stirner's most significant work, *The Ego and Its Own*. It shows uniquely how the topics covered by Stirner and his critical, historical method reflect Hegel's own thinking. What divides Stirner from Hegel is also disclosed to highlight crucial features of Hegel's notion of the individual and the natural and cultural worlds. The self-enclosed and all-powerful image of the ego entertained by Stirner is contrasted with Hegel's affiliation of the ego with the entire pattern of thought determinations embracing natural and cultural formations.

If the impetus for Stirner's critique of prevailing society is shown to derive from his dislocation of the individual ego from Hegel's intricate interweaving of the ego with a wider web of meaning, Marx is depicted in the two following chapters as departing from Stirner and Hegel in seeing individuals as enmeshed and thwarted within patterns of social interaction. Marx's account of alienation and the disordered reproduction of social structures is examined by exploring his diagnosis of the tensions within historic and contemporary capitalist modes of production.

Chapter 6, '*The German Ideology*, Stirner and Hegel: The Theory of History and the History of Theory', reviews the development of Marx's materialist theory of history in terms of his polemical engagement with contemporary young Hegelian theorists, notably Stirner. Marx's critique of Hegelian ideas, however, is not taken to constitute a definitive break with Hegel's characteristic holistic conceptualisation of history and society. Marx's notion of alienation, which is shown to rest upon Hegelian foundations, is in turn identified as informing his account of history. Chapter 7, 'Good and Bad Infinites in Hegel and Marx', highlights the methodological and conceptual affinities between the theoretical standpoints of Hegel's *Logic* and Marx's *Grundrisse*. The connections which are established in these chapters between the *Grundrisse*, *The German Ideology* and *The Economic and Philosophical Manuscripts* on the one hand and a range of Hegels writings on the other hand, exemplify the continuity of Marx's theoretical standpoint, consisting in his deployment of a distinctively Hegelian, holistic style of theorising.

Chapter 8, 'New Leviathans for Old: Collingwood, Hobbes and the Spirit of Hegel', connects Collingwood's restatement of liberalism with Hegel's *Philosophy of Right*. Collingwood's *New Leviathan* is shown to be deeply paradoxical in terms of its combination of an unremitting hostility towards Hegel and its deployment of a conception of intellectual history and a revamped version of the social contract that closely resemble Hegel's own notions of the development of political philosophy and social ethics. Collingwood's restatement of liberalism, insofar as it rehearses an Hegelian standpoint, is a reminder that Hegel cannot be dismissed as illiberal due to his recognition of the social and historical construction of individuality.[22]

Chapters 9 and 10 relate Hegel to Lyotard and Rawls respectively, and in so doing bring Hegel face to face, so to speak, with important strands of recent political philosophy. Chapter 9, 'Lyotard, Hegel and the Dialectic of Modernity', compares theorists who at first sight share no common ground. Lyotard is either celebrated or denigrated for popularising a postmodern break from modern predecessors. He repudiates holistic thinking and declares unremitting scepticism about 'Hegelian' claims to detect an overall pattern to historical development. His rejection of grand narratives of modernity is explicitly directed against Hegel, who is taken to epitomise the totalising theorist, whose perspective Lyotard declares to be redundant. The sharpness of this opposition between Lyotard and Hegel, however, is instructive on the development of the postmodern turn in philosophy and on what is at stake in its conflict with preceding styles of thought. The very core of Lyotard's thought, his scepticism about the possibility of a metalanguage to appraise other forms of thought and activity, is shaped by his own active engagement with Hegel and his disenchantment with the political possibilities of the Hegelian tradition in its Marxist variant.

Rawls's *A Theory of Justice*, on its publication in 1971, did much to relieve the prevalent scepticism about the power of theory to generate first-order responses to problems of the ethical and political world. Rawls articulated a conception of justice that harmonised with the mood of the times and exhibited hard-edged analytical power. The substance and style of Rawls's theorising were seen as hostile to Hegel. Nonetheless, in response to criticism from a variety of quarters, Rawls's subsequent major work, *Political Liberalism*, in its respect for history and the dependence of liberal theory upon an appropriate social and political context represented an accommodation of Hegel. The penultimate chapter of this volume, 'Hegel and Rawls: The Reasonable and the Rational in Theory and Practices', recognises affinities between Hegel and Rawls that remain underplayed in critical commentary. Rawls and Hegel, however, are taken as remaining divided by significant differences between their styles of philosophising and the substantive characters of the liberal political communities they theorise.

The essays in this book may be read separately, reflecting their provenance in papers written separately either as articles or for delivery at conferences. The original papers have all been reworked, however, so as to consolidate their collective and interconnected elucidation of Hegel and his place in the history of political thought. They are intended to show how a range of political philosophies exhibit crucial affinities with and differences from Hegel. The political theories of Collingwood and Marx, for instance, are thoroughly imbued with Hegelian patterns of thought, while aiming to break decisively from Hegel. An ambitious aspiration of this book is to develop a critical vantage point whereby Hegel's political philosophy can be evaluated in the light of the several political theories to which Hegel's political philosophy is related.

The final chapter undertakes an evaluation of Hegel's substantive political thought, drawing upon the preceding studies and the revisionary Hegelian conception of the history of political thought that has been advanced in this Introduction. Hegel is not seen as the consummation of political philosophy. The hubris of the Hegelian claim to completion, and the partial, accommodatory character of his substantive political thought are recognised. Hegel, though, within the critical perspective provided by a range of historical and contemporary political philosophers, is shown to offer a complex and finely balanced political theory, which remains of value despite its partiality and misguided absolutism. While contemporary politics is not to be comprehended through an unrevised Hegelian perspective, Hegel's dialectical concern to trace and connect a plurality of values within a reasonable pattern of modern social and political practices is an exemplary model for contemporary theorising.

2 Plato and Hegel: Reason, Redemption and Political Construction

INTRODUCTION

The political philosophies of Plato and Hegel can be compared and contrasted in relation to three distinct but connected arguments. First, Plato and Hegel share a common recognition of the significance of the social world for the development of individuals. Second, they both outline political communities that are held to be able to organise social life so as to overcome the alienation and disharmony that they see as common and persistent problems of social interaction. Third, their respective political solutions for these social problems are radically different as they have distinctive conceptions of reason and its role in social life. The originality of this study resides in its focus upon the specificity of Plato's and Hegel's approaches to what they took to be the task of political theory, the articulation of a political community resolving the problems and tensions of social practice. Hegel self-consciously attempted to supersede Plato's ideal community by allowing for freedom of the individual within his rational state. However his political theory is distinguished from Plato's most dramatically by his effort to redeem the negativity of political experience by unveiling the inner rationality of the modern state, whereas Plato, contrary to Hegel's interpretation of the *Republic*, sought to construct an ideal political community that was wholly removed from the tensions and negativity of contemporary states.[1]

Plato and Hegel are united as philosophers by the emphasis they place upon the social foundations of experience and the extent to which they locate an individual's thought-patterns, values and attitudes within a social setting. Inwood has perceptively distinguished Plato and Hegel from contract theorists who take the supposedly presocial individual as the basic element of social and political analysis by noting that for Plato and Hegel, 'It is rather the socialised man who is the essential man.'[2] For both Plato and Hegel, self-awareness and personal integration are social rather than natural attributes.

16

While a rational political community fosters these attributes, alienation and a divided mind are the experiences of those individuals within communities which are imperfect. Hence for both philosophers the community assumes great significance in positive and negative senses. Their delineation of ideal political communities derives its point from the negative possibilities of social interaction explored in their writings.

Plato's *Republic*, the supreme statement of Plato's political theory, involves a critique of the values enshrined and encouraged within the contemporary Greek *polis*.[3] The urgency in the argument of the *Republic* arises out of its recognition of the individual's dependence on the community, coupled with the insight that in the prevailing social atmosphere even the best individuals are corrupted and prevented from realising their potential. For Plato, the goal of philosophy is to establish the true patterns of reason and then to turn to political practice so that a political community can be constructed so as to provide spiritual shelter for the lost and alienated souls he depicts in various images in the *Republic*.

Hegel, like Plato, was very much aware of the power of social forces; for Hegel the individual considered outside a social context is an abstraction.[4] While Hegel's *Philosophy of Right* begins with the individual, this is because he purposely begins with the abstract and ends his examination in the concrete world of political communities in which the bare individual is at home.[5] Self-knowledge, Hegel explicitly argues, is a function of social life and if a community designates an individual a 'dependent' person, a slave, then that individual is, in effect, debarred from achieving the self-realisation that he is a free, independent subject.[6] According to Hegel, individuality and perceptions of individuality, vary from social context to social context. Again, like Plato, central to the inspiration behind the entire Hegelian philosophy is a recognition of the 'negativity' of social life; in both his early and late writings Hegel strikingly brings out the alienation involved when social life appears as a foreign power dominating and distorting the individual's aspirations. For Hegel a slave-owning society maintains a pattern of social life that inhibits an individual from coming to terms with his own identity. But for Hegel, unlike Plato, the task for philosophy is not to rescue the individual from social alienation by prescribing a new political order. Rather, the philosopher is to redeem the negativity of the present by recognising the inner rationality that underlies the surface appearance of social fragmentation and justifies the dissonance and discordance exhibited by past social formations. In contrast to Plato, reason, for Hegel, is not external to experience; it is a complex process of development evident in the vicissitudes of human interaction. Hegel argues that the philosophical articulation of the principles of a rational state is dependent upon its prior achievement in political practice. Moreover the rational state of Hegel is predicated upon the actual power of each individual to know himself as a rational agent by freely relating himself to others in the various social practices composing the political community. Hence, while Plato and Hegel drew philosophical inspiration from the common recognition of the power of social forces and, in particular, of the alienation engendered by social conditions, their political philosophies involve different solutions to the problems they identify.

Comparative studies of the political theories of Plato and Hegel have tended to neglect the distinctiveness of their respective standpoints. Hegel, in the *Philosophy of Right* and in lecture courses on politics, philosophy and history, argued that Plato's political philosophy foreshadowed his own in its adherence to traditional concerns and practices.[7] Foster, in his book *The Political Philosophies of Plato and Hegel*, urges that Plato and Hegel are closely linked as political philosophers, notwithstanding Hegel's concern to incorporate a modern concern for a variety of forms of freedom, in that they both assume that an ideal political association is not a free creation of individuals but is based upon an objective, 'natural' order of reason.[8] In a self-conscious contrast to Foster, Hall, in an article entitled 'Plato Hegel and Subjectivism', links Plato closely to Hegel by arguing that both theorists frame accounts of politics that allow for individual happiness and freedom.[9] These studies can be criticised in terms of the details of their interpretations of Plato and Hegel. Hegel assumes that the provisions for the guardian class apply to all citizens of Plato's ideal commonwealth. Foster disregards the systematic character of Hegel's philosophy and Hegel's genuine concern to theorise politics in relation to freedom, while Hall understates the authoritarianism of Plato's ideal state. More seriously, however, these interpretations abstract from the distinctiveness of the respective solutions to social tensions offered by Plato and Hegel. Plato's imaginative construction of an innovative political community, predicated upon the separation of theory from practice, involves a radical break with tradition whereas Hegel's conception of the dependence of theory upon practice encourages him to conceive of the tensions and discord of social life as being redeemed by the rationality implicit in actuality.

PLATO

The *Republic* testifies in several ways to the enormous power for good and ill that the social environment exerts over the individual. Plato prescribes wholesale changes in the organisation of social life as he is convinced that these radical measures represent the only means of rescuing individuals from the pernicious grip of corrupt social practices. These measures include massive state censorship, the propagation of persuasive but untruthful state propaganda, the abolition of the family for the ruling classes and state control of property, extending to a complete ban on private property for the ruling classes.[10] Such measures have prompted commentators as diverse as Hegel and Popper to condemn the *Republic* for denying the individual the freedom essential to his nature.[11] While this criticism is justified, it is important to recognise that Plato gives the state such power because of his fundamental assumption that the individual's character and actions are deeply influenced by social practices. Hall, for instance, in criticising Hegel, is right to point to Plato's explicit concern for the individual. He is wrong, however, to underplay the authoritarian character of the state Plato envisages as requisite to permit the flourishing of individuals.[12] Indeed Plato emphasises the overwhelming obstacles that lay in the path of an individual seeking enlightenment in the prevailing social atmosphere; he runs grave risks by pursuing a goal that is fundamentally at odds with public aspirations.[13]

A consistent theme throughout the *Republic* is the social and political nature of man; the range of human capacities and virtues are only envisaged as flourishing within a community. The ideal state outlined in the *Republic* is developed out of a primitive community that Plato conceives as emerging logically and naturally out of the interplay of human needs: 'My notion is, said I, that a state comes into existence because no individual is self-sufficing; we all have many needs.'[14] The political community, for Plato, is rooted in basic human needs; it is not an adventitious accretion to human life, it is central and basic to the human condition. This picture of the role of the state in the economy of human existence is reinforced by the entire analysis of justice conducted in the dialogue. Plato postpones an analysis of justice in the individual until he has located it in the community. The symmetry that is thereafter established between justice in the individual and justice in the state, coupled with the symmetry between the varieties of unjust state and the varieties of unjust individual, assumes and confirms that the individual is inextricably bound up with the state. Indeed the analogy between the individual and the state involves an organic conception of the state that, in itself, suggests that the individual cannot be independent of the state. The extent to which Plato conceives the individual to be dependent upon the state had been revealed in the *Crito*. In that dialogue Socrates had acknowledged the authority of the community in condemning him to death, despite its manifest shortcomings, as he recognised the variety of ways in which his life had depended upon the sustaining ethos of the *polis*.[15]

While the *Republic* emphasises the supreme status of the community in human affairs, it also presents a devastating indictment of the contemporary patterns of social and political life. The cave is an image of the human condition designed to point up the distorted values and perverse priorities of the contemporary political community. The illusory, dream-like social attitudes that sustain a community in the darkness of ignorance are graphically represented as chains binding the community to the perpetual nightmare of a subterranean existence. The prevailing preoccupation with the world of objects and their images fosters an uncritical acceptance of opinions that can only be exchanged for knowledge by the scrutiny of ideas. In this image of the cave Plato advances as far as any theorist in his recognition of the extent to which an individual's values are shaped and in this case distorted by the prevailing direction of a community's way of life. Cushman has commented on this aspect of the cave allegory: 'He (Plato) recognises that the character of human thought concerning reality is powerfully conditioned by the climate of opinion, the prevailing mind-set in which the individual participates from childhood.'[16] The social reinforcement of illusion is conceived as so powerful that in the event of an attempt being made to liberate the cave dwellers, 'if they could lay hands on the man who was trying to set them free and lead them up, they would kill him'.[17] Within the cave contemporary politicians and sophists are assigned the role of carrying puppets along the parapet; and it is the shadows of these objects that preoccupy the citizens of the cave. The citizens themselves are viewed as contributing to their own condition as they pride themselves in disputing about these shadows.[18] This social preoccupation with shadowy images solicits and corrupts the rare individual whose nature equips him to aspire to truth and wisdom. Nor is the cave an isolated image; its message is confirmed by other powerful images. Plato likens the dead hand of ill-informed, casual public opinion to the fancies of a great beast whom the sophists are depicted as flattering and humouring.[19] Against this suffocating background, a potential philosopher will hardly be able to hold out. Indeed Socrates' own travesty of a trial at the hands of unthinking politicians, so movingly dramatised in the *Apology*, is never far from Plato's mind when he recounts the injustice obtaining in the contemporary p*olis*.[20]

Given this savage critique of his own political culture, added to his assessment of the unavoidable significance of social life, it is unsurprising that Plato advocates that control of the state should be removed from the hands of career politicians who know nothing of the true principles of politics. Socrates' recommendation, however, that it is only philosophers to whom political power can be entrusted, is a move that astonishes his interlocutors. It is a political manoeuvre that marks a radical break with Greek tradition as philosophy had only been taught privately to individual citizens and philosophical expertise was not a quality evident in political life.[21] It is a logical development, however, from Socrates' remark at his trial that 'the unexamined life is not worth living'.[22] According to Plato, the unthinking, self-interested behaviour fostered by contemporary political life locks the community into an unexamined alienation from a life that is truly concordant with reason.[23] Plato's disinterested pursuit of philosophical wisdom leads him to conclude that the rational pattern for human life can only be achieved by philosophical enquiry. Hence philosophers are to assume control of the political community and rule on behalf of the vast majority of citizens who are considered incapable of achieving an understanding of absolute, philosophical knowledge bequeathed by a vision of the Good. Plato's resolution of the human predicament that arises out of the alien goals pursued in contemporary society is one that is foreign to the traditions of Greek experience, as the criteria invoked to evaluate social and political life are removed from experience. For Plato, reason is a procedure of dialectical criticism that has no commerce with the world; hence the rational political community outlined by Plato is the product of a logical analysis of abstract ideas rather than a reflection on empirical data.

The philosophical justification of the political community recommended in the *Republic* turns upon the consistent exploration of the principle of the division of labour, which initiates Plato's analysis of the idea of justice. The rigorous examination of the implications of this principle leads on to a rigid class division within the ideal community between those psychically equipped to be rulers, those suited to be auxiliaries and the remainder who consent to engage in production and trade. In the subsequent discussion of the distinctive requirements of the ruling class of guardians, Plato establishes that the guardians will need a sophisticated and arduous form of higher education in order to comprehend the Forms, the ideal principles of reason. The thrust of this education is to turn the interest of the philosophical guardians away from the experimental world of change and movement towards a concern for the dialectical examination of thought itself, which ultimately leads to an understanding of the idea of the Good, the source of all knowledge, being and value. These characteristics of reason provide the theoretical justification for Plato's recommendation of an authoritarian state whereby a select few impose standards of conduct and styles of education on a citizenry whose freedom is radically curtailed. As Hare has observed, 'Given Plato's views about knowledge of the Good and about the role of education in making possible a good life, it is easy to see how he came by his highly authoritarian political doctrines.'[24]

Plato's separation of the principles of reason from the changing world of experience, however, casts doubt on the practicality of the ideal state. Plato explicitly remarks that practice, by its very nature, is recalcitrant to theory: 'Is it not in the nature of things that action should come less close to truth than theory.'[25] While Plato's thoughts on this matter are ambiguous, as Annas has recognised, he affirms that at least an approximation to the ideal state is feasible in practice.[26] Nonetheless his understanding of the necessary imperfection of practice leads him to conclude that even an approximation to the ideal state could not survive in the instantial world. He articulates a theory of history tracing the decline of the ideal state through the increasingly imperfect states of timocracy, oligarchy, democracy and tyranny. The doubts expressed in the *Republic* about the feasibility of translating the theoretically rational political community into practice give rise to Plato's later political dialogues, the *Statesman* and the *Laws*. In the *Statesman*, Plato's reflections on the imperfections of practice receive a more prominent and spectacular expression. Plato rehearses a myth that the universe itself, due to its material composition, is subject to great reversals of motion that bring imperfection in their wake. The record of contemporary governments is held to reveal the imperfection of the contemporary era. Pending the arrival of a true statesman, Plato now urges that any law-abiding, constitutional state should provide at least a measure of relief from the disordered practices of contemporary political communities. But Plato maintains that if a true statesman were to appear, he should be given absolute power to mould the citizens according to the dictates of reason.[27]

The *Laws*, to a greater extent even than the *Statesman*, discloses Plato's readiness to engage in theorising the conditions of admittedly imperfect remedies for the troubles attending contemporary politics. Plato only permits himself a brief reference to the ideal of an enlightened autocrat having a completely free hand to arrange the political community along rational lines. This would involve a thoroughgoing communism in which all traces of individualism were extinguished.[28] The actual state that Plato concentrates on recommending in the *Laws* makes concessions to the domain of practice. It is characterised by rigid adherence to the rule of law and a mixed form of sovereignty. This second-best state is the product of Plato's pragmatic review of the Greek political tradition.[29] However, as Saunders observes, the overt caution and pragmatism of the *Laws* does not completely dominate Plato's concern that the political community should be aligned to the abstract principles of philosophical reason.[30] The ultimate supervision of this second-best state's welfare is to be entrusted to a nocturnal council, which will devote itself to the exhaustive study of philosophy and theology so that it can change and amend the law as reason requires. Hence Plato's later political thought is an uneasy compromise between the ideal community of the *Republic* and the requirements of practice.

HEGEL

According to Hegel, all routes leading to an understanding of reality must focus upon the social construction of reason and reality. The crucial concept in Hegel's system is Spirit (*Geist*); 'The Absolute is Spirit – this is the supreme definition of the Absolute.'[31] Like every other concept in the Hegelian system, Spirit derives its meaning from that to which it is opposed. Indeed Spirit, for Hegel, 'opposes' itself to nature both cognitively and practically, hence 'the manifestation of itself to itself is, therefore, itself the content of Spirit'.[32] This theoretical and practical manipulation of natural phenomena is achieved by conscious, thoughtful activity undertaken by subjects (men) situated in a natural environment. Men, by their mastery of nature supersede the merely natural, but they do not fully appreciate their spirituality until they engage in social interaction with other subjects. It is only in social activity that a mirror is held up to the individual subject, so that he recognises his own particular ability to think and practically determine his life by rational activity as the mark of his generic, universal identity that is Spirit.[33] Hegel argues that the logical conditions of this achievement in self-consciousness consist in a series of competitive and cooperative modes of social interaction. However it is only through the reciprocal recognition of one another as free subjects integrally related through the practices of a rationally organised political community that men recognise themselves as free, independent spirits who at the same time have universal, social ties to one another. As Singer has observed, 'In the end mind can only find freedom and self-understanding in a rationally organised community. So minds are not separate atoms, linked together by the accidents of association. Individual minds exist together, or they do not exist at all.'[34]

The fact that social transactions and their rational political organisation are essential for individual self-awareness in Hegel's thought does not blind him to the possibility of disharmony and alienation in social and political life. Plant has urged that Hegel's philosophy was inspired by social and political problems he identified in his youth: 'it seems to me that the whole of Hegel's work has a social and a political dimension, that his whole philosophy, and not merely his explicit political and social theorising, was a response to certain problems in social and political experience'.[35] Hegel's early writings testify to his sense of the enervation and alienation endemic in contemporary social, political and religious experience. Men are held to be bereft of social ties that could integrate the atomised individuals who bestow their own spiritual status on an alien God. Hegel observed in his Tübingen essay of 1793, 'Our religion aims to educate men to be citizens of heaven whose gaze is ever directed thither so that human feelings become alien to them.'[36] By the completion of his mature system, however, Hegel had come to consider that in essence the contemporary social and political practices composing the modern state were rational. But this reconciliation with reality, which Hardimon has made the focus of a lengthy study of Hegel's social thought, does not mean that negative aspects of social experience are ignored.[37]

Hegel's mature conception of reason is one that seeks to redeem the world and man from an agonising confrontation with discord and suffering by understanding the role of negativity in the economy of salvation.[38] The mature Hegel saw Christianity as a mythical representation of his own philosophy, and Christ's personal redemption of the world is transposed into the redemptive powers of reason in Hegel's system. Hegel observed in the Preface to the *Philosophy of Right*, 'To recognise reason as the rose in the cross of the present and thereby to enjoy the present, this is the rational insight which reconciles us to the actual.'[39] Hegel's mature system therefore redeems the failures and frustrations of social life by viewing them as integral to the achievement of human freedom and rational self-knowledge. In the section of the *Philosophy of Spirit* dealing with the dialectic of self-consciousness, Hegel discusses intensely competitive and destructive modes of social interaction that are nonetheless seen as playing a positive role in the human drama, not merely because they exist, generally, as subordinated, sublimated aspects of more complex patterns of social intercourse, but also because they are seen as vital to the growth of self-consciousness. The life and death drama of one individual engaged in recognitive struggle with another testifies to the intensity of the individual's need to prove his own universal status by eliciting its concrete recognition from another individual who will thereby confirm his spiritual identity. This thirst for spiritual recognition is also exemplified by the master–slave relationship. This relationship is inherently unsatisfactory as the slave is reduced to the mere object of the master's desires, and the master cannot receive the spiritual acknowledgement he needs from the slave, whom he himself degrades.[40] The longing for spiritual recognition, which even in this disordered form is a timeless component of the human condition, can only be satisfied and so mastered by a reconciliation with the negative aspects of this need for recognition.

The redemptive role of reason in Hegel's treatment of past human experience does not underplay the negative aspects of experience.[41] Hegel is acutely conscious of the appalling misery and apparent pointlessness of the historical process as the fortunes of the men and women of past nations and states are examined. He is, however, impelled to view this misery as serving some purpose that can justify it: 'But even as we look upon history as an altar on which the happiness of nations, the wisdom of states and the virtue of individuals are slaughtered, our thoughts inevitable impel us to ask to whom or to what ultimate end have these monstrous sacrifices been made.'[42] The ultimate end which Hegel sees the historical process as promoting is the development of freedom and reason. While oriental tyrannies submerged the individual within the state, and the middle ages witnessed the alienation of human power and freedom, the social formations of these eras are nonetheless viewed as stepping stones to human freedom. The necessary telos of human history is seen as the achievement of a rationally organised political community that expresses human freedom and which provides the social platform for the absolute awareness of freedom and reason in artistic, religious and philosophical conception.[43]

Hegel's commitment to redeem the negativity of experience therefore, prompts him, to impose a rational goal on the historical process that derogates from the very freedom he imputes to the process.

Hegel's understanding of history as exhibiting the progressive development of freedom within increasingly rational political frameworks, entails that the ideal rational political community outlined in the *Philosophy of Right* is based upon the type of state already in existence in Northern Europe.[44] Hegel considers that reason is internal to experience and the philosopher has no licence to construct fanciful imaginary states that have no reference to practical experience. He declares, 'It is just as absurd to fancy that a philosophy can transcend its contemporary world as it is to fancy that an individual can overleap his own age, jump over Rhodes.'[45] The philosopher, however, is not considered to be merely photographing contemporary facts. Hegel is concerned to show how, despite its exhibition and sublimation of profound social tensions, the essential features of the modern state are rational.[46]

Hegel's conception of the universal, social nature of Spirit underpins the sense of community and individual commitment to intersubjective practices that characterise his rational state. The citizen's participation in social practices and his acknowledgement of the general claims of the community express his practical recognition of his own universal, inevitably social identity. At the same time Hegel's ideal state is not envisaged as dwarfing the individual. Hegel recognises that each individual by his 'spiritual' nature is free, as each is capable of stepping back from the particular desires and impulses that press in upon his will to direct his life freely according to rational considerations.[47] The rational political community in the *Philosophy of Right*, Hegel claims, balances the universal social claims of the community against the rights of the self-directed individual. While there is evidently scope for tension and disharmony in the fulfilment of these claims, it should be recalled that for Hegel the individual only has meaning in a social context.

The rational state outlined by Hegel incorporates a high degree of individual freedom for its citizens, who are conceived as directing their own affairs. The individual in Hegel's state will have the right to be respected as a person, handle his own property, engage in family life and, insofar as circumstances permit, enter the occupation and class of his own choosing. At critical stages in the argument of the *Philosophy of Right*, and in the lecture courses on the *Rechtsphilosophie*, Hegel highlights the significance of this autonomy for the individual by contrasting it with the dependence of the individual citizen upon the dictates of the ruling class of guardians in Plato's *Republic*. Hegel considers that Plato reacted to the disruptive and novel assertion of individual freedom and particular interests in the late fifth century BC by reasserting in aggressive terms the claims of the traditional *polis* over the individual. In the section on civil society in the *Philosophy of Right*, Hegel remarks:

> in his *Republic* Plato displays the substance of ethical life in its ideal beauty and truth; but he could only cope with the principle of self-subsistent particularity, which in his day had forced its way into ethical life by setting up in opposition to it his purely substantial state. He absolutely excluded it from his state, even in its very beginning in private property and the family, as well as in its more mature form as the subjective will, the choice of a social position and so forth.[48]

For Hegel the universal claims of the state must not be upheld at the expense of individual freedom, and individuals, to establish their own identities and fulfil their particular aspirations, need to hold personal property, maintain diverse family connections and freely enter into particular types of work and social class. Hegel stresses that the individual in modern society differs markedly from his ancient counterpart in the freedom he has to develop his particular skills and talents and satisfy his diverse needs in civil society, where the market fosters a variety of enterprises and social positions.[49]

While Hegel is critical of Plato's neglect of individual freedom, he is at pains to emphasise that a rational state must integrate individual freedom with the universal claims of the community. In the *Philosophy of Right* he is reported as declaring, 'Similarly, it might seem that universal ends would be more readily attainable if the universal absorbed the strength of the particulars in the way described for instance in Plato's *Republic*. But this, too, is only an illusion since both universal and particular turn into one another. If I further my ends, I further the ends of the universal.'[50] For Hegel, the exercise of individual freedom is conditional upon the practices of a well-ordered state, and in the rational state he outlines, the citizens are envisaged as exhibiting a sense of community testifying to the universal ties sustaining their individual development. Hegel considers that participation in family life and in the classes and corporations of civil society will engender in the citizens a readiness to display this sense of community. Although Hegel, unlike Plato, allows the individual to exercise his own initiative in joining a particular class, he sees all three classes of his state as fostering in the individual an awareness of his community of purpose with other individuals. In this respect, Hegel's understanding of class relations differs from Plato's. Although Hegel's universal class of civil servants are depicted as being concerned with the public good in a way that matches the disinterested concern for the common good of Plato's guardians, Hegel's class of civil servants is not presented as exclusively determining the nature of social and political life and the other classes of his state, the business and agricultural classes, are seen as promoting an appreciation of man's universal ties.[51]

Hegel also considers the political arrangements of his state to be important in ensuring that the individual identifies with the political community. The individual will have the right to be governed and protected by laws that he can conscientiously obey as they will be framed according to rational procedures involving publicity given to debates within the legislature and the public accessibility of the codified system of laws. Furthermore, although Hegel does not espouse popular sovereignty, the individual citizen of his state will be represented through representatives of his estate in the Assembly of Estates, which considers and agrees to legislation, and there will be freedom of expression. The apex of the state is the hereditary monarch who, though reliant on advisors, supplies an unambiguous focus of authority and who, according to Hegel, serves as a living symbol of the individual's spiritual freedom as the monarch's authority is seen as arising solely from his natural inheritance of the spiritual qualities that each man possesses by the mere fact that he is born a human being.

Aspects of the practices and institutions of Hegel's state suggest either an uncritical endorsement of particular, contingent arrangements of his era, or, as Ilting has suggested, a more reprehensible accommodation to a reactionary regime.[52] Nonetheless, Hegel sees his state as supremely rational in its promotion of individual freedom and in its exhibition of a public patriotism testifying to a communal recognition of the universal, social side of man's spiritual nature.[53] But consistent with Hegel's view that reason redeems rather than abolishes negative aspects of experience, he acknowledges that his ideal state harbours imperfections and discordant features. The rational state is not thought to eliminate the general destructive and competitive tendencies of the human spirit, as exemplified by his analysis of the life and death struggle and the master–slave relationship. Indeed Hegel goes so far as to view war as an heroic expression of the citizens' patriotism.[54] In the detailed discussion in the *Philosophy of Right*,

Hegel alludes to significant problems and tensions arising from the operations of civil society. He was perturbed, as Henrich has rightly observed, by the problems of overproduction, which create a rabble of paupers who are denied the means of satisfying the social needs thrown up by the very processes that leave them destitute.[55] Particularly disturbing for Hegel is the prospect that their poverty will alienate them from the universal life of the community.[56] Furthermore, in its very nature civil society expresses a selfish concern with individual aims or particular allegiance to specific classes and organisations. 'It is the system of ethical order split into extremes and lost.'[57] According to Hegel, this appearance of selfishness and fragmentation is, however, redeemed by the sense of community displayed in civic patriotism, the achievement of which is outlined above.

CONCLUSION

Plato and Hegel are united as political theorists by their focus upon the significance of the social context in their understanding of human affairs. According to both thinkers man cannot and should not be seen outside this context; an individual's values and aspirations are shaped comprehensively by the political community he inhabits. The 'natural' habitat for Plato's 'democratic' man is the democratic state; just as the citizen of his ideal state would be out of his element if he ventured into the cave. Similarly Hegel recognises that there is an unbridgeable gap between the ancient Athenian citizen and the individual citizen who inhabits the modern state.[58] This gap is constituted by the differing social and political contexts. Given their recognition of the significance of changing social contexts, it is unsurprising that both Plato and Hegel develop a philosophy of history to supplement their analyses of the state. The possibilities of social and political life examined in their philosophies of history give depth and meaning to their political theories. Furthermore Plato and Hegel share a common inspiration for their political philosophising; they were both prompted to theorise by the need to understand and overcome the dissonance and disharmony they perceived in social life. Hegel's entire philosophy can be read as a sustained attempt to come to terms with the 'negativity' of experience, which, unlike many other philosophers, he took to be inevitably social in character. In his first published masterpiece he observed that 'Spirit gains its truth only by finding itself in absolute dismemberment. The Spirit is this power only by looking the negative in the face and abiding with it.'[59] And the centrepiece of Plato's *Republic* is his eloquent plea, 'Unless, that is to say, political power and philosophy meet together, while the many natures who now go their several ways in the one or the other direction are forcibly debarred from doing so, there can be no rest from troubles my dear Glaucon, for states nor yet, as I believe, for all mankind.'[60]

Hegel and Plato also see the task of political theory as being the delineation of a rational political community, which resolves the social and political predicament exhibited in their writings. But the manner in which the two philosophers fulfil this task is profoundly different. Hegel considers Plato's approach to political philosophy to resemble his own in that he interprets the *Republic* as disclosing the inner rationality of an actual form of political experience. In the Preface of the *Philosophy of Right* he remarks, 'Plato's *Republic* which passes proverbially as an empty ideal is, in essence, nothing but an interpretation of Greek ethical life'.[61] More specifically, Hegel construes the *Republic* as an uncompromising reaffirmation of the authoritative claims of the traditional *polis* to subdue the nascent individualism and cynical pursuit of particular interests that were subverting the order and harmony of Greek political life in the late fifth century BC.[62] Hegel argues that these novel disruptive forces were so powerful that they could not be countered by a reversion to traditional political forms.[63] Plato, however, is not criticised by Hegel for his traditionalism, as philosophy, according to Hegel, cannot theorise the conditions of an imaginative political experiment but can only understand an actual political tradition. Hegel's rehearses this interpretation of Plato's political philosophy in his several lecture courses on the *Rechtsphilosophie*. This repeated alignment of political theory to an actual tradition suggests that Hegel, even in his lecture courses on the *Rechtsphilosophie*, maintained a political position that was not fundamentally at odds with the famous epigrammatic formulation of his conception of political philosophy expressed in the Preface to the published version of the *Philosophy of Right*: 'When philosophy paints its grey in grey, then has a shape of life grown old. By philosophy's grey in grey, it cannot be rejuvenated but only understood. The owl of Minerva spreads its wings only with the falling of the dusk.'[64]

Contrary to Hegel's interpretation of Plato's philosophical intentions and practice, however, in the *Republic* Plato prescribed a novel ideal state designed to eliminate the gross imperfections of actual states, which marked a radical break with the Greek political tradition.[65] In his theory of history, Plato designates the actual political traditions of Sparta and Crete as examples of the imperfect regime of timocracy, and his revulsion against the Athenian democratic tradition inspires the acerbity of his strictures against democracy in the *Republic*.[66] Indeed, throughout the *Republic* Socrates' imaginative pursuit of theoretical political perfection is conditioned by his implicit acceptance of Thrasymachus' statement in the opening book that the ruling parties in actual states merely promote their own interests.[67]

The sharpness of Plato's break with traditional political practices is explained by the standards of rational criticism he invokes to evaluate the traditional Greek *polis* and establish an ideal political community. The Forms, rightly seen by Kraut as crucial to the whole ethical argument of the *Republic*, are conceived as unchanging, unqualified principles of reason wholly removed from experience.[68] In direct contrast, Hegel sees reason as woven into the fabric of experience. Man, for Hegel, is inherently rational; man's ability to think and act rationally is seen as the dynamic force of reason itself. The notion, the key category of reason in Hegel's *Logic*, is explained as the abstract form of man's self-consciousness.[69] The contrast with Plato is clear-cut, for Stanley Rosen is justified in observing that there is no adequate depiction and explanation of the activity of self-consciousness in Plato's philosophy.[70] It is Hegel's conception of reason as being internal to experience that enables him to see the historic modern political state as itself displaying the essential characteristics of reason, despite the many imperfections and tensions it exhibits.

Reason, for Hegel, unlike Plato, is 'the rose in the cross of the present'.[71] The distinctive conceptions of reason held by Plato and Hegel entail that the rational political communities they outline vary significantly in character. Because reason is removed from experience, according to Plato, and is only accessible to philosophers, Plato's ideal political community entrusts power to a philosophical elite who will take whatever steps are necessary to align the state with the principles of reason. The freedom of all the citizens of Plato's ideal state is to be restricted so that the antisocial desires and preferences of individuals are not allowed to undermine the public good. Even the rulers of Plato's ideal state must acknowledge the absolute priority of the community over the individual. This priority assigned to the community is insufficiently recognised in Hall's interpretation of the relationship between Plato's and Hegel's political philosophies, in which both philosophers are seen as catering unevenly for individuality.[72] In marked and self-conscious contrast to Plato, Hegel's rational state is grounded in the freedom of the individual, whose capacity for reason entitles him to be treated as a person and not a thing.[73] While a sense of community and civic obligation are just as important in Hegel's thought as they are in Plato's, for Hegel this sense of community must redeem rather than abolish the egoistic perspective of civil society.

The divergent standpoints of Plato and Hegel on reason and its relation to experience raise significant questions about the status and viability of their political theories. Plato's conception of reason encourages him to develop the logical form of a state, squaring with his abstract idea of justice, which is presented and developed without reference to concrete political practice or actual historical development. The simple notion that justice entails that each individual should undertake the job for which he is suited, coupled with Plato's views on the divergent psychic capacities of individuals, leads to the formulation of an authoritarian, hierarchical state that is profoundly different from the actual states of Greek political experience. While Plato's abstract assumptions may be questioned, partly due to their very abstractness, the separation of the process of reasoning from concrete political experience allows the theoretical construction of a community that puts adherence to principle before egoism, expediency and the seductive power of the status quo. But the strictness of the separation of theory from practice engenders doubts in Plato's own mind about the viability of the community he outlines, so he engages in second thoughts on the question of politics in the *Statesman* and the *Laws*; the very radicalism of Plato's rationalism threatens to make his political theory irrelevant to practice. Indeed, even within Plato's more practical political dialogues there is still a commitment to the achievement and application of philosophical knowledge, as attested in divergent ways by Saunders and Strauss in their commentaries, which render even their relevance to practice questionable.[74] There are no corresponding doubts in Hegel's mind about the viability of his rational state. Indeed his very project of redeeming the frustrations and failures of the world by recognising the fundamental rationality of actual experience allows him to discover the outlines of the rational state in the contemporary world. As Hardimon has noted, 'the real [for Hegel] is not a Platonic, ontological "beyond".'[75] Hence for Hegel the philosophy of history expresses the progressive development of freedom, whereas for Plato it merely charted the imperfections of practice.

Hegel's location of philosophical reason in the intersubjective norms of practical life, the product of mutual recognition and misrecognition, has received much subsequent support from philosophers.[76] His ready endorsement of particular political arrangements, such as hereditary monarchy, as being the supremely rational necessary outcomes of a process of historical development, however, subordinates the independence of reason to the requirements of political sociology, as Walsh has implied, and undermines the redemptive role of reason in Hegel's thought.[77] In divergent ways, commentaries on Hegel's political philosophy by Brod and Tunick observe the questionable nature of Hegel's justification of contingent social and political institutions.[78] Hegel argues that a hereditary monarch provides a definite focus of authority and symbolises the spiritual freedom of man by his natural inheritance of power. But if human beings are to achieve recognition of their universal spiritual status by identifying with the political organisation of their social interaction, then surely popular sovereignty and a democratic form of rule would be more effective instruments for securing this end than vicarious reliance on political symbols drawn from a particular historical period. Hegel's endorsement of the particular political forms of his age suggests that his claim to go beyond religion in providing a rational understanding of reality is questionable. In the Introduction to his *Lectures on the History of Philosophy*, Hegel distinguishes philosophy from religion by its capacity to transcend metaphor and myth (*Vorstellung*), to present in purely conceptual terms the rationality of reality. 'Philosophy thinks and conceives of that which religion represents as the object of consciousness, whether it is as the work of the imagination or as existent facts in history.'[79] The redemption offered by Hegel's philosophical system, however, which sees the particular political forms of his age as representing the supremely rational teleological goal of history, demands as much faith as belief in Christ's salvation of the world on the cross, the myth it was conceived as rationally restating.[80]

3 Hegel's Plato: The Owl of Minerva, Political Philosophy and History

INTRODUCTION

Hegel considers that Plato's political theory, as articulated in the *Republic*, constitutes a retrospective philosophical endorsement of the traditional Greek *polis*, which was disintegrating in Plato's lifetime under the impact of novel, individualistic, disruptive forces. For Hegel, Plato is reasserting what Hegel takes to be the preeminent characteristic of the Greek *polis*, evident in both Athens and Sparta, namely the vital, harmonious integration of the individual into the ethical practices of the community.[1] This understanding of the *Republic* reflects Hegel's well-known declaration in the *Philosophy of Right* proclaiming the dependence of theory upon the prior achievements of practice. 'When Philosophy paints its grey in grey then has a shape of life grown old. By philisophy's grey in grey it cannot be rejuvenated but only understood. The Owl of Minerva spreads its wings only with the falling of the dusk.'[2]

Hegel's interpretation of the *Republic* as an imaginative reformulation of the structure of a disintegrating political culture focuses attention perceptively on Plato's undeniable hostility to contemporary political practices and attitudes, but it is fundamentally at odds with Plato's own frank admission that what he is proposing is startling and paradoxical in the context of traditional Greek political assumptions.[3] Hegel's failure to recognise the novel radicalism of Plato's political thought is reflected in subsequent commentaries on the relationship between Plato and Hegel. Foster and Ware, for example, follow Hegel in seeing Plato's political thought as rehearsing Greek political traditions.[4] The disruptive and innovative character of Plato's political thought, however, is captured by Inwood in an article analysing Hegel's and Plato's political theories. 'The main reason for Hegel's failure to criticise Plato's state effectively was perhaps his reluctance to concede that Plato was an innovator, proposing an ideal which was not put into practice.'[5] Again, Hegel's conception of Plato as a philosopher systematically rehearsing the ideal of harmonious order exhibited by the ancient Greek *polis* presupposes that Plato was a thinker with a settled, clear-cut body of doctrines, which jars with the apparently unresolved dilemmas and allegorical allusiveness of the dialogues.[6]

By exploring the implications involved in viewing the *Republic* from an Hegelian perspective, this analysis of Hegel's Plato clarifies the nature of Plato's political philosophy. Additionally, it raises questions about the validity of Hegel's historical appreciation of past philosophies and his claim to have incorporated them into his own philosophical system. The questions that are thereby raised can be used to interrogate the claims of Hegel's philosophy, which are sweeping and often resist effective criticism. Hegel claims that the configurations of natural phenomena and the theoretical and practical activities of man, past and present, must be seen as contradictory, dependent aspects of experience, fundamentally incoherent unless viewed as invoking the all-encompassing, rational perspective of the Hegelian system. The very power and range of this Hegelian vision have often subverted critical evaluation either by exciting uncritical acceptance or by provoking unthinking rejection, as is revealingly endorsed in the following observation by Gellner: 'Nothing could be more pointless than some kind of sober, moderate interpretation and assessment of Hegel . . . . He is everything or he is nothing or, following what he said, both at once.'[7] Partisanship, however, does not promote philosophical awareness and one route to the achievement of a sober, balanced assessment of Hegel is to compare an aspect or branch of his system with the empirical material it is designed to explain. Plant has noted that Hegel himself recognised that his system's coherence with empirical observation was one of the tokens of its validity:

> The final internal criterion of adequate explanation which can be extrapolated from some of Hegel's *obiter dicta* and also from his practice is that a philosophical explanation of a mode of experience, a form of life or of an institution must cohere with what is known on empirical grounds about such modes, forms and institutions.[8]

An examination of Hegel's Plato therefore represents a valuable case study in the critical evaluation of the explanatory power of Hegel's system. Plato's dialogues can be examined evidentially to check Hegel's claim that his system accounts for and assimilates theoretical perspectives other than his own without distorting them in the process. While there is an hermeneutical circularity to Hegel's idea of critical interpretation, he recognises that the past is falsified to the extent that it is a mere repository of the ideas of the interpretive present.

HEGEL AND THE HISTORY OF PHILOSOPHY

To appreciate fully Hegel's interpretation of Plato's political philosophy presupposes an awareness of the significance of history within Hegel's philosophy. In his first major work Hegel emphasised that truth was not a static, timeless formula external to the process of achieving it. 'Everything depends on grasping and expressing the ultimate truth not as substance but as subject as well.'[9] The key concept in the truth that Hegel's system reveals is 'Spirit', and his philosophy construes all aspects of reality as forming a series of interrelated conditions for the self-awareness of Spirit. Spirit is the intersubjective world of meaning and freedom evident in the practical and theoretical activities of men. Men, according to Hegel, become increasingly self-conscious of their 'spiritual' status over time and this historical dimension in their recognition of their inherent freedom entails that Hegel's system has a philosophical understanding of history embedded within it.

As has been emphasised by Forbes and O'Brien, however, Hegel's philosophical understanding of history does not ignore the works of empirical historians in perceiving world history as the concrete realisation of and insight into the freedom integral to Spirit.[10] In the Introduction to his *Lectures on the Philosophy of History*, which traces the development of political and cultural freedom, Hegel distinguishes between 'original' history and various kinds of 'reflective' history and shows how philosophical history emerges out of the conceptual tensions disclosed in the practice of these historians. The original historian is limited to relating events with which he is immediately familiar, whereas reflective historians deal with events of an epoch other than their own, but in doing so are inexorably distanced from the attitudes and beliefs revealed in those events. In his discussion of the discord involved in reflective history, Hegel observes that 'Whatever [the age] we live in, we can [immerse ourselves] as fully as we like in the life of Ancient Greece – which is congenial to us in many respects – yet we shall never be able to sympathise in the most important issues of all.'[11]

This gulf between past and present ways of life and forms of thought is only overcome, for Hegel, by his own philosophical understanding of the connections linking the rational political achievements of the present with the past forms of life out of which they have emerged. Philosophy, in conceiving of the world as rational, unites all aspects of the world, past and present, to the achievement of reason. The philosophical understanding of world history developed by Hegel consists in the progressive development of political freedom, which his system discloses to be the achievement of the Northern European political communities of his contemporary world. The despotisms of the oriental world and even the beautiful, integrated world of the Greek *polis* were not based upon the freedom of the individuals who comprised those communities.

For Hegel, the crucial events in the emergence of the freedom characterising his contemporary world were the objective system of rational law established by the Roman state and the advent of Christianity and its emphasis upon the intrinsic value of the individual soul, which received its supreme expression in the Reformation. Hegel's philosophical appreciation of the significance of the progressive development of freedom in the political communities that have succeeded one another in world history underpins his interpretation of Plato's political theory. For Hegel, all of men's activities are related to the common character or 'Spirit' that informs the community, so that a philosophical understanding of politics will be directly related to the political community that forms the background for such an understanding. As Houlgate observes, Hegel's subtle linking of questions of truth, freedom and history to the development of distinct political cultures turns upon his plausible conception of the essentially mediated character of human activity and thought.[12] A philosophical articulation of the principles of political freedom is held to be necessarily linked to the emergence of the modern state. Hence, for Hegel, Plato's political philosophy cannot be an expression of political freedom as the traditional Greek *polis* was not organised to promote freedom. Indeed Hegel considers the breakdown of the Greek *polis* to have occurred in the late fifth century BC, due to the strain imposed by the novel assertion of individual rights and interests.

While Hegel's understanding of the progressive development of political and cultural freedom is contained in his *Lectures on the Philosophy of History*, his most detailed discussion of Plato's political theory lies within his *Lectures on the History of Philosophy*. In his Introduction to the latter, Hegel argues that to engage in the history of philosophy necessarily evokes philosophical questions concerning the relationship between past and present ways of thinking that are similar to those the philosopher raises in reviewing political history and the problems posed by the standpoint of reflective historians. Past philosophies are taken to express ways of viewing reality that are alien to contemporary modes of thought, and hence can be seen as external and essentially unrelated either to one another or to current achievements in philosophy.

Hegel's resolution of these philosophical questions consists of systematically relating these past philosophies to the present achievement of his own philosophy in discursively articulating the rationality of reality. Emphasising the relevance of past philosophies, Hegel observes that 'every philosophy has been and still is necessary. Their principles are retained; the most recent philosophy being the result of all preceding and hence no philosophy has ever been refuted.'[13] Hegel therefore argues that a work of philosophy derives its point and significance from the place it occupies in the philosophical tradition and that the overall meaning of this tradition has been revealed by the Hegelian system. Hegel's contextual reading of philosophy evidently links him to the relativistic philosophical perspectives of contemporary philosophers such as Rorty, Kuhn and Macintyre, but his claim to comprehend the truth of these contextually limited perspectives distances him from the limited claims of these current perspectives.[14]

Hegel holds, however, that his philosophical understanding of the history of philosophy does not force past philosophies into rigid, schematic patterns determined by the dictates of his own system. In his introductory remarks on the nature of the history of philosophy he notes, 'what can be said in this Introduction is not so much something that can be stated beforehand as what can be justified or proved in the treatment of the history'.[15] Just as Hegel's philosophical understanding of political and cultural development is predicated upon the research of original and reflective historians, so his history of philosophy is held to be based upon an empirical, textual study of the works of past philosophers. Indeed previous historians of philosophy are criticised for 'burdening philosophers with deductions and assertions which were neither made nor thought by them'.[16] It is for such a failure to achieve the requisite objectivity in interpreting past philosophies that Brucker and Tennemann are castigated, for they are held to have anachronistically attributed the premises and conclusions of Wölff and Kant respectively to past philosophies.[17]

Hegel's sensitivity to the dangers of importing present ideas into a distinct past testifies to his profound sense of history. As he observes, 'we are too apt to mould the ancient philosophers into our own forms of thought'.[18] But further introductory comments on the historical pattern of philosophical development suggest that this sense of history has overtones of an historicism that subverts contingency in that his concern to see his own system as the logical culmination of the progressive development of past cultures and philosophies leads him to view historical developments as following a necessary, unalterable pattern. Just as the modern state is seen as necessarily superseding earlier forms of political organisation, so what comes first in philosophy is taken as being necessarily the most abstract and shallow, while the most modern philosophy is the richest and deepest.[19]

HEGEL'S PLATO

Hegel's interpretation of Plato's political philosophy, as recorded in the *Republic*, is developed most comprehensively in his *Lectures on the History of Philosophy* and rests upon his location of Plato in the political and philosophical traditions of Ancient Greece. Plato's entire philosophical outlook is seen by Hegel as informed by the peculiar ethos of the traditional Greek *polis*. More specifically, he considers Plato's *Republic* to be reasserting in troubled times the authoritative claims of the traditional *polis* to wield effective power over the individual to ensure a settled ethical pattern of social life. As Pelczynski notes, 'the fundamental presupposition of the *Republic* and ancient Greek political thought generally [Hegel argues] was the absolute priority of the community over the individual'.[20] While Hegel sees the content of Plato's political philosophy as arising out of his reflection on the practice of Greek politics, he relates Plato's style of philosophising to his immediate philosophical predecessors. He understands Plato's practice of philosophy as emerging out of his rigorous cultivation of the Socratic commitment to scrutinise the bases of beliefs and attitudes. Hegel argues that Plato and Aristotle are crucial in the formal development of philosophy as they digested and systematically explored the implications of Socrates' realisation that truth resides in consciousness and reality is constituted by thought. For these reasons, Hegel declares, 'Plato and Aristotle above all others deserve to be called teachers of the human race'.[21]

   The crucial proposal in the *Republic*, which is seen by Plato as vital for the achievement of justice in the community, is the recommendation that philosophers should be entrusted with absolute power. The philosophical rulers are envisaged by Plato as governing in a novel and radical fashion. Education is to be rigidly supervised; art will be censored severely; the family, gender inequality and private property will be abolished for the ruling classes, whose breeding, additionally, will be subject to ruthless control. The novelty of these political arrangements is highlighted by the inclusion of an educational curriculum for the ruling class that includes mathematics and dialectic. Hegel, however, abstracts from the novel political expedients contained in the *Republic*'s quest for political perfection, to construe it as reasserting the traditional order of Greek political life. Hegel observes, 'When we thus study the content of the Platonic Idea, it will become clear that Plato has in fact represented Greek morality according to its substantial mode for it is the Greek state-life which constitutes the true content of the Platonic *Republic*.'[22]

Hegel's standpoint on the *Republic* as a principled restatement of a tradition of political life is advanced throughout the series of lecture courses he gave on politics at Heidelberg and Berlin. In the lectures on *Rechtsphilosophie* at Berlin in 1819–20, for instance, he observes that 'Plato has recognised the actual nature of his world.'[23] Hegel's interpretation of the *Republic* depends for its plausibility on the symmetry he establishes between the authoritarian power exerted over the individual by Plato's philosophical rulers and the traditional submersion of the individual in the ongoing life of the *polis*. For Hegel, the priority of the community over the individual was only challenged in Greek political life in the fifth century BC, in the generation immediately preceding Plato. This challenge is held to have taken the form of individuals putting their own interests before that of the community and subjecting the claims of the *polis* to their own conscience. Hegel maintains that it was Plato's abhorrence of these novel developments that led him to outline an aggressively authoritarian political community in the *Republic* that effectively prohibits all forms of individual freedom. 'But this moment, this movement of the individual, this principle of subjective freedom is sometimes ignored by Plato and sometimes even intentionally disparaged because it proved itself to what had wrought the ruin of Greece and he considers only how the State may best be organised and not subjective individuality.'[24]

It is therefore the need to counteract recent developments that Hegel sees as explaining the radical and novel aspects of the *Republic* such as the curtailment of family life and artistic expression.[25] Implicit in Hegel's argument is the recognition that Plato's *Republic* contains novel features, but for Hegel it is to be understood as a novel reformulation of a traditional political pattern of life, rather than as setting out a radical, innovative political doctrine. Hegel's understating of the novel elements in the *Republic* is echoed in subsequent Hegelianised accounts of Plato's political philosophy. Ware and Hardimon, for instance, in vindicating Hegel's standpoint on Plato, take the *Republic* as representative of the Greek political tradition insofar as it is seen as reflecting Plato's concern to revivify a moribund tradition.[26]

Hegel's interpretation of the *Republic* is undoubtedly perceptive in the manner it relates its argument to the historical context. Indeed Plato's theory of Forms, which conceives reality as conforming to a rational structure set apart from the activities of the knowing subject, mirrors the general dependence of the individual on the order and structure of the ancient *polis*.[27] There is also an abundance of evidence in the dialogues to show that Plato's political philosophy is a self-conscious reaction to the cynical pursuit of self-interest and the moral relativism that were being practised and advocated by Sophists in Plato's lifetime. Scholarly studies of Plato such as those by Irwin and Klosko emphasise the significance of this context.[28] Those monsters of Plato's literary imagination, Polus and Thrasymachus, incarnate the tendency for self-assertion to override community responsibility in the contemporary political atmosphere against which he was reacting.[29] But the purified political community recommended in the *Republic* is not seeking to restore the values of a fading political tradition; Plato is prescribing a novel political experiment.

By the criteria invoked in the *Republic*, the traditional *polis* does not represent a significant political achievement as it was not predicated upon the truths revealed by philosophical enquiry. Moreover it is fundamentally misleading to characterise the *Republic* as representing a reformation of a political tradition when its crucial proposal, the union of philosophical knowledge and political power, is entirely foreign to the Greek political experience. Annas, in her study of the *Republic*, points up the variety of ways in which Plato departs from prevailing ethical and political traditions in the course of his argument.[30] Plato's distinctive philosophical and political perspective allows him to condemn even the most respected representatives of the Athenian political tradition, Themistocles and Pericles. Even in Plato's later political dialogues, which Hegel does not consider, the *Statesman* and the *Laws*, where the Greek political tradition is explicitly drawn upon to support the project of theorising the conditions of admittedly imperfect remedies for the contemporary political predicament, Plato emphasises that an ideal solution would break with traditional practice. In the *Statesman* he argues that if a true statesman were to appear, he would dispense with laws and devote himself to eugenics and education, and in the *Laws*, in the brief vision of the ideal community he allows himself, he entertains the prospect of a thoroughgoing form of communism that has never been exemplified in practice.[31]

The originality of Plato's political vision is therefore dismissed by Hegel in his vision of the *Republic* as a restatement of the values of the Greek political tradition. Hegel's interpretation of Plato's political philosophy also suffers from its imputation to Plato of the settled systematic style of philosophising needed to frame his image of the *Republic* as a coherent, unambiguous reformulation of the traditional form of Greek political life. Hegel argues that Plato's dialogues can be made to yield a clear-cut set of doctrines despite Plato's frequent recourse to allegory and imagery and the enigmas presented by the dialogue form itself. Hegel's vision of 'Platonism' turns upon the theory of Forms, which is taken by Hegel to represent the unwavering achievement of conceiving reality as an interconnected pattern of ideas. In fact Hegel conceives Plato's philosophy as a system resembling his own in that the theory of ideas is held to articulate a set of abstract categories, which are then shown to provide the logical order exhibited by natural phenomena and the standards by which human affairs should be organised. For Hegel, the classical exposition of the theory of Forms is in the *Parmenides*, the underlying order of nature is revealed in the *Timaeus* and the supreme expression of the principles by which human affairs should be governed is contained in the *Republic*. In a sentence that unmistakably betrays his reading of Plato in the light of his own system, Hegel observes, 'If the *Parmenides* be taken along with the *Republic* and the *Timaeus*, the three together constitute the whole Platonic system of philosophy divided into three parts or sections – Logic, Mind and Nature.[32]

Hegel's characterisation of Plato as a systematic philosopher is an anachronistic importation of his own style of philosophising into a previous age. Plato's philosophy is not susceptible of formulation in neat, summary terms. Rather than being an unambiguous component of a system, each dialogue is an individual expression of a search for truth depicted frequently in irreducibly artistic images. Plato was motivated by a quest to discover a set of truths untainted by association with sense experience and undiminished by trading on presuppositions. The dialogues themselves, however, do not record a stabilised, final version of such truth. J. Glenn Gray has commented perceptively on Hegel's failure to allow for the artistic impulse evident in the dialogues: 'In his quarrel with tradition Hegel certainly went too far in separating

Platonic content from Platonic form. He could not realise that Plato was artist as well as philosopher.'[33]

While Hegel does not discuss the *Parmenides* and the *Timaeus* at any length, the contention that these dialogues are constituent elements of a fixed, philosophical system appear inherently problematic. In the opening part of the former dialogue, Parmenides taxes Socrates over the relationship obtaining between the Forms and their instances, and the dilemmas that are thereby posed are not resolved in the remainder of the dialogue. Again, at the beginning of the *Timaeus* the significance and status of what follows is deprecated.[34] In the *Republic* itself Plato emphasises that he cannot himself offer the certainty he takes to be the terminus of the philosophical quest for truth. While Plato declares that the idea of the Good is the ultimate source of being, value and knowledge, he confesses that he cannot give a theoretical account of it.[35] Plato's resort to imagery to convey the significance of the Good points up a paradox that runs throughout the *Republic*. While the *Republic* recommends dialectic as the means of achieving philosophical truth, analogy and imagery are the instruments that are actually used to advance the argument. As Robinson has observed on the middle dialogues as a whole, 'what the middle dialogues really rely upon in order to persuade us and apparently also to intuit the truth is analogy and imagery'.[36] Perhaps the insistent urgency with which Plato recommends the establishment of his philosophical state derives from its wholesale commitment to the study of philosophy, which offers the prospect of realising his quest for philosophical certainty.

CONCLUSION

Hegel's interpretation of Plato's political philosophy is not detachable from the organising principles of his own system. Hegel postulates the teleological goal of the historical process to be the absolute self-awareness of Spirit allegedly furnished by his own philosophy. Previous philosophies are held to be inexorably tied to the historic political communities in which they were developed and are viewed as constituting necessary, indispensable stages in the progressive development of truth. The interpretative perspective provided by this system ensures that the *Republic* is located in its historical context and that intelligent connections are made between Plato's philosophising and the cultural values of the traditional *polis*. Hegel argues plausibly that Plato's entire philosophical outlook reflects the emphasis on order and harmony rather than the individual freedom and self-expression that was characteristic of the ancient *polis*. The plausibility of this argument is underlined by Taylor in his influential work *Hegel*, in which he urges that there is a sociologically conditioned epistemological break between ancients and moderns on the question of the self. 'On this [ancient] view there is no notion of the self in the modern sense, that is of an identity which I can define for myself without reference to what surrounds me and the world in which I am set.'[37]

Hegel's historical perspective also alerts him to Plato's hostility to the novel, disruptive forces evident in his contemporary *polis*; he links the aggressively authoritarian character of the political community constructed in the *Republic* to Plato's revulsion for the contemporary trends of egoism and the cynical disregard of the public good. Ware's general reading of Hegel's conception of philosophy and its history is exemplified by Hegel's reading of Plato. Ware rightly emphasises the Hegelian recognition of the tendency for philosophical reflection to recognise fully the force of a tradition at the very time it is being superseded.[38]

Hegel's determination to view political and intellectual developments as tracing necessary historical patterns conforming to the principles inscribed in his own system, however, leads him to simplify and distort the complexity of the relationship between the *Republic* and the historical culture in which it is written. Plato's political philosophy is not an elegiac rehearsal of a moribund political tradition but the imaginative advocacy of a radical political experiment. Hegel implicitly admits that there are novel elements in the state outlined in the *Republic* but sees these novelties as expedients to revive a fading tradition in troubled times. The entire emphasis of the *Republic*, however, is upon the self-consciously original pursuit of perfection, political and philosophical, not on the restoration of a disintegrating political tradition.

Again, Hegel's interpretation of Plato's political philosophy suffers from its imputation to Plato of a style of philosophising that is held to prefigure his own systematic practice. Hegel does not acknowledge the frank recognition of philosophical paradox and puzzlement expressed in the dialogues and the irreducibly artistic expression of an unended quest for certainty. Strauss is surely commenting on the Hegelian understanding of Plato when he observes that 'the individual dialogue is not a chapter from an encyclopedia of the philosophical sciences or from a system of philosophy, or still less a relic from Plato's development.'[39] Criticism of Hegel's reading of Plato retains significance as the tendency to misrepresent Plato's thought by viewing it in Hegelian terms is not confined to Hegel himself. Indeed the distortion involved in such an approach can be seen more clearly in the following observation by Findlay: 'Platonism and Hegelianism are, in my view, the same philosophy with differences of emphasis and elaboration which make Hegelianism, all in all, its richer and more satisfactory expression.'[40] The subsequent influence of the Hegelian reading of Plato is also evident in Foster's comparative study of Plato and Hegel, which abstracts from the decidedly distinct characters of Plato's and Hegel's projects to appraise Hegel as superseding Plato to the extent that he accommodates a series of individual freedoms.[41] Other, more recent reviews of the relation between the political philosophies of Plato and Hegel likewise tend to assume an identity between their formal approaches to philosophising. [42]

Hegel's Plato, then, must be analysed cautiously and critically. Whereas Hegel's recognition that the *Republic* is intimately related to the cultural norms and practices of Ancient Greece is instructive, his assumption that Plato's political philosophy is a systematic reformation of preceding political patterns is highly questionable. Indeed its incongruity with the nature of the community recommended in the *Republic* suggests that the Hegelian system's assimilation of distinctive theoretical perspectives is only achieved by distorting them to trace patterns determined by the logic of its own organising principles. Plato's philosophy, in form and content, however, can only be construed as lacking freshness by abstracting from its innovative, paradoxical radicalism so that it subscribes to a preconceived vision of political philosophy as necessarily backward looking and descriptive. The externality of this Hegelian vision of Plato casts doubt on a prevalent, current reading of Hegel in which he is interpreted as framing an 'open' system, the dialectical patterns of which are seen as arising out of internal linkages between concepts and areas of experience rather than being dictated by a preconceived schematic model. The essays by Wartenberg and Forster in *The Cambridge Companion to Hegel* warn that non-metaphysical readings of Hegel tend to play down unduly the strong claims that Hegel makes about dialectical reasoning and the necessary structure of thought and being. [43] A considered review of Hegel's reading of Plato reinforces the point that Hegel's metaphysical claims induce him to misrecognise the distinctness of intellectual projects that are 'other' than his own.

4 Hobbes, Hegel and the Modern Self

INTRODUCTION

Hobbes and Hegel are political theorists whose general approaches to the philosophical understanding of political life are in significant ways distinct from one another. Peperzak and Siep have rightly emphasised the opposition between Hobbes's naturalism and Hegel's idealism.[1] The major texts by Hobbes and Hegel on political theory, *Leviathan* (1651) and the *Philosophy of Right* (1821), express divergent conceptions of philosophy and political association. Nonetheless Hobbes and Hegel are at one insofar as they recognise that the world of values and social interaction in which human beings can be at home is a world that depends crucially upon the inventive, constructive powers of human beings. They share an understanding of the world in which the self is seen as above all a self-defining subject and in which political authority derives from the capacities of human beings.

Although comparative studies on Hegel and Hobbes have not focused on the notion of the self, Buchwalter identifies Hobbes and Hegel as distinctively modern thinkers insofar as they employ constructive modes of reasoning. This common mode of reasoning informs the self-defining conception of the self that is central to the thought of Hobbes and Hegel and distinctive of modernity.[2] The argument of this chapter highlights this affinity between Hobbes and Hegel, while recognising divergencies between their conceptions of the self. The self, for Hegel in contrast to Hobbes, will be shown to be self-developing as well as self-defining. Hobbes's self is essentially particular, pursuing an individual felicity, whereas for Hegel the self is inherently universal and expresses its capacities by developing ties with other selves.

Ancient and medieval metaphysics located man in a meaningful cosmic order, where objective values and obligations set limits to man's inventiveness. Hobbes and Hegel, however, see the values, rights and obligations that define man's ethical world as being established and defined by man himself. This locus for ethical and political values in man's creative powers is a distinctively 'modern' view of the self, in that the crucial problems and possibilities for politics are related to the self-defining character of the self.[3] While the psyche, for Plato, derives its values and political orientation from an objective world of forms and, for Aristotle, is linked teleologically to the *polis*; the self, for both Hobbes and Hegel, is involved in the radical task of forging for itself a world of values.

The 'modern' self-defining view of the self shared by Hobbes and Hegel, however, is not entertained by all modern theorists. Modern thinkers such as Locke, Paine, Wollstonecraft and Burke understand the individual as tied to sets of values that are not forged and defined by man himself, even if man is necessarily implicated in their translation into practice.[4] Locke, Paine and Wollstonecraft are all distinctively modern thinkers. The conceptual language of their political theories includes modern notions such as individual rights, natural reason and representation of the people. Democratic theory, rights and freedom are all distinctively 'modern', but none of these theorists defends the rights of the individual and the people solely in terms of their derivation from and authorisation by man's creative powers. Rather they look to an objective normative order of reason, natural law and natural right, just as Burke in reacting against these views, defends the old order by invoking providence and natural development.

Whereas these other modern theorists see human beings as interpreting but not creating a natural order, Hobbes and Hegel clearly specify that all obligations, rights and values flow from man's creative powers. While they are not the only modern theorists to do so, Hobbes and Hegel, at the threshold of the modern era, provide clear but distinct accounts of social and political life framed upon a conception of human self-creating powers. Hegel saw both Hobbes and himself in this light; he recognised their common self-conscious employment of modern notions of human creativity.[5]

Hobbes and Hegel, then, subscribe to a version of the modern self and its powers, in which a self-defining self authenticates other paradigmatically modern features of social and political life, such as individual rights and political representation. They differ, though, in the way they perceive man's self-defining powers as operating. For Hobbes, an individual person's desires and choices cannot be evaluated or judged by anyone else, and there can be no sense of self-development. The body politic, and its obligations and rights, enables man to follow the purposes he has defined for himself, but neither adds to nor alters the meaning of those purposes. For Hegel, on the other hand, the individual is capable of self-development as well as self-definition, and the political world is seen as a development of the self and as a construction that widens the perspective of the self. This distinction between Hegel and Hobbes can be understood in the terms offered for a general comparison of the two thinkers by Taminiaux in his essay 'Hobbes et Hegel', whereby Hegel is seen as building upon Hobbes's work but correcting his empiricist standpoint by adopting a speculative philosophical perspective.[6] Hence Hegel's developmental view of the self can be seen as speculative in the way its conception of the self is irreducible to the empirically observable. Rather, a self is seen as inexorably inhabiting a world of cultural meaning so that it must be understood 'speculatively', whereby the integral connections between the self and a wider world of meaning are understood.

Thus this focus on Hobbes and Hegel points up what is central to their common notion of a self-defining subject as a 'modern' self, and what is different in their two versions. This focus also illustrates what Taylor, in his *Sources of the Self – The Making of the Modern Identity*, has referred to as the 'full complexity and richness of the modern identity'.[7] Taylor highlights what the present chapter brings out in a concentrated fashion, namely the diversity and richness of the 'modern' identity, which renders the task of either going beyond or repudiating modernity a more demanding one than is presumed in many postmodernist essays.[8]

HOBBES AND MODERNITY – REASON, SELF AND ARTIFICE

In *Leviathan* Hobbes repudiates the Aristotelian notion that the natural and human worlds display an inherent, essential, rational purposiveness, which can be objectively and unconditionally grasped by the exercise of human reason.[9] Reason – that is, philosophical method – is seen by Hobbes not as a teleological realisation of virtue, but as a procedural technique deployed to comprehend a mechanistic world composed of bodies in motion. As Malcolm has observed, Hobbes decisively rejects the notion of reason 'intuiting natural teleological values'.[10]

The self in Hobbes's conception of reason is initially conceived of materialistically as but a body whose behaviour is explained by internal movements generated by the motion of the external bodies with which it is in contact. For Hobbes the explanation of human action turns fundamentally upon the passions generated within a particular self by its contact with external bodies. While reason can calculate the consequences of social interaction undertaken by individuals engaged in securing their ever-changing desires and suggest procedural rules for ameliorating the insecurity of an apolitical situation, it does not disturb the mechanistic and individualistic picture of human behaviour. This Hobbesian conception of the self is compatible with the later celebration of human artifice as a necessarily cooperative but not communal project. Hobbes's initial conceptualisation of human beings as natural, particular individuals materially distinct from one another, and necessarily pursuing individual, private objectives, underpins his recognition of the possibilities of discord and the problems of establishing security.[11]

Smith observes in *Hegel's Critique of Liberalism* that Hobbes's notion of the self, in contrast to Hegel's, does not allow for an evaluative discrimination of the self and its motivations. Whatever the self desires is to be accepted, the self is not to be judged by its activities.[12] Reason, for Hobbes, derives it's political point from the imperative of self-preservation, hence its recommendations are instrumental to providing a secure framework for self-motivated behaviour. An on-going concern on the part of individuals for the nature and operation of the rules and laws of a political association and subsidiary social practices, is not seen by Hobbes as being more commendable than any other individual concern. Indeed, insofar as popular involvement in political affairs might generate discord in policymaking, Hobbes precludes subjects from exercising sovereign power.[13] Hobbes did not envisage human beings as collectively maintaining a moral community. Individual selves, for Hobbes, lack a coordinating moral purpose or even what Goldie terms the 'acquired, habituated, and experiential moral knowledge which society historically accumulates which becomes "second nature"'.[14]

Hobbes, in explaining the rationale of a political commonwealth in *Leviathan* thus begins with a study of the bodies of which it is composed, which are also seen as its artificers. Hobbes sketches a picture of man as matter in motion, in which individual selves seek to satisfy their discrete desires occasioned by contact with external bodies. Rather than men naturally aggregating into communities to pursue a common good, as Aristotle maintained, good and bad are seen as correlative to the distinctive and separate desires of men.[15] Men, as depicted in a natural state, are seen as pursuing the power to ensure continual success in achieving their desires, which in turn leads to conflict and competition between men. This predicament constituted by a continual disposition for war in the absence of the state is seen by Hobbes as native to the internal momentum of a natural 'self'. Hobbes's depiction of this predicament invokes the independence of human judgement: conscience, the supposed inner voice of the self, is categorised by Hobbes as contentious private opinion.[16] The moral judgement of the self, then, is not to be related to an external normative order.

In this state of nature imagined by Hobbes, contracts regulating property and the family and organised civil activities such as the arts and industry are unviable, given the insecurity involved in the generalised 'natural' right of every self to use its own power to do whatever is necessary to preserve its life. If the problematic of the state of nature is generated by the momentum of the natural self, the resolution is a product of the procedural reason of the same self reflecting upon the generalised insecurity of the state of nature.[17] The natural self is moved to seek peace by making a special contract with fellow selves whereby natural rights are transferred to a sovereign power external to the mutual covenant between them, who thereby has the power to enforce civil peace. The dictates of reason motivating the procedures to ensure civil peace, Hobbes terms laws of nature.

While men even in the state of nature are envisaged as motivated to follow the laws of nature, which are prudential dictates suggesting ways of preserving one's life through the establishment of peace, they are only conceived as binding obligations in conditions of settled political life where it is safe to forego one's natural right to all things. Hobbes observes that the laws of nature can be seen as emanating from God in his capacity as the first cause of all motions in the world. This characterisation of the laws of nature, together with an idiosyncratic interpretation of scripture in the latter parts of *Leviathan*, which result in doctrinal authority and Church organisation being assigned to the sovereign, has led State, in a recent work of careful scholarship, to locate Hobbes within a long-standing tradition of theistic natural law.[18] While Hobbes may thereby be located plausibly within a natural law tradition, he nonetheless occupies a distinct place within this diverse, developing tradition. What must not be obscured is Hobbes's originality and modernity in framing and developing an account of the state from the natural propensities and procedural reasoning of a human self, characterised without reference to a suprahuman defining normative order of reason. Hobbes can indeed be placed in many different contexts (as can any thinker) without conflicts necessarily arising between them; Hobbes's work touches upon many different intellectual currents, and highlighting a location within one context depends upon what question is being asked about Hobbes's thought and drawing out the significance of the answer gained. The point of this chapter is to bring out the modernity of the conception of the self entertained in the *Leviathan*. The self, as artificer, creates a settled political association. The voluntary formation of the commonwealth is seen by Hobbes as the necessary means by which individual selves can execute for themselves peaceful, settled conditions. The purpose of the commonwealth is precisely to create settled public and private spaces in which self-defining selves can operate freely. This is the only purpose of the state; there is no other common good, and there is no *common* will in Hobbes.

Hobbes's conception of artifice redeems the chaos, delivers man by his own makings from the parlous natural condition of mankind. It is the response to and resolution of the predicament posed by the state of nature. As Flathman notes:

> Because artifacts such as words, conceptions, and theories (as well as actual products like the State) make rather than present or represent 'things', for Hobbes they themselves cannot be fabrications in the sense of lies or deceits (albeit he was intensely aware that language enables lying and that lies are often told and deceptions frequently perpetrated concerning artifacts). For the same reason...for those who oppose this Hobbesian view they will be fabrications in the pejorative sense and will never be without a taint of falsification.[19]

Thus Hobbes's self is a unified, autonomous self, which is a natural self in the Oakeshottian sense of arising from the (non-depraved) nature of man, and a creative self in that the state is made purely by its artifice.

HEGEL AND MODERNITY – REASON AND SELF-DEVELOPMENT

Hegel, in a clear contrast to Hobbes's radical individualism and materialism, embraced absolute idealism and emphasised the significance of 'community' in political life. For Hegel, what is ultimately real is thought, and more specifically, reason, which understands thought itself. Bodies, of course, exist for Hegel. Indeed Hegel contrives to establish their philosophical necessity, but awareness of bodies is taken as invoking the thinking and rational activity of human agents who, as Findlay and Wartenberg observe, are thereby assigned a higher teleological status.[20] For Hegel, unlike Hobbes, the universals of thought are the prime constituents of human identity and an individual human being if he or she is to achieve self-recognition must see him/herself as a universal being. Hegel's conception of thought as constitutive of human identity underpins the political theorising undertaken in the *Philosophy of Right*. The rationality of the political community delineated in the *Philosophy of Right* resides in the recognition on the part of its citizens of the ethical ties linking them together and in the universal public authority of the community's laws.[21]

For Hegel, then, the self doesn't simply define itself and construct a state. Rather the self itself develops and a rational development is one in which the self recognises and expresses itself in a political world that reflects its rational, universal character. An index of the differences between Hegel and Hobbes on the self and its development are the different stories they tell in their mythical pictures of the primordial struggle between human beings that lies beneath the surface of civilised behaviour. Hobbes's state of nature is a stripped-down version of the human condition in which all individuals, without the security of a civil association in which a sovereign can ensure civil peace, pursue their own ends and in so doing promote a general insecurity by each aiming for power over others. The basic psychology of self-interest evident in this scenario does not change in the light of the achievement of a civil commonwealth; the law and the authority of the sovereign guard against catastrophe but individuals still seek their own ends without reference to any shared perspective with others.

Hegel, in contrast, in the *Phenomenology of Spirit* sets out the process of a dialectical struggle for recognition between individuals as part of the story whereby consciousness can be seen as realising the truth of its own processes of conscious awareness. In tracing the story of how consciousness comes to understand the processes of its own activities, Hegel highlights the significance of how the self of self-consciousness recognises its own status. Hegel sees this process of recognition as necessarily social, and as part of this process he identifies a life and death struggle between individuals. This struggle is not conducted by strictly independent selves. The energy of the struggle, for Hegel, testifies to a relationship where each is seeking recognition from the other, and it thereby betokens a development of the self that is not envisaged by Hobbes. In Hegel's account of the dialectic of recognition, one self will submit to another self but the resulting master – slave relationship is unsatisfactory because the freedom and subjectivity of consciousness is not truly recognised. The story is not in fact complete until the end of the *Phenomenology of Spirit*, where selves mutually recognise one another in their actions, within the setting of a spiritual religious community.[22]

Throughout Hegel's writings the self is seen developmentally so that individuals are not recognised as coherent and integrated until they recognise their freedom and generic nature by cooperating with and respecting one another as free agents. For Hegel, the self doesn't simply define itself and act to achieve individual ends, it develops and a rational development is one in which the self recognises and expresses itself in a political world that reflects its rational, universal character. The development of the self for Hegel is a process that must be understood synchronically and diachronically; it is one that is implicit in social practices and takes place over time. History, for Hegel, is a story of progress in which freedom has been achieved progressively; slavery and despotism are signs of an immaturity and unfreedom that is superseded in the modern world, where the culture expresses the value of freedom and individuality and the state can be seen as uniting all citizens in a common recognition of freedom.[23] While Hegel sees history as a story of progress, he acknowledges it to be painful and disturbing. History gives the appearance of being irrational and affords a spectacle of human misery that can only be redeemed by philosophical insight into the unintended results of human activities.[24]

The historical development of the self is disturbing, but Hegel also recognises that the 'rational' world of the modern state in which the self can realise freedom is by no means unproblematic. At the outset of the *Philosophy of Right*, Hegel takes the self as an inherently free, self-determining being that determines its actions by the universals of thought. This identification of the self is sufficient to establish the rights of individuals to life, liberty and property. These rights, however, are considered abstract insofar as they cannot be upheld in isolation from a network of social practices and institutions and ultimately the sustaining authority of the state. The abstractness and fragility of a self conceived in isolation from a supportive social context is highlighted by Hegel's recognition that an appeal to an individual's conscience to be the arbiter of right and wrong involves similar tensions and destructive possibilities as those observed by Hobbes.[25] A social setting, an intersubjective ethical framework sustained by the norms and laws of a political community, is seen by Hegel as furnishing the supportive context in which an individual can express and register the universal character of freedom.[26] In the *Philosophy of Right* Hegel sees the relationship between individual and public aspects of freedom as being complex, however, in that the 'modern' self-defining individual is taken as requiring a social and economic context in which he can pursue specific interests, as well as recognising common ties with other human beings.

In his account of civil society, which Hegel takes as being a distinctive feature of the modern world, the vigorous pursuit of particular, individual interests is seen as constitutive of a variety of social and economic relations. This focus on the pursuit of individual interest is seen by Hegel as an essential component of the 'modern' identity of the self as a free being that determines the shape of its own life. Hegel recognises, however, that the concentrated pursuit of individual interest generates tensions in and between selves. As a consequence society becomes fragmented and those incapable through poverty of satisfying their particular interests tend to act like a rabble in that their poverty in juxtaposition to the wealth of others inspires hopelessness, resentment and alienation.[27]

The problems of the modern world associated with the vigorous pursuit of self-interest are not to be seen as being definitively resolved in Hegel's thought. Nonetheless the *Philosophy of Right* envisages that the individualistic perspective of civil society is superseded, if not abrogated, by selves who recognise ethical ties with fellow citizens by respecting laws and political institutions regulating the practices of civil society. Civil society itself, for Hegel, is fundamentally a social world in which the interdependence of individuals is affirmed in market transactions. But a full practical recognition of the universal character of the self is envisaged by Hegel as only being achieved in a general, conscientious adherence to the laws enacted by a well-structured state. The self that is aware of its freedom and universality by seeing itself as a member of an ethical political community is a self that not only defines itself, but also develops a public, social perspective.

This development of the self envisaged by Hegel distinguishes his political thought from that of Hobbes. In his *Lectures on the History of Philosophy*, Hegel respects Hobbes's derivation of political authority from the character of the human self and appreciates his recognition of the dependence of individual activities upon a political regime, artificially constructed by men.[28] But Hegel deprecates Hobbes's identification of the construction of the state with the common fear of human selves concerning the likelihood of death. Hegel remarks, 'Thus their (Hobbesian men) similarity is not derived from their greatest strength; it is not as in modern times founded on the freedom of the spirit or on an equality of merit and independence'.[29] For Hegel it is insufficient for a political association to allow men freely to define and undertake their objectives. Rather Hegel maintains that a rationally ordered state must allow selves to recognise and identify with an intersubjective framework of norms and practices.

HOBBES, HEGEL AND MODERNITY

Hobbes's and Hegel's shared concern with describing the self as a self-defining subject, a self-generating subject unlimited by a given moral order, is recognised in the proliferation of recent academic commentaries that see their political theories as 'modern' political projects.[30] This standpoint on Hobbes and Hegel is given additional support by Hobbes' understanding of himself as a theorist breaking new ground and Hegel's self-conscious recognition of himself as a theorist of the modern state.[31]

Hobbes's and Hegel's depiction of the self and its relations to political order have been picked out in various studies of Hobbes and Hegel as exemplifying key elements in their 'modern' identity as political theorists. Kraynak for instance, in his book *History and Modernity in the Thought of Thomas Hobbes*, suggests that 'This notion of autonomous or self-reliant thinking is the basis of Hobbes's project for scientific Enlightenment. It enables him to construct a new edifice of science . . . and a political science of absolute sovereignty.'[32] Tuck, in his book *Hobbes*, sees Hobbes as developing his thought in relation to modern scepticism about the self and its relation to the natural and social worlds.[33] And it is the theme of Goldie's paper, 'The Reception of Hobbes', that Hobbes was certainly taken by his (intellectual) contemporaries as outlining a theory of the self-defining subject that was radical and outrageous, in shedding the theological premises of all and every area of intellectual life, premises that 'remained highly visible in the political theory of Hobbes's contemporaries'.[34] Flathman, in a book on Hobbes in a series devoted to modernity and political thought, also places significance upon the role of the self-defining subject in Hobbes's theory, invoking the language of 'making' and 'artifice'. 'Placed by God in a universe that is largely devoid of meaning', Flathman observes Hobbes as recognising 'the kind of artificing that matters most is the making of individual selves and their lives.'[35] And Flathman, in emphasising the modern self-defining character of the Hobbesian self, deprecates 'The commentators who argue that Hobbes thinks we are or should be made by something other than ourselves, by God, Nature, Reason, Our Community, and so forth.'[36]

For Flathman, 'the primary unit of Hobbes's thinking is the individual person and her makings, unmakings and remakings of herself and her worlds, the primary objective of his political and moral thinking is to promote and protect each person's pursuit of her own felicity as she herself sees it'.[37] Oakeshott also explicitly aligns Hobbes's theory of the self (absolute will and voluntary artifice are the terms he uses) to modernity. It is precisely this part of Hobbes, he says, 'that allied him to the future' and shows a clear 'breakaway from the great Rational–Natural tradition ... which ... found embodiment in the Natural Law theory'.[38]

Likewise Brod, in his influential study *Hegel's Philosophy of Politics – Idealism, Identity and Modernity*, observes the significance of Hegel's recognition of a new conception of the self and its relation to politics in the modern era. He notes that 'The key factor in Hegel's analysis of history is his claim that the modern era has come to be essentially characterised by the emergence of a new form of rational universalist consciousness, which finds expression in the *Philosophy of Right* and the modern attempt to found political institutions on the self-consciousness of the members of those systems.'[39] Again, in his introductory but insightful work on Hegel, *Freedom, Truth and History*, Houlgate sets out to trace the systematic connections which Hegel establishes in trying 'to develop the true conception of the freedom and self-determination to which modern consciousness now lays claim'.[40]

Hegel and Hobbes, then, are both seen by recent commentators as theorists of modernity and the 'modern' character of their thought is traced most notably to the self-defining nature of the selves entertained in their social and political theories. Both thinkers incorporate within their social and political thought key features of modern political life such as a recognition of individuality as a significant element in human interaction and the linking of sovereignty to the powers and opinions of subjects. Their distinct versions of individualism and popular sovereignty are predicated upon a common understanding of the source of political authority and values as residing in the powers of construction and artifice possessed by human beings. This affinity in their thought entails that the differences between them should not be exclusively emphasised, as is the case in the comparative studies of their thought conducted by Peperzak and Siep.[41] Hegel himself picked out this aspect of Hobbes's thought as being crucial in characterising his status as a 'modern' thinker. In his *Lectures on the History of Philosophy* Hegel remarks 'Before this [that is Hobbes] ideals were set before us or Holy Scripture, or positive law was quoted as author-itative. Hobbes, on the contrary, sought to derive the bond which holds the state together, as that which gives the state its power, from princi-ples which he sees within us, which we recognise as our own.'[42]

The self-defining character of human beings exhibited in Hobbes's and Hegel's political thought distinguishes their standpoints from pre-modern thinkers such as Plato and Aquinas who invoke supra-human standards and values to condition the range of human inventiveness. Again, their common derivation of moral and political values from human powers and actions distinguishes them from other modern thinkers such as Locke and Paine who see political life in terms of its linkage to a pattern of natural law ultimately determined by a God distinct from the world of human artifice.[43] While Hobbes and Hegel are therefore united as theorists in at least one crucial respect, they are separated by the distinct ways in which they conceive of man's self-defining powers. For Hobbes, the powers and attributes of human beings are to be known by an effort of introspection combined with rational deduction as the nature of man does not change in the course of history. Man in Hobbes's calculation has a fixed nature and hence the nature of the self and politics can be determined definitively by a perspicuous effort of thought. Political authority is demanded by the insecure character of human interaction in a 'natural' world where individuals are the sole arbiters of right and wrong, and the traumas of a state of nature are an ever-present possibility if the lines of political authority should be snapped. For Hegel, in contrast, the human self is not fixed; man's nature is not to be defined outside of an historical perspective. Men, according to Hegel, develop over time and, crucially, in terms of their social interaction with others. Indeed the significance of politics for Hegel resides ultimately in its capacity to furnish a setting in which individuals can develop a social/public per-spective whereby they can recognise and express their generic identity as inherently universal creatures. Whereas both Hobbes and Hegel see man as self-defining, Hegel is distinguished from Hobbes by the self-developing character he imputes to human beings.

POSTMODERN AND MODERN SELVES

While Hobbes and Hegel differ in the way they depict the self-defining nature of man, they are at one in seeing this nature of man as supplying an overall perspective or framework for considering social and political life. Lyotard, in his book *The Postmodern Condition: A Report on Knowledge*, however, articulates a radical scepticism about such universal claims, which is symptomatic of much recent thought. He takes it to be a consequence of developments in the allegedly postmodern age, such as the increasing complexity and mobility evident in communication networks that a metanarrative – that is, a philosophical system – purporting to provide an overall, summative and objective account of human activities is rendered redundant. He observes, 'A self does not amount to much, but no self is an island; each exists in a fabric of relations that is now more complex and mobile than ever before. Young or old, man or woman, rich or poor, a person is always located at "nodal points" of specific communication circuits, however tiny these may be.'[44] These distinctive circuits or language games are local and heterogeneous. He specifically dismisses the Hegelian enterprise in remarking 'that only the transcendental illusion (that of Hegel) can hope to totalise them [language games] into a real unity'.[45]

Rorty, in his essays in *Contingency, Irony and Solidarity*, maintains a standpoint related to Lyotard's, in seeing the present situation as novel in the contemporary philosophical disposition to part company from classic Enlightenment notions that truth is to be 'discovered'. For Rorty there is no 'outside' to the contours of language; language provides the content in which selves and political orders are continually being invented. Language develops through new metaphors that gradually become literal in their usage as their place in a language game becomes familiar. The evolving language games develop contingently, for Rorty, and are not to be understood teleologically as progressively approximating 'truth'.[46] In his essay 'The Contingency of Language', Rorty remarks that 'The line of thought common to Blumenberg, Nietzsche, Freud and Davidson suggests that we try to get to the point where we no longer worship anything, where we treat nothing as quasi divinity, where we treat everything – our language, our conscience, our community – as a product of time and chance'.[47] In the essay entitled 'The Contingency of a Liberal Community', Rorty urges that the values of a liberal political culture, to which he is committed, are best served by abandoning aspirations to universalism and the attempt to provide philosophical foundations. In contrast he urges narrative redescriptions of current institutions and practices that do not affect to adopt a position outside of a contingent language.[48]

Lyotard's and Rorty's strictures against metanarratives purporting to provide universal foundations for the self, politics and society, reflect back interestingly on the projects on which Hobbes and Hegel were engaged. Hobbes's and Hegel's political theories aim to establish philosophical foundations for a systematic diagnosis of the political condition that is taken as admitting a resolution that can be justified on rational grounds. The distinctiveness of their respective positions, however, should serve as a reminder that the 'modern' standpoints deprecated by Lyotard and Rorty are not all of a piece. Indeed the political theories of Hobbes and Hegel can be seen as incorporating in distinct ways a recognition of the diversity and dispersal of identity in the social world that is symptomatic of much postmodern thought.

The relevance of Hobbes's political thought to postmodern preoccupations is highlighted by Gray and O'Sullivan.[49] O'Sullivan neatly brings out the postmodern sense of Hobbes's political theory by fixing on the significance of difference in Hobbes's diagnosis of the interaction of self-defining selves in a state of nature: 'his [Hobbes's] state of nature is, in effect, a "deconstructed" condition, in which no individual or perspective is privileged, and all differences are validated.'[50] The Hobbesian state of nature can be seen as a graphic metaphor for a postmodern account of the human condition in which there are no defining and objective ties between selves and the self itself is only a contingent site for the pursuit of evanescent objectives. The self, after all, 'does not amount to much'.[51] For Lyotard and Rorty the dispersal of identity characteristic of a postmodern age takes place within the context of distinct language games or practices. This emphasis upon social context, however, does not in itself generate a solution to the Hobbesian nightmare of a collision between separate, distinct values where there exists no overreaching authority or power to determine political allegiance. The attractiveness of a Hobbesian and authoritarian solution to the problems arising out of their dispersal of identity in a world that admits of no overreaching system of values has been identified by O'Sullivan.[52] Indeed Giddens, in his book *Modernity and Self-Identity*, signals how aspects of the late modern world compound the problems of the human condition identified by Hobbes. The late modern world, for Giddens, sees the self as enmeshed in a range of distinct, abstract, self-referential systems that distance the self from any merely local and natural roots.[53] These self-referential systems, testimony to the power of globalising forces, collectively generate a high risk culture in which the Hobbesian nightmare of a state of nature is replaced by the prospect of diverse routes to global destruction. Given this bleak prospect, the Hobbesian manoeuvre of avoiding the prospect of war engendered by the collision of distinct, separately defined values and objectives by accepting a common political authority to achieve the rationally agreed minimum of peace and stability remains relevant.

The attractiveness of Hobbes's solution to the political predicament arises out of its profound recognition of diversity and the 'subjectivity' of values. The 'metanarrative' of a concomitant, generalised, universal insecurity that generates an artifical solution to this predicament is interesting and relevant to postmodern thought in that this general recognition of insecurity does not override the radicalism of the subjectivism Hobbes sees as necessarily part of the self-defining human condition. The very attractiveness and relevance of Hobbes's political thought for the late modern or postmodern world should, however, give cause for concern. Hobbes's solution to the diversity he saw as intrinsic to the human condition is notoriously problematic. The sovereign is necessarily distinct from the selves over whom (s)he rules. There are no qualifications to the unbridled use of power save an ultimate right of self-defence, and the self over whom rule is exercised does not develop sustaining and defining ties with other members of the political community.

Hegel, in contrast to Hobbes, sees the development of a rational political community as enabling the self to recognise a community of purpose and identity with others, hence ensuring that more than peace and stability are secured. Human beings in the Hegelian metanarrative of politics see themselves as characters in a story of human progress and self-development. This characterisation of Hegel's political theory seems to confirm its adherence to a notion of truth and universality that is fundamentally at odds with the sceptical perspectives of Lyotard and Rorty. But the postmodern reading of historical development in which modern, rational, holistic and totalising perspectives give way to a contemporary recognition of fragmentation, partiality and irreducible conflict is indeed a partial perspective. Dallmayr, in *G. W. F. Hegel: Modernity and Politics*, observes that what is omitted in such a perspective is a recognition of the complexity of Hegel's thought. He notes 'Hegel's role as both instigator *and* critic of the discourse of modernity'.[54] The general unity of reason established in Hegel's philosophy, like the sense of community generated in his state, does not replace the dissonance and fragmentation he identifies in the modern world. Hegel predicates his conception of the political community on the self-defining powers of the self, and he sees this essentially 'modern' self as developing its individuality and pursuing particular, local aims that threaten to undermine the bases of political and cultural unity. Dallmayr remarks, 'In mounting their various attacks, critics frequently can be shown to move along paths that Hegel had sketched out long ago. Thus, to take the case of post-structuralism, the emphasis on differentiation and local particularity is precisely the point that Hegel actually had directed against the abstractness of Enlightenment thought (including its Kantian variant)'.[55]

Hegel incorporates diversity and particularism into his conception of reason and community. The self for Hegel, unlike Hobbes, is a developing self that has developed a sense of individuality and particularity by participating in the complex and differentiated modes of market activities in the modern world. Hegel, however, traces the presence of a countervailing unity amidst the particularism and fragmentation of the modern world. The self for Hegel is self-developing and self-defining; its development and definition invoke a social context of interaction. This context of social interaction serves as a mirror to reflect the disparities amidst individual aims and values, but also points up common ties linking together individuals.

Hegel sees the political community as expressing shared public values and laws holding together individuals. He envisages individuals developing a sense of respect for these values and hence for one another. Without such a developing sense of community in public life, there would be alienation and rootlessness. The dangers of alienation and rootlessness are aspects of the modern identity that have not been superseded by the achievement of a 'postmodern' identity. They signal the continuing relevance of an Hegelian metanarrative that looks to the political arena to develop a complex sense of unity in order to mitigate the potential isolation of a self-defining self.

CONCLUSION

The modern world is a complex one that contains many patterns of thought. One influential pattern of thought that, as Habermas notes in *The Philosophical Discourse of Modernity*, is characteristically modern, is that that sees the self as a self-defining subject.[56] To see the self as a self-defining subject, however, is not to define the self exhaustively. The self-defining selves of Hobbes and Hegel are radically distinct. The distinctness of these selves highlights the differences within and between 'modern' conceptions of the world that are played down in postmodern critiques of modernity.

Hobbes and Hegel are not to be swept aside. They offer theoretical perspectives that are relevant to contemporary theoretical paradigms.

Hobbes's sceptical cast of mind, envisaging a fragmentary world composed of selves recognising no common or universal values, expresses a possible destination for the contemporary turn against unity and universalism. The global spread of technology and weaponry adds extra urgency to the need to avoid a breakdown of social and political order. Hegel's dual recognition of a 'modern' self susceptible to the alienation and rootlessness of fragmentary, conflictual modes of social interaction gives point and credence to the achievement of social and political unity. The metanarratives of both Hobbes and Hegel are not to be easily dismissed, for the problems to which they were conditional responses are still part of our self-constituted identities.

5 Stirner's Critique of Hegel: *Geist* and the Egoistic Exorcist

Stirner's thought is recognisably Hegelian while at the same time constituting a determined assault on the principles of Hegel's system. His thought represents what Toews has styled 'the transformative translation of Hegelian terms'.[1] The radicalism of Stirner's critique of Hegel's standpoint, coupled with his creative development of Hegelian notions of alienation, historical and social forms of conflict and the intrinsic freedom of the human ego, provide an ironically unique insight into the bases of Hegelian thought. The irony referred to above derives from Stirner's celebration of the unique, flesh and blood individual, which he contrasts with what he sees as Hegel's false perspective in which, for Stirner, the human ego is emasculated by being taken as meaningful solely in terms of its involvement in general patterns of thought. Stirner is trenchant in his critique of spiritual notions, which he sees as so many forms of alienation that restrict the creative powers of the human ego.

Hegel's philosophy conceives of reality as testifying to the unificatory, universal powers of *Geist* or spirit. A person, for Hegel, is alienated to the extent that he perceives himself to be set apart from the rest of reality, be it nature or other men and women. The spiritual capacity to think and act rationally, for Hegel, links men with other men and the world they inhabit and expresses the generic identity of human beings. For Stirner, the concrete individual ego is everything, and concern for what is generically human is a fetter, or what he terms a spook or ghost. Hegel's system is, for Stirner, a ghost that needs to be exorcised. Stirner begins *The Ego and Its Own* with a pithy statement of his position, which pointedly criticises Hegel:

> What is not supposed to be my concern! First and foremost the good cause, then God's cause, the cause of mankind, of truth, of freedom, of humanity, of justice; further, the cause of my people, my prince, my fatherland; finally, even the cause of mind (Geist) and a thousand other causes. Only my cause is never to be my concern. 'Shame on the egoist who thinks only of himself!'[2]

Stirner's opposition to Hegel is clear and its forceful expression challenges the reader to reflect upon the relative merits of Stirner's and
Hegel's philosophical positions. The trenchancy of Stirner's critique of
Hegel, however, should not obscure the extent to which Stirner's work
discloses an understanding of Hegel's philosophy. Stirner, in subjecting
Hegel's philosophy to criticism, maintains that Hegel's thought, insofar
as it privileges ideas and the common attributes of human beings,
resembles religion in that it derogates from the autonomy and creativity of the unique ego. This critique of Hegel, however, assumes that
Hegel's philosophy is not a mere reiteration of religion. Stirner does
not read Hegel's philosophy as maintaining that an independent God
is the prime mover in reality and the cause of historical and social
development. In an essay of 1842, 'Art and Religion', Stirner makes
clear that he does not see Hegel as a religious theorist in this sense by
observing, 'Who will deny that Philip II of Spain is infinitely more
godly than Joseph II of Germany, and that Hengstenberg [a Lutheran
pietist critic of Hegel and the Young Hegelians] is truly godly, whereas
Hegel is quite not.'[3]

   This chapter will explore positive links between Stirner and Hegel
and Hegelianism, and assess Stirner's polemical critique of Hegel and
affiliated Hegelian standpoints. In so doing the relevance of Hegel and
the Hegelian tradition for Stirner's thought will be demonstrated.
Recognition of the relevance of the Hegelian tradition for Stirner's
thought runs counter to Ferguson's interpretation of Stirner's philosophy. She observes, 'While the question of Stirner's relation with
Hegel is of some historical interest, the focus on the correct placing
of his ideas within this historical tradition is to sidestep an actual
confrontation with his arguments.'[4]

STIRNER'S HEGELIANISM

If Stirner is concerned to exorcise the ghost of Hegel in *The Ego and Its
Own*, he conducts this exorcism by Hegelian means. While Hegel's
philosophy is subtle and complex, one of its major themes is that reality
is to be understood as essentially thought, so that in thinking man is at
home with himself. For Hegel this recognition of the status of thought
is not immediately apparent to human beings, but is an historical and
social achievement. *The Phenomenology of Spirit*, Hegel's first major
work, introduces the theme of the achievement of truth through modes
of alienated consciousness and signals the formation of a distinct

tradition of theorists who explore the human world and the attainment of social harmony and personal equilibrium in terms of pathways of social and personal alienation. Bruno Bauer, Ludwig Feuerbach and Karl Marx are distinctive Hegelian theorists who all conceive of the human world as displaying patterns of alienation whereby the productive, creative agency of human beings is misrepresented in alien ways of thinking and acting and needs to be affirmed and reclaimed by social theory. Stirner, in common with and in conscious opposition to these Young Hegelian theorists, develops an account of reality in which egoism is central but is subject to theoretical and practical forces of alienation. Stirner's thought is misrepresented if it is seen, as McLellan suggests, as far removed from the standpoint of Hegel's system.[5]

The Phenomenology of Spirit depicts a succession of ways in which consciousness apprises its situation.[6] The experience of consciousness in making sense of the world is tracked, and what emerges as central to this narrative of the phenomenal forms of consciousness is that consciousness always plays a formative role in apprehending the world. Consciousness in apprehending the world distinguishes between the act of consciousness and the truth, which is the object of consciousness. Hegel, however, sees this distinction as a distinction within consciousness that does not override the unity between knower and known.

Comprehension of the unity between knower and known is the outcome of the journey undertaken in *The Phenomenology of Spirit*. It sets up the basis of speculative knowing and hence the Hegelian system of philosophy. The preceding primitive and historical modes of consciousness reviewed in *The Phenomenology of Spirit*, insofar as they maintain a split within consciousness and divide one consciousness from another, express the fragmentation within experience and the social diremption that constitute alienation. The philosophical consciousness, for Hegel, must traverse this highway of despair to develop its conception of the unity of knower and known, thought and being. It does not liquidate the alienated forms of consciousness that it has reviewed. For Stirner there is no common link between the unique ego and general patterns of thought, and therefore it is not a question of reorienting the self to its contextual setting so that it recognises itself in the other. Rather the self must assert itself and break with all supposed common ties. Stirner's opposition to Hegel's standpoint of speculative knowing is stark and runs counter to Stepelevich's suggestion that Stirner should be seen as aiming to complete the project of Hegel's *Phenomenology of Spirit*.[7]

Speculative philosophy, then, for Hegel does not abolish alienation. It does, however, provide a perspective within which experience is understood as integrated and practical religious and social life in the modern world is taken by Hegel as providing a culture in which human beings can live in a relatively harmonious and integrated fashion, superseding the most glaring historical examples of alienation. In his systematic, mature, philosophical system, which self-consciously builds upon the insights of *The Phenomenology of Spirit*, Hegel understands the whole of reality as expressing the unity of Spirit. Within his synoptic philosophical perspective, ushered in by artistic and religious experience, Hegel conceives of nature as permeated with the unity of thought that scientists and philosophers can apprehend. Thought within nature, though, is external to itself; nature is an objective world that is alien to human beings and does not possess inner self-determination. It can be construed as the alienation of spiritual self-determination. In social and historical experience, for Hegel, the freedom of human beings is expressed and developed, but not without the pain of specific forms of social interaction in which freedom is denied and man is alienated from a sense of his own freedom.

In reviewing the practical, expressive and theoretical dimensions of human experience Hegel sees forms of alienation within, for example, a renewed phenomenological understanding of the travails of consciousness, and in the record of human history. History, for Hegel, is the story of freedom, but it is a narrative that recognises the human misery intrinsic to historical experience and the evident imperfection of historical social formations such as Oriental Despotism and Medieval Feudalism. While history is the story of progress for Hegel, the gradual development of political freedom, so that it embraces all members of a political culture, does not efface the experiences of slavery and serfdom.

Hegel, however, sees unity and reconciliation in a rational state that affords an integrative sense of community for individuals who are able to pursue private interests. The dialectic between the individual and the social in Hegel's political philosophy is subtle but evokes a savage critique from Stirner, in whose philosophy there can be no accommodation of the self with the social setting. Hegel sees the rights of individuals, notably property rights, as socially recognised rather than natural attributes. He also places much importance on the role of a community's law in shaping an individual's obligations to others and promoting a shared sense of freedom. The individual and the community are nicely balanced in Hegel in that the workings of a free political economy are seen as instrumental to the achievement of individual satisfaction, but the intervention of the political administration is necessary to achieve social cohesion. Again, Hegel perceives the epitome of the political state, the hereditary monarch, as symbolising the freedom of each individual within the state.

In *The Phenomenology of Spirit*, as noted above, Hegel follows and appraises consciousness in its modes of apprising reality. Pinkard has emphasised the crucial role of dialectic of recognition in this appraisal of consciousness for it highlights the ineliminably social nature of experience.[8] Selves in their struggle with one another misrecognise their unity, but the very struggle attests to the social dimension of consciousness. To understand oneself, for Hegel, presupposes seeing oneself in relation to others. Stirner likewise sees the self as necessarily pitted in conflict with other selves. At the beginning of the first part of *The Ego and Its Own*, entitled 'A Human Life', Stirner intimates a close philosophical and methodological affiliation with Hegel:

> Accordingly, because each thing *cares for itself* and at the same time comes into constant collision with other things, the combat of self-assertions is unavoidable. *Victory or defeat* – between the two alternatives the fate of the combat wavers. The victor becomes the *lord*, the vanquished one the *subject*: the former exercises *supremacy* and 'rights of supremacy', the latter fulfils in awe and deference the 'duties of a subject'.[9]

Stirner, then, from the outset of *The Ego and Its Own* follows Hegel in seeing conflict as intrinsic to development. He even self-consciously evokes the famous dialectic of recognition in *The Phenomenology of Spirit* to highlight his assessment of the importance of struggle and opposition in establishing the identity of the authentic ego. Stirner is at one with Hegel in seeing social life and the meaning of history in terms of struggle and development. Stirner, in addressing the questions how an individual ego can establish an authentic existence and how historical development has prepared the way for the flourishing of egoism, turns to the notion of a man's life to provide a structure for his developmental account of the person and history.

For Stirner the child is captive to his or her sociological context, the youth sets itself against the immediate world of family by developing a world of ideals and principles, but these very principles are the conditions the mature ego must break from if it is to establish an authentic unique existence. Historical development, for Stirner, runs according to the same conceptual scheme. The ancient world is a time of childhood, where individuals are immersed in their immediate contexts, but this gives way to a period of youth in which men become bewitched by their own thoughts and ideals. This spiritual age embraces the religiosity of the medieval world and the strident humanism of Young Hegelian successors to Hegel such as Bruno Bauer and Feuerbach. In Stirner's image of his contemporary age, man is entering maturity and the age of egoism, in which individuals break free from all the ideals and ghosts of their imagination and concentrate on pursuing their own ends.

In the first part of *The Ego and Its Own* Stirner deals with the history and sociology of the alienation of the ego, but in the second part of the book he develops an account of ownness, a positive analysis of what is involved in authentic egoism. In this account Stirner endeavours to resist enshrining egoism in a set of ideals or principles. 'Ownness includes in itself everything own, and brings to honour again what Christian language dishonoured. But ownness has not any alien standard either, as it is not in any sense an *idea* like freedom, morality, humanity and the like: it is only a description of the – *owner*.'[10]

In explaining what is involved in ownness, Stirner is at pains to distance the authentic egoist either from subscription to ideals or absorption into a social practice. He is ready to acknowledge an association of egoists, but such an association must be determined by the free choice of egoists. If an egoist decides against continuing an association, then the association is at once at an end. For Stirner, there can be no question of obligation for an egoist. An obligation derogates from the freedom and authenticity of the egoist. In outlining how an egoist owes no allegiance to social practices and moral principles, Stirner clarifies his position by discussing principles and practices that Hegel reviews in his *Philosophy of Right*.

Leopold, in his Introduction to a recent edition of *The Ego and Its Own*, observes how Stirner sees the state as exercising mastery over the individual in a manner evocative of Hegel's account of the master–slave relationship in *The Phenomenology of Spirit*.[11] The entire account of the egoist's rejection of the obligatoriness of moral principles and social practices, however, is to be understood as following and rejecting Hegel's account of the state as expressing and developing man's universality. Stirner discusses property, the law, the market, public administration, crime, conscience and the monarchy, and in each case gives a different account from Hegel's. Hegel is concerned to see these practices and principles as requiring effective social cooperation and coordination for them to be successful, whereas Stirner sees the accumulation of power in social institutions and practices, which are taken as prescribing forms of conduct as unacceptable to a free egoist. The differences between Stirner and Hegel, however, should not obscure the methodological and thematic affinities in their thought. Both theorists see man as progressing through stages of conflict and alienation, and both understand freedom in contemporary society as explicable in terms of an individual's orientation to a set of moral principles and social and practices.

STIRNER CONTRA HEGELIANISM

Stirner's philosophy takes autonomy as its goal and alienation as its defining alter ego. Its critique of historical modes of life and current political and social ideologies resembles Hegel's diagnosis of distorted forms of consciousness that do not recognise the active and constitutive role of consciousness in experience. For Stirner, however, Hegel's critique of modes of consciousness that posit truth as something distinct or alien from consciousness remains implicated in the alienation of the power and autonomy of the ego. For Stirner, Hegel's philosophical understanding of reality, whereby the thought of consciousness is taken as pervading reality, derogates from the ego in that the assertiveness of the ego is alienated by limiting it to what can be universalised in thought. This commitment to universality is taken by Stirner as tantamount to denying the supremacy of the actual, particular ego. Stirner observes:

> With him [Hegel] reality, the world of things, is altogether to correspond to the thought, and no concept is to be without reality. This caused Hegel's system to be the most objective, as if in it thought and thing celebrated their union. But this was simply the extremist case of violence of thought, its highest pitch of despotism and sole dominion, the triumph of mind, and with it the triumph of philosophy.[12]

For Stirner, Hegel's system subordinates the actual man, the egoist, to the despotism of thought, just as it subjugates the world to a procession of categories. Stirner rejects this in favour of what Brazill has termed 'an extravagant titanism in which the ego became in effect its own absolute'.[13] Stirner sees all attempts to frame ideals and principles to order and restrain the self-assertiveness of the ego as so many forms of alienation. For Stirner, Hegel's philosophy, and the theories of his Young Hegelian successors such as the Bauer brothers and Feuerbach, resembles religion in that true freedom in their theories is taken to be adherence to general patterns of thought and conduct. The absolute independence of the individual is denied. Just as religion subordinates the ego to the demands of an alien God, Stirner sees Hegel's thought as subordinating actual men to ideas and Spirit (*Geist*). The ego, for Stirner, generates its own commitments; subscription to another's code or to a political scheme that allocates an individual a specific role justified by general criteria fractures the sense of integrity and whole-ness of the egoist. Alienation is the inevitable fate of any compromise with the world and others.

In the second part of *The Ego and Its Own*, in which Stirner discusses his own positive philosophy of ownness, there is a running critique of Hegel's political philosophy in that Stirner discusses and criticises key elements of Hegel's political thought, notably property, rights, con-tract, morality and forms of ethical life – the family, civil society and the state. Stirner makes plain his disagreement with Hegel's entire enterprise in *The Philosophy of Right* by completely disavowing the notion of 'right' on a social basis. He observes:

> Right is the *spirit of society* . . . . All existing right is *foreign law*; some one makes me out to be in the right, 'does right by me'. But should I therefore be in the right if all the world made me out so? And yet what else is the right that I obtain in the state, in society, but a right of those *foreign* to me.[14]

For Stirner, a perspective that sees human beings gaining freedom by assuming ethical obligations in social intercourse is one that abrogates the freedom of the ego. While Hegel sees rights of personality and property as being maintained and confirmed in a social setting under-pinned by the authority of the state, Stirner sees the dependence of the individual on a social organisation such as the state as highlighting the alienation involved in these 'rights'. For Stirner, the legal context of property rights undermines the individual who is not free to do what he will with his property. The egoist, for Stirner, will not and should not suffer the state to interfere in the slightest with his property. Mediation of the state between an individual and his property in Stirner's per-spective abrogates the autonomy of the egoist.

Stirner's unequivocal refusal to see freedom in the authority of the state leads him to deny the obligatoriness of the law. Whereas Hegel sees crime as a signal of the individual's freedom to choose, which ultimately points in the direction of community laws that must be obeyed if the individual is to be free, Stirner denies the immorality of crime. For Stirner, crime is a social designation for an act the egoist need not recognise. The state, for Stirner, acts like a master and the internal organisation of the state, which Hegel takes to be important in that a constitutional monarchy for him is supremely rational, is of no importance. For Stirner, 'Every state is a despotism, be the despot one or many'.[15] Likewise Stirner puts no faith in Hegel's estimate of the state's capacity to ameliorate the problem of pauperism. Pauperism, for Stirner, depends upon the state for market operations, and unequal property holdings are promoted by the state's maintenance of the social and legal context for economic transactions. Stirner is equally sceptical of socialist or communist projects for the redistribution of property. Reliance on the state, for Stirner, is the problem rather than the solution.

Against the power and authority of the state Stirner poses the power of the unique individual ego. The authentic egoist, for Stirner, admits of no binding ties with others. The individual egoist might enter into a union with other egoists but he will not submit to a 'common' will. If at any point he wishes to break with the conditions of union at any point he will do so. Just as Stirner is against the state and its laws, so he is against all social institutions that call for ethical commitments from individuals that condition their conduct. Notably, he opposes the family, which Hegel sees as playing an important educative role in preparing individuals for ethical commitments. For Stirner, the family constricts the individual. Marriage, for Stirner, in theory and practice is not a binding commitment or a 'love' that transcends individuality; it is a relationship entered into by an individual to promote his or her interests and desires. Likewise he is against all practices and institutions that cultivate individuals into accepting binding ethical commitments.

While much of the force of the arguments in *The Ego and Its Own* is directed against Hegel and his philosophy, Stirner also takes issue with rival Young Hegelian theorists, who also aspired to develop Hegel's thought so that they theorised the conditions of human freedom in a way that banished all traces of alienation. For Stirner, however, Young Hegelians such as Bruno Bauer and Ludwig Feuerbach still conceive of real human experience in essentialist, universal terms that are just as fanciful and distorting of actual experience as Hegel's idealism. Stirner's break with Hegel's thought led him to emphasise his separation from contemporaries who retained what he considered to be an untenable Hegelian essentialism.

Toews observes that Stirner sees Bruno Bauer's privileging of the play of critical self-consciousness as illicitly universalist in that it represents 'the final form of the domination of real human existence by culturally produced "objective," "universal" values'.[16] Stirner also plays the transformative method, coined and operated by Feuerbach, against Feuerbach himself in his absolute rejection of all heteronomy. Feuerbach had seen religion and religious language as constituting an inverted world whereby the active creative powers of man were transposed to a God external and supposedly responsible for human beings. He sought to transform this situation through the transformative method where what affected to be subject (including thought in Hegel's philosophy) would be transformed into the object and *vice versa*. Hence man, the species, would assume the role of subject of its own destiny. But for Stirner, this evocation of the powers of the species, mankind as a universal, derogated from the powers of actual men and women. He observes,' Man is something only as my quality like masculinity or femininity'.[17] In 'Stirner's Critics', a riposte to Feuerbach's criticisms of *The Ego and Its Own*, Stirner undertakes a powerful critique of Feuerbach's standpoint. 'Because he is this unique Feuerbach, he is also at the same time a male, a human being, a living being, a Frenchman and so forth. But he is also more than all that.'[18]

Just as Stirner criticises Feuerbach for his continuing entanglement in an essentialism whereby the individual is alienated, so he castigates Bruno Bauer for his continued play with the ghosts of essentialised man. He takes a critical perspective on Bauer's review of the Jewish question just as Marx does, though from a different angle. He notes that Bauer wants to do away with the particularism of racial allegiances and uphold instead a formal equality of man. In regard to Bauer's standpoint, Stirner observes that

> *Man is man in general*, and in so far every one who is a man. Now everyone is to have the eternal rights of man, and, according to the opinion of communism, enjoy them in the complete 'democracy', or, as it ought more correctly to be called – anthropocracy. But it is I alone who have everything that I – procure for myself; as man I have nothing.[19]

STIRNER AND HEGEL

A study of Stirner's egoism is instructive about Hegel. It reveals what is assumed about Hegel by a Young Hegelian, well-versed in Hegel's philosophy, as well as what is seen as objectionable in Hegel's thought to the same well-informed critic. It also discloses the Hegelian roots of Stirner's own philosophy. Hegel is assumed by Stirner to identify human beings in terms of their reflective capacity and to envisage their freedom as the goal of the historical process. Stirner criticises Hegel for identifying human beings in terms of their general reflective capacities rather than focusing upon the pure individuality of a particular individual.

Stirner sees it as his critical task to expose the alienation involved in identifying individuals in general conceptual terms so that he can signal the path towards authentic individual freedom. The methodological rationale of Stirner's most famous work is to expose and explain the history of alienation and chart the development of freedom by criticising the major social institutions and practices of the contemporary world. The course of *The Ego and Its Own* thereby exhibits an affinity with Hegel in its concern to trace the story of the historical emergence and development of freedom, amidst discordance and alienation.

Analysis of Stirner's critique of Hegel and assorted Young Hegelians also raises important questions about the nature of human freedom and social and political practice. Stirner's critique of each and every ethical and social obligation challenges the communitarian standpoint of Hegel and many subsequent theorists. Hegel's identification of freedom with subscription to the practices of a rationalised version of the modern state is repudiated directly in Stirner's disavowal of any commitment that is not the absolute and retractable choice of a particular individual.

Stirner's process view of the self, which is of a piece with Hegel's own account of subjectivity, captures how an individual self resists being categorised exhaustively in terms of social roles. A self is always something more than its particular activities; it is itself a source of creativity. This creative dimension of the self does not square with features of Hegel's rational state. A patriarchal family denies the creativity of women and children, a non-democratic state undermines self-determination and the supervisory role allocated the civil service in clearing up the loose ends of market transactions derogates from the powers of agency to be enjoyed by ordinary individuals.

Critics from Marx onwards, however, are surely right in observing that Stirner does not allow sufficiently for the sociality of human beings. The next chapter of this book examines the impact of Stirner upon Marx, both in terms of Marx's awareness of the power of Stirner's critique of other Young Hegelians and in respect of his critique of radical individualism. Another Young Hegelian, Feuerbach, stung by the acerbity of Stirner's critique of his 'essentialist' humanism, offered a telling retaliatory strike in '*The Essence of Christianity* in relation to *The Ego and Its Own*'. Feuerbach emphasises the unsustainability of Stirner's individualism in observing, 'I am dependent on Thou. No Thou – no I.'[20]

Stirner's egoism represents a *reductio ad absurdam* version of radical individualism. An individual's subscription to a set of particular social practices and principles is an appropriate object of criticism. Social commitments, however, are not reducible to those which are acceptable to changing perceptions of individual interest. If individuals universally appraised their commitment to practices and principles according to estimates of their own fluctuating interests, there would be no effective basis for social cooperation. In turn the conditions for the cultivation of individuality would be undermined. The dialectic of recognition rehearsed in Hegel's *Phenomenology of Spirit* highlights the intersubjective character of the expression of individual agency. The relationship of mastery and slavery, which Stirner invokes as testifying to the inherently conflictual social world of self-assertive egos, is shown by Hegel to be contradictory. For Hegel, self-recognition involves the identification of key human attributes, which can only be achieved by observing transpersonal human qualities in human interaction. A slave is treated as an object not a person and the master's power is not recognised by an equal. True freedom requires recognition of one's freedom by equals. Hegel's dialectic of recognition testifies to the social character of human freedom; it is neither a matter of physical power nor individual skill. It is a social condition in which individuals express their freedom in reciprocal recognition of one another's qualities.[21]

6 *The German Ideology*, Stirner and Hegel: The Theory of History and the History of Theory

INTRODUCTION

In this chapter it will be argued that *The German Ideology* should be analysed and interpreted as an integral whole. Its various sections, which have tended to be taken as detachable in previous interpretations, share a community of purpose and character. In design and practice *The German Ideology* is a work devoted to the history of theory. The character of the project upon which Marx and Engels are engaged in *The German Ideology* is clearly conveyed in the subtitles of its two volumes, 'Critique of Modern German Philosophy according to its representatives, Feuerbach, B. Bauer and Stirner', and 'Critique of German Socialism according to its various prophets'.[1] The sections on Feuerbach, Bauer and Stirner, which constitute volume 1, criticise the respective philosophical positions of these Young Hegelian theorists by relating them to one another and tracing their derivation from Hegel's absolute idealism. The second volume, dealing with German socialism, criticises the attachment of German socialists to the language and concepts of philosophers in the Hegelian tradition analysed in the first volume. The pressing concern of *The German Ideology* to rebut rival contemporary theories shapes its well-known statements on materialism, historical method and alienation. The work can best be understood as a polemical contribution to a debate between Young Hegelians within an Hegelian tradition of discourse.

Marx and Engels composed *The German Ideology* between 1845 and 1846, during which time they revised drafts and rearranged passages. This process of reordering the text should warn commentators that the sense of any particular passage in the text might depend on sections removed from that location in the last draft. Significantly, Marx and Engels reworked the opening section on Feuerbach to include material developed initially in the course of their critique of Stirner, which forms the third section of the first volume. Carver, in an informative discussion of *The German Ideology*, emphasises that this process of textual revision was never formally completed: 'the text *The German Ideology* was never revised to the point that the discussion was properly organised and clean copy prepared'.[2] While Marx and Engels made repeated if unsuccessful efforts to secure publication of the text, only the section on Grun in the second volume was published in their lifetime.[3] This precedent of publishing separately part of *The German Ideology* has been followed subsequently, notably in the distinct focus upon the opening section, on Feuerbach, in English-language versions of excerpts from the complete text.[4]

The conventional practice of critics has likewise been to concentrate upon the opening section, virtually excluding the remainder from consideration. This focus of critical attention runs counter to the relative lengths of the sections. The section on Stirner constitutes two thirds of the entire work. An exclusive focus upon the opening section of *The German Ideology* therefore underrates this devotion of attention to Stirner and neglects the provenance of parts of the opening section that arose from critical reflection upon Stirner. Moreover the critical significance of Stirner on Marx has been signalled by Arthur and Kolakowski in perceptive studies of Marx's intellectual development, and by Thomas in his study of Marx and anarchist theorists.[5] McLellan, in his study *The Young Hegelians and Karl Marx*, while generally dismissing the section on Stirner as arid, nonetheless refers to the influence of Stirner on Marx's criticisms of Feuerbach.[6] In the brief, retrospective summary of the development of his ideas outlined in the Preface to *A Contribution to a Critique of Political Economy*, Marx himself, far from isolating and highlighting the opening section of *The German Ideology*, refers to it instead as a text composed of two volumes that is devoted to the overall theoretical task of criticising post-Hegelian philosophy, in which he and Engels were resolved 'to settle accounts with our erstwhile philosophical conscience'.[7]

A token of the intensity of the critical orthodoxy concentrating interpretative commentary upon the opening section of *The German Ideology* is the adherence of both Althusser and Avineri to this conventional practice, notwithstanding their profound disagreement over the extent to which *The German Ideology* constitutes a 'break' in Marx's intellectual development.[8] Ironically, given his awareness of the impact of Stirner on Marx's thought, this critical orthodoxy is epitomized by McLellan in his *Karl Marx: His Life and Thought*, and in his *Karl Marx: Selected Texts*, in which he observes, 'By far the most important part of

The German Ideology is the unfinished section on Feuerbach'.[9] McLellan's identification of the source of this section's significance as residing in a self-contained exposition of a theory of history is equally uncontroversial. McLellan takes this theory of history as being developed out of the following elements: 'a general statement of the historical and materialist approach in contrast to that of the Young Hegelians, a historical analysis employing this method, and an account of its immediate future – a communist revolution'.[10] This reference to the contrast between the materialist and historical approaches of Marx and Engels and that of the Young Hegelians, however, signals the problems associated with the prevalent way of reading *The German Ideology*. The development of a 'theory of history' in the opening section is not readily detachable from the ongoing, wider context of a history of theory in which the process of settling accounts with post-Hegelian ideologies, undertaken throughout the work, provides the polemical and conceptual, discursive setting for the formulation of a distinctive theoretical standpoint.

This chapter aims to establish the importance of reading *The German Ideology* as an integral whole, in which the opening section, like the later ones, is best understood by observing and recognising its connections with the other sections. This reading will be explored in a number of interrelated ways. The elaboration of the overall approach to historical study undertaken by Marx and Engels is in fact charged and informed by the entire work's criticism of the theories of history formulated by Young Hegelian theorists. In particular, its characterisation of the division of labour as involving alienation, which is to be superseded by means of a communist revolution, is shown to involve patterns of thought and a normative conception of man that is resumed and explicated in the subsequent section on Stirner. Ironically the impact of this conception of man upon the conception of history outlined by Marx and Engels in the opening section is shown to run counter to their professed concern to frame a view of history without reference to such a standard. The entire account of communism in the opening section resonates with a protracted engagement with the specification of an individual, and the conditions and character of an individual's activities undertaken in the section on Stirner. The interpretative possibilities of a reading of *The German Ideology*, which takes its constitutive sections as being linked by an ongoing engagement in the history of theory, are further demonstrated by relating the materialist approach to history, sketched in the opening section, to the operational character of the history of theory undertaken throughout the work. The viability and implications of the sketch of a materialist approach to history are explored by investigating the apparent independence of thought assumed by Marx and Engels in their practice as historians of theory and by examining the explanation offered by them in the section on Stirner for the apparent detachment of German theoretical thought from material conditions. Finally, evidence of the considerable and complex impact of Hegelian and Young Hegelian theories, drawn from all sections of *The German Ideology*, is assembled to investigate the claims of divergent interpretations of how *The German Ideology* is related to Marx's intellectual development.

MATERIALISM, HISTORY AND THE YOUNG HEGELIANS

In articulating their method of approach to history in the opening section of *The German Ideology*, Marx and Engels develop for the first time a materialist conception of history that focuses theoretical and revolutionary attention upon the material record of historical development, envisaged as being shaped by and exemplified in the practical engagement of men in their productive activities. In generally characterising their outlook on history, however, Marx and Engels portray ideas and consciousness in striking and highly controversial terms. Ideological conceptions are deprecated as mere reflexes and echoes and are portrayed as derivative and inconsequential, historically. The language of Marx and Engels is challenging and unequivocal: 'The phantoms formed in the human brain are also, necessarily, sublimates of their material life-process which is empirically verifiable and bound to material premises. Morality, religion, metaphysics, all the rest of ideology and their corresponding forms of consciousness thus no longer retain the semblance of independence.'[11] This is a radical statement, and the severity of its reductionist standpoint requires explanation. An explanation can be provided in the character of the enterprise upon which Marx and Engels are continuously engaged throughout *The German Ideology*: a polemical encounter with a number of Young Hegelian theorists. Just as Miller in *Analyzing Marx: Morality, Power and History* has remarked that the extreme model of productive force determinism presented in the Preface to *A Contribution to a Critique of Political Economy* is to be explained by Marx's polemical concern to highlight industrial development, in pointed contrast to Proudhon and the Utopian Socialists, so the extreme materialism presented in *The German Ideology* is to be explained by its polemical contrast to the abstract formulations of the Young Hegelians.[12]

The general, polemical characterisation of the Young Hegelian theorists employed in the Preface to *The German Ideology* approximates closely to some of the terms in which thought and consciousness are subsequently portrayed in the opening section's presentation of its historical outlook, and in so doing suggests that the thoroughly reductionist character of those terms is a product of the hostility of Marx and Engels to Young Hegelian ideas. In the Preface, Marx and Engels characterise the Young Hegelians in the following terms: 'The products of their brains have got out of their hands. They, the creators, have bowed down before their creations. Let us liberate them from the chimeras, the ideas, dogmas, imaginary beings under the yoke of which they are pining away.'[13] Bauer, Stirner and prophets of German socialism, following Young Hegelian practice, are specifically inveighed against in subsequent sections of *The German Ideology* for undertaking accounts of history manufactured by the mechanical operation of abstract thought determinations that effect no purchase on the empirical world.[14] The point of the trenchantly provocative expression of the 'materialist' standpoint in the opening section of *The German Ideology* resides in the determination of Marx and Engels to highlight their opposition to Young Hegelian reliance upon abstract, philosophical speculations to order and shape their accounts of history.

Indeed Marx and Engels, both in the section on Stirner and elsewhere in *The German Ideology*, are at pains to distance themselves from the kind of historical enterprise undertaken by Stirner in his own highly polemical contribution to the Young Hegelian philosophical debate, *The Ego and Its Own*, published in 1844. The absurdly abstract and ahistorical categories deployed by Stirner can be seen as evoking the vigorous materialism expressed in *The German Ideology*. Stirner's model of historical development follows Hegel, who had envisaged the process by which the conditions and presuppositions of Spirit, the universality and freedom inherent in intersubjective experience, are expressed as being one of historical progress culminating in his own philosophising. Stirner likewise presents his account of the Egoist as the culmination of an historical process. The individual of the past is presented as having failed to recognise himself as the unique source of value, enslaving himself to nature and its laws in antiquity and to spiritual conceptions in the modern world.

Stirner encapsulates the course of world history within the suggestive but categorially insubstantial notions of childhood, youth and manhood. These concepts form the master categories of a review of history that receives a more specific, if equally idiosyncratic analytical classification. Childhood and youth are seen by Stirner as representing respectively the ancient and modern worlds, which in turn are taken as exemplifying negroidity and monogloidity. He observes:

> The history of the world whose shaping properly belongs altogether to the Caucasian race seems till now to have run through two Caucasian ages, in the first of which we had to work out and work off our innate negroidity; this was followed in the second by mongoloidity (chineseness which must likewise be terribly made an end of).[15]

Stirner's categorisation and explanation of history in terms of a metaphorical conceptualisation of a man's life, upon which is superimposed a racial scheme, invokes the concentrated ridicule of Marx and Engels in the section on Stirner in *The German Ideology*. His enterprise is discussed and dismissed in the following terms: 'We spoke above of the German philosophical conception of history. Here in Saint Max [Stirner], we find a brilliant example of it. The speculative, the abstract conception, is made the driving force of history and history is thereby turned into the mere history of philosophy.'[16] Stirner is held to develop his conception of egoism and offer a history of its development that abstracts from all concrete developments in its reduction of the social and material foundations of experience to the 'unique' consciousness of an egoist. Likewise Bauer and the True Socialists following Feuerbach are seen as substituting a procession of abstract thought determinations for concrete historical development. The imputed reductionism in this process of abstraction forms an exact counterpart to the vigorous statement of a materialist standpoint at the outset of *The German Ideology*, and thereby serves to highlight its character as a polemical riposte.

The polemical concern of Marx and Engels in *The German Ideology* to combat Young Hegelian and, in particular, Stirner's ideals, is evident in their emphatic determination to deny a goal or *telos* to the historical process derived from a philosophical conception of man. In criticising Stirner, Marx and Engels are at pains to point up the absurdity of this teleological notion. Stirner is held to have written history backwards so that the standpoint of the egoistic 'man' determines the nature and activities of the historical 'child'. For instance they criticise Stirner's retrojection (i.e. projecting backwards) onto Christianity of a hidden atheism and criticism, which thereby hastens the next stage of historical development. Marx and Engels condemn this illicit ascription of a teleological purpose, namely the achievement of egoism, to the historical process, by remarking, 'In this way it is infinitely easy to give history "unique" turns, as one has only to describe its latest result as the task which in truth it originally set itself.'[17]

This pointed and critical review of Stirner's false teleological perspective on history is the most elaborated criticism of a teleological view of history in *The German Ideology*. But Bauer and the True Socialists, Semmig and Grun, are similarly condemned for viewing historical change in terms of its achievement of a final, normative, purpose. Semmig receives especially bitter criticism, for in his concern to show Feuerbachian humanism as both the foundation of socialism and the *telos* of historical development, he is depicted as presenting an amateurish pastiche of Stirner.[18] The pointed and critical reviews of false, teleological readings of history in subsequent sections tellingly reflect the opening section's opposition to the use of terms such as 'man' and 'species', which Marx had deployed in earlier writings. In the opening section Feuerbach's equation of the existence of man with his essence or species is condemned as an unwarrantable abstraction from specific social and historical circumstances, which, in masquerading as a justification of communism, is seen as vulnerable to Stirner's own strident critique of 'spiritual' conceptions as enslaving the ego. The opening section's hostility to the invocation of the term 'man', however, is especially severe as it is perceived as lending itself to the expression of the antihistorical, teleological construal of history that is mercilessly exposed in the subsequent sections. Indeed, in explicitly eschewing a causal, teleological role for 'man' in the presentation of their own conception of history, Marx and Engels, in the opening section, are specifically concerned to separate themselves from what they designate a philosophical view. This philosophical view evidently refers to the True Socialists' parading of a Feuerbachian philosophical perspective, Bauer's convoluted reading of history in terms of the development of self-consciousness and Stirner's account of the egoistic man, who, while denying defining ties with other men and declaring the death of 'man', is nonetheless seen metaphorically and teleologically as the goal of the historical process.

Marx and Engels observe:

the whole process [of history] which we have outlined has been regarded by them [philosophers] as the evolutionary process of 'man' so that at every historical stage 'man' was substituted for the individuals existing hitherto and shown as the motive force of history. The whole process was thus conceived as a process of the self-estrangement of 'man' and this was essentially due to the fact that the average individual of the later stage was always foisted on to the earlier stage.[19]

The objection to the deployment of the term 'self-estrangement' here, like the opposition to the term 'man', derives from its putative role as a causal factor in a teleological reading of history which over-rides a focus upon actual historical conditions in specific modes of production. Marx and Engels, then, in the opening section of *The German Ideology* explicitly disavow a teleological reading of history in which 'man' functions as the motive evolutionary force in overcoming forms of self-estrangement. They are also concerned to present their postulates or premises of historical study as neither imputing nor implying a teleological purpose to the historical process. Nonetheless, despite what Marx and Engels assert so prominently at the beginning of *The German Ideology*, the view of historical development set out in the opening section, when related to the expanded, normative conception of human nature developed in the subsequent section on Stirner, will be shown to be affected by a reading of prior historical develop-ment in terms of a normative conception of man to be established under communism. While this normative conception of man is not always operative, it licenses the opening section's references to aliena-tion in the division of labour, and in so doing imparts an implicitly teleological character to its conceptualisation of the historical process in that historical development is conceived in terms that diagnose societies prior to communism as derogating from a normative standard that is to be realised under communism.

HISTORICAL DEVELOPMENT, LABOUR AND HUMAN NATURE

In characterising the premises of their historical method, Marx and Engels, in the opening section of *The German Ideology*, are at pains to deny that they are employing a philosophical conception of man be-tokening a teleological reading of history. They are, after all, explicitly concerned to distinguish their position from the absurdities they diag-nose as vitiating rival Young Hegelian standpoints. They observe:

When the reality is described, a self-sufficient philosophy loses its medium of existence. At the best its place can only be taken by a summing-up of the most general results, abstractions which are derived from the observation of the historical development of men. These abstractions, in themselves, divorced from real history have no value whatsoever. They can only serve to facilitate the arrangement of historical material, to indicate the sequence of its separate strata. But they by no means afford a recipe or scheme, as does philosophy, for neatly trimming the epochs of history.[20]

Accordingly, even in the highly condensed, polemically reductionist treatment it sometimes receives, much of what they have to say in specifying the premises and overall character of their approach to history does not entail that past events are identified in terms of the future realisation of a normative conception of man.

Human beings, as presupposed by their study of history, are taken as natural beings whose language, consciousness and needs are seen as reflecting their natural status. The satisfaction of needs and man's language and consciousness are also seen as inherently social, as is the organisation of the practical process of production to satisfy needs. This process of satisfying needs is seen as an ongoing process, and it is the sphere of production, in particular the aggregate of productive forces available to men, that is seen as shaping the condition of society in distinct historical epochs. In their considered reflection upon the development of history, seen from this standpoint, Marx and Engels observe the tendency for these productive forces to develop and they highlight the tremendous development of the productive forces under capitalism as a precondition for the achievement of communism. While the development of the productive forces is thereby linked to the goal of communism, Marx and Engels are concerned to distance themselves from a teleological interpretation of this growth in productive capacity. They note, 'Thus the communists in practice treat the conditions treated up to now by production and intercourse as inorganic conditions without, however, imagining that it was the plan or the destiny of previous generations to give them material and without believing that these conditions were inorganic for the individuals creating them.'[21] Moreover a characterisation of historical development that observes the growth of forces of production in relatively uncontroversial empirical terms is a feasible project, and it does not, in itself, commit Marx and Engels to a reading of past events in relation to a normative conception of man to be realised in a future form of society.

Indeed for the most part the analysis of actual historical development, which concentrates on the transition from feudalism to capitalism that is offered in the opening section of *The German Ideology*, is not imbued with a teleological conception of man. This account is characteristically concerned to describe in non-normative terms the growth of productive forces in response to burgeoning demand and trade. The rise of manufacturing is correlated to the accumulation of capital by merchants on the one hand and increasing population, trade and political security on the other. Thereafter capitalist relations of production increasingly predominate and the extension of markets into a world market stimulates the development of big industry, initially in Britain but subsequently, through competition, in other countries. Centrally involved in this account of history, however, is a focus on the increasing division of labour and interspersed in the account of this process are references to the activity of labour that presuppose a normative frame of reference. For instance the medieval craftsmen's preoccupation with a particular task and the modern worker's indifference to his work are disparaged in the following quotation: 'every medieval craftsman was completely absorbed in his work, to which he had a complacent, servile relationship, and in which he was involved to a far greater extent than the modern worker whose work is a matter of indifference to him'.[22] Likewise big industry is held to make the process of labour unbearable, which is explicated subsequently as involving, through the intensification of the division of labour, shutting off the proletarian from all self-activity, which is explicitly contrasted with post-revolutionary complete individuals who cast off all natural limitations. Arthur has emphasised the significance of this conceptualisation of labour and has pointed up the radicalism of the projected abolition of labour under communism.[23]

Marx and Engels acknowledge the centrality of the division of labour in their conception of history by providing a generalised account of its role and meaning in historical development. In so doing they highlight its character in expressing and intensifying the alienation of man in that 'as activity is not voluntarily, but naturally, divided, man's own deed becomes an alien power opposed to him, which enslaves him instead of being controlled by him'.[24] While Marx and Engels do not explicitly present communism as a teleological goal of historical development, they nonetheless compose an arresting image of communist life in which the individual is held to be able to cultivate his gifts in all directions. Marx and Engels pointedly and revealingly contrast the alienation endemic to social formations sustaining a division of labour with an arresting image of communist society:

For as soon as the division of labour comes into being, each man has a particular, exclusive sphere of activity – he is a hunter, a fisherman, a herdsman or a critical critic... While in communist society, where nobody has one exclusive sphere of activity but each can become accomplished in any branch he wishes, society regulates the general production and thus makes it possible for one to do one thing today and another tomorrow.[25]

This vivid contrast between communist man and his historical predecessors has exercised subsequent commentators, and well-informed, thoughtful commentators on Marx, such as Carver, McLellan and Arthur, have seen it as a parody, either of Fourier in the view of Carver and Arthur, or Stirner according to McLellan.[26] To suggest a parody, however, is not as Thomas avers to dismiss its serious intent nor to deny its role in positively displaying the normative conception of man entertained in *The German Ideology*, the negative side of which informs its depiction of the division of labour as a condition of alienation.[27] Stirner, as well as Fourier, is suggested in this image, for Marx and Engels are subsequently concerned, in their section on Stirner, to pour scorn on his notion that the unique individual can create himself by assuming a particular, peculiar quality or interest by the exertion of an act of will.

Indeed the subsequent critical discussion of Stirner's conception of the individual and his related activities in *The German Ideology* expands upon and confirms the normative image of the many-sided social individual of communist society suggested in the opening section. It thereby underlines its relevance as a conceptual reference point for the alienation taken as being evidenced in the division of labour and highlights its significance for inspiring practical revolutionary action. Detailed consideration of this discussion justifies Kolakowski's suggestion that 'questions of personality and personal freedom are treated in *The German Ideology* in the form of a polemic with Max Stirner'.[28]

In their discussion of Stirner, Marx and Engels are highly critical of Stirner's conception of the reflexive powers of the individual to step back from any particular vocation or interest, such as a critic, by making it his own as a particular, peculiar act by a unique individual. To Stirner's celebration of particularity and the unique individual, Marx and Engels counterpose the all-round development of the individual who fulfils his many-sided potentialities. The fixation of a passion or interest so that it assumes an isolated and abstract character is held to confront the individual as 'an alien power', which recalls the characterisation of the division of labour in the opening section of *The German Ideology* as resulting in a situation in which 'man's own deed becomes an alien power opposed to him'.[29] The process of the fixation of passions and interests, in the section on Stirner, is indeed held to depend on the actual conditions and relationships facing the individual, namely the division of labour. Marx and Engels press home their criticisms of Stirner by unfurling an apposite, if brutal *ad hominem* argument. 'In the case of a parochial Berlin schoolmaster or author...whose relations to this world are reduced to a minimum by his pitiful position in life it is indeed inevitable that his thought becomes just as abstract as he himself and his life and that thought confronts him in the form of a fixed power.'[30]

Geras, in his study *Marx and Human Nature:, Refutation of a Legend*, reflects upon the opening section of *The German Ideology* but draws upon material in the section on Stirner, and observes that the work as a whole presents an account of human nature. He acknowledges that the most contentious need that Marx and Engels ascribe to human beings in *The German Ideology* is 'the need of people for a breadth and diversity of pursuit and hence of personal development'.[31] The section on Stirner is in fact notable for its evocation of this normative conception of the individual. In a significant passage Marx and Engels invoke the term universality to depict the character of unalienated human activity:

> In the case of an individual, for example, who embraces a wide circle of varied activities and practical relations to the world and who, therefore, lives a many-sided life, thought has the same character of universality as every other manifestation of his life. Consequently it neither becomes fixed in the form of abstract thought nor does it need complicated tricks of reflection when the individual passes from thought to some other manifestation of life. From the outset it is always a factor in the total life of the individual, one which disappears and is reproduced as required.[32]

The intrinsic connection between the individual and his universal 'social' activities posited by Marx and Engels runs directly counter to Stirner's claim in his own response to critics that 'Work has no value whatsoever in itself and is an honour for no man.'[33]

Marx and Engels' account of man and his activities in the section on Stirner recalls Marx's description of man as a species-being in the

Economic and Philosophical Manuscripts of 1844, where man's character as a species-being is identified by Marx in the following terms:
'Man is a species-being...because he looks upon himself as a universal
and therefore free being.'[34] Productive activity in the *Economic and
Philosophical Manuscripts* is held to be reflective of man's species-
being due, among other features, to its universal application and its
capacity to be undertaken freely.[35] Notwithstanding the criticism in the
opening section of *The German Ideology* of the projection onto the
term species of self-generating historical powers, its discussion of
the individual and the supersession of the division of labour and
alienation involves the conceptual world of the *Economic and Philosophical Manuscripts* of 1844. This linkage is exemplified by the section
on Stirner, which emphatically confirms a reading of the opening
section that acknowledges the continued significance of normative
assumptions about man and communism. The total absence of a discussion of the section on Stirner is notable in, and perhaps explanatory
of, Kain's interpretation of *The German Ideology* in his book *Marx and
Ethics*, in which he asserts, 'in *The German Ideology* Marx's discussion
of communism, as he himself points out, shuns any discussion of
"man" or the human essence. Instead, it proceeds in a wholly empirical
and materialist way.'[36]

The notion of the individual and his 'universal' activities, entertained
by Marx and Engels throughout *The German Ideology* and developed
explicitly in the section on Stirner, suggests their close involvement in
a thoroughly Hegelian mode of theorising. Hegel, in *The Philosophy
of Right*, in an argument to which Marx and Engels refer obliquely
in the second volume of *The German Ideology*, discusses the will in
terms of its relations to individuality, particularity and universality.[37]
Hegel's dialectical development of these relations turns upon his
employment of the notions of 'good' and 'bad' infinity, which are
invoked at strategic moments throughout his *Logic*.[38] The good infinite
is figuratively represented by a circle as it is the concept whose object is
not outside itself and hence is not forever presupposing a limit or
barrier to itself. In terms of the will, Hegel argues that if the will
becomes determinate and gives its universality an appropriate, objective specification, 'its object is itself and so is not in its eyes an "other"
or "barrier"'.[39] Marx and Engels, in *The German Ideology*, view the
division of labour in terms redolent of Hegel's discussion of the will.
The division of labour erects a series of socially constructed barriers
between the individual and his free adoption and expression of universal activities.

HISTORY AND THEORY

The Hegelian overtones of the discussion of the individual and his activities undertaken by Marx and Engels in the section on Stirner reflects their characteristically close concern with Hegel and the development of his ideas in different directions by Young Hegelian theorists throughout *The German Ideology*.[40] Indeed, somewhat surprisingly in the light of the vigorously materialistic recommendations for historical method entertained at the outset of the work, *The German Ideology* develops a history of theory that consists for the most part of a close textual study of a number of theoretical texts. This textual analysis is supplemented by a plausible account of how these texts can be seen as influencing one another and how they can all be seen as developing aspects and sides of Hegel's general philosophical approach. Connections and judgements are made, incorporating a recognition of similarities and differences, progress and decline, at some distance from a consideration of material circumstances, reflecting back uneasily upon the work's uncompromisingly reductionist opening salvos and thereby pointing up their polemical character. In tracing the interconnections between the Young Hegelian theorists and their common lineage in Hegel, Marx and Engels display an appreciation for the complex ways in which theoretical ideas can be developed by thinkers sharing a common language of conceptual thought.

Their sensitivity to the nuances of intellectual influence is evident in their treatment of Stirner in *The German Ideology*, for they relate Stirner's thought in a multitude of ways to their source in Hegel. Seven of Hegel's works are invoked to shed light on Stirner's manner of philosophising, and the content as well as the form of Stirner's philosophy is shown to derive and derogate from Hegel's practice of philosophising.[41] Both Kolakowski and McLellan have suggested that the content of Stirner's philosophy departs radically from Hegel's philosophical conception of Spirit.[42] Marx and Engels, however, connect Stirner's conception of the ego to Hegel's enterprise in the *Logic*, where his key term, the Notion, which expresses the self-reflecting character of thought, is linked to the absolute negativity of the ego.[43] The core of Stirner's thought, therefore, is closely associated by Marx and Engels with Hegel's philosophical system and this is a more plausible reading of their relations than the 'break' assumed by McLellan. In *The Philosophy of Spirit* Hegel explicitly links the development of Spirit's achievement in self-awareness, registered in cultural and intellectual activities, to what he terms 'The universality of the I [that] enables it to abstract from everything, even from its life.'[44] Again Stirner's historical understanding of the emergence of egoistic man is related to Hegel's conception of the realisation of Spirit in history. Likewise, in their discussion of Bauer in the second section of *The German Ideology*, Bauer's concern to portray self-consciousness as the teleological truth of historical development is related to its historical source in Hegel's *Phenomenology of Spirit*.[45]

Marx and Engels also note that the criticisms of Feuerbach entertained by Bauer derive from Stirner's criticisms of Feuerbach and Bauer in *The Ego and Its Own*.[46] In that work Stirner had been a severe critic of all forms of thought and practice that he took as masking or thwarting the creative, authentic powers of the ego. Hence he was as scathing about Feuerbach's dissolution of the notion of God into its predicate, an essentialised and spiritualised conception of man and Bauer's assimilation of men to their common 'freedom' in self-consciousness, as he was about the practices of liberalism and socialism, which he saw as sacrificing individual autonomy on the altar of political and social regulation. Marx and Engels point to the provenance of Bauer's strictures against Feuerbach's essentialism and his postulation of man as something holy in the following passage: 'Bauer's criticism of Feuerbach, insofar as it is new, is restricted to hypocritically representing Stirner's reproaches against Feuerbach and Bauer as Bauer's reproaches against Feuerbach.'[47] Throughout *The German Ideology*, in fact, Marx and Engels show themselves to be highly sensitive to the power and force of Stirner's criticisms of Feuerbach and are also at pains to distance themselves from Stirner's criticisms of communism. In the opening section, as noted previously, they criticise Feuerbach's characterisation of himself as a communist. In so doing they employ Feuerbach's transformative method against his own theorising, for they maintain he identifies 'communist' as a predicate of the subject Man and thereby deprives communism of its specific social and political foundations.[48] They explicitly observe that a most serious consequence of Feuerbach's reduction of communism to an abstract humanism is that it allows Saint Bruno and Saint Max (Bauer and Stirner) to 'put in place of the real communist Feuerbach's conception of the communist'.[49] The influence of this Feuerbachian notion of communism and its unfortunate results are analysed by Marx and Engels in considerable detail in the second volume of *The German Ideology*, where the German socialist movement is held to be in thrall to highly abstract philosophical notions of 'man' and his teleologically determined development, which fuse

Feuerbach and Hegel and also reflect Stirner's teleological approach to history.[50]

In their historical treatment of the Young Hegelian theorists, Marx and Engels therefore show how theoretical developments can be comprehended and explained by relating them to theoretical debates and intellectual influences. They appear to assume a level of independence for theory and intellectual argument that contradicts the trenchant materialist reductionism of their opening counterblast to the Young Hegelians and does not square easily with the assumption of the causal primacy of the mode of production that is maintained throughout the opening section of *The German Ideology*. In the course of their treatment of Stirner's discussion of liberalism in the third section of *The German Ideology*, Marx and Engels pay head to the specific conditions of historical development in Germany that are held to have promoted an abnormal, moralistic independence of the bureaucracy, and the apparent independence of the state and German theoreticians whose theories are not straightforwardly consonant with bourgeois interests. German development since the Reformation till the 1840s is held to have displayed a completely petty bourgeois character, and the German theoretical engagement with political forms is consequently seen as assuming a more abstract form than that prevalent elsewhere.[51]

While these comments on German historical development do not fully address the implications of their practice of the history of theory, they do interestingly reflect on a qualification they attach to one of their statements of the causal primacy of the mode of production in the opening section of *The German Ideology*. In this statement, while the mode of production is said to be the basis of all history, explaining the state and different theoretical products, the rider is added that 'by which means of course the whole thing can be depicted in its totality (and therefore, too, the reciprocal action of these various sides of one another)'.[52]

THE GERMAN IDEOLOGY AND THE DEVELOPMENT OF MARX'S THOUGHT

Reflection upon *The German Ideology* as a work in the history of theory helps to clarify the character of Marx's intellectual development. *The German Ideology* has been taken by a variety of critics, including Althusser and Cowling, to signify a decisive theoretical discontinuity in Marx's development. Its criticisms of Feuerbach are held to reflect

Marx's decisive break with the Hegelian and Feuerbachian influences evident in the *Economic and Philosophical Manuscripts* and to register his abandonment of the theory of alienation.[53] The significance of an Althusserian interpretation of *The German Ideology* cannot be dismissed lightly, despite the current unfashionability of Althusser's writings, for as Callincos has observed, Althusser's notion of a radical break between an early 'Hegelian' Marx and a later 'non-Hegelian' one cleared the conceptual space for the currently influential analytical Marxists.[54] In *The German Ideology* Marx and Engels are certainly critical of notions of species, 'man' and 'estrangement', which had previously been assigned key roles in Marx's thought. This criticism is evidently inspired by Stirner's strictures against such language, the susceptibility of socialism and communism to criticism when it is expressed in such concepts, and their professed polemical concern to counter the practice of ordering history according to highly abstract, teleological categories.

The German Ideology, however, does not signal a break from Marx's involvement in the Hegelian tradition. Its discussion of Stirner's conception of the individual, when related to its earlier discussion of the division of labour, makes it evident that, like the *Economic and Philosophical Manuscripts*, it operates with a normative conception of human nature. This normative conception of human nature, emerging clearly in the critique of Stirner, provides the elaborated conceptual reference point for the opening section's account of the materialist view of historical development and for the all-round development of communist man. Its linking of past and future in terms of the negative and positive possibilities of individual and social action relates uneasily to the opening section's repudiation of a teleological goal to the historical process as the past is discussed intermittently in terms of its derogation from a standard to be realised in future communist society. Marx and Engels may be concerned to distinguish their position from philosophers who 'have only interpreted the world, in various ways', but their call for practical action is informed by a general, normative understanding of human capacities.[55] The ambivalence of the characterisation of the historical process in *The German Ideology* resembles the ambiguity of the language of the *Economic and Philosophical Manuscripts*, where history is seen as an unfurling of human capacities realised in communism but 'communism is not as such the goal of human development'.[56]

The German Ideology, then, for a variety of reasons should not be read as a work whose interest resides in a theory of history economically advanced in an opening section that represents a decisive break with a philosophical past. Rather it should be read as an integral whole, whose thoroughgoing commitment to a history of theory represents an incisive historical review of the distinct and interrelated directions in which Hegelian ideas had been taken, that is both massively informed and revealingly informative. This continuous engagement in the history of theory provides the appropriate context in which the opening section's statement of its overall approach to history, its actual analysis of historical development and the character of its portrait of communist society should be assessed. In this light, its polemical concern to counter highly abstract, idealist modes of thought, its express purpose of countering teleological views of history and its continuing involvement in a tradition of thought embracing such standpoints all influence, without being explained by, its expression of a general viewpoint on history and its development. The enterprise of settling accounts with an erstwhile, philosophical conscience should be construed as a process actively informing the formulation of a counterposing view, rather than as the mere reporting of superseded standpoints quite external to the presentation of a new viewpoint.[57]

7 Good and Bad Infinites in Hegel and Marx

This chapter reveals the conceptual affinities between Marx's *Grundrisse* and Hegel's *Logic* by examining the works in the light of Hegel's notion of good and bad infinites. The dynamic of concepts in these works will be shown to turn upon the negative, unsatisfactory character of conceptualisations (bad infinites), which run up against external barriers, and the positive pull of progressively more satisfactory conceptualisations (good infinites), which treat seemingly external barriers as internal moments of their own specification. In sum, the hallmark of a rich and inclusive explanation for Marx, as it is for Hegel, is one that leaves nothing merely presupposed or external. Hence they maintain a paradigm of reflexive, totalising explanation.

The close conceptual affinity between the explanatory procedures of the *Grundrisse* and the *Logic* also intimates a close theoretical linkage between the overall theorising of Hegel and Marx. A focus upon the *Grundrisse*'s reworking of Hegel's notion of good and bad infinites admits an understanding of the conceptual underpinning of its account of alienation, which in turn allows for an appreciation of the links between the *Grundrisse* and the account of species-being articulated in the *Economic and Philosophical Manuscripts*. The upshot is that a close conceptual connection can be established between the early and the late Marx.

Marx's deployment of arguments concerning good and bad infinites in the *Grundrisse* manifests a close theoretical link with Hegel. In the *Grundrisse* and elsewhere, it will be argued that Marx, like Hegel in a number of his works, employs the argumentative logic of good and bad infinites to develop synchronic systematic arguments.[1] Moreover the notion of infinity for both Marx and Hegel by virtue of its specification in terms of good and bad, where the good involves the removal of barriers to free development and the bad an endless rehearsal of limits, entails that evaluative language cannot be divorced from descriptive language.

This chapter pursues what has been set out above. Initially Hegel's notion of infinity in its good and bad forms will be explored by explaining its formal characterisation within the *Logic*, thereafter it's deployment in the *Phenomenology of Spirit* and the *Philosophy of Right*

93

will be analysed. Having set out Hegel's understanding of good and bad infinites and their role in conceptual understanding, Marx's overall argumentative strategy in the *Grundrisse* will be shown to reflect Hegel's understanding of both good and bad infinites. Finally, the continuity of the *Grundrisse* and Marx's *Economic and Philosophical Manuscripts* will be explained.

GOOD AND BAD INFINITES IN HEGEL

Hegel's *Logic* is a notoriously difficult book to read, but an argumentative guiding thread running through the book is the notion of infinity. The notion of infinity is formally and explicitly addressed at the end of Chapter 2, but it also informs transitions throughout the work. Discussion of the infinite in the *Logic* emerges out of the argumentative impasse arising out of the preceding examination of the nature of Being. Being is the conceptually primitive affirmation of reality commencing the *Logic*. Its very poverty, however, is shown to evoke the category of nothing, and the uneasy oscillation between Being and Nothing in turn is taken as yielding a further conceptual specification in terms of determinate being. Determination, however, is held to imply limits and finitude and an urge to supersede barriers of the finite. For Hegel, though, it is a mistake to conceive of the finite as distinct from the infinite. 'Contrasted with the finite, with the sphere of affirmative determinateness, of realities, the infinite is the indeterminate void, the beyond of the finite, whose being-in-itself is not present in its determinate reality.'[2] For Hegel, true infinity is neither opposed to nor beyond the finite, rather it is a way of conceiving the finite as in itself infinite, conceptually united and rendered coherent by a totality of conceptual connections. Hegel expresses the contrast between his conceptions of good and bad infinity by likening the true infinite to a circle where a series of determinate concepts meet with one another, whereas the bad, untrue infinite is represented by a straight line that goes on forever, stretching beyond the points at the end of the line: 'the image of true infinity, bent back into itself, becomes the circle, the line which has reached itself, which is closed and wholly present which is beyond beginning and end'.[3]

An important implication of Hegel's notion of infinity is that the subject of his *Logic* cannot be a suprahuman 'infinite' subject that is beyond finite human beings. The infinite for Hegel is not opposed to the finite, an infinite subject has no extra-finite powers to propel human history or conceptual development. The *Logic*, on this reading, is not the story of how abstract, suprahuman thought creates its own logical conditions for a world, but is an examination of the general categories of human thought by which reality is to be conceptualised. The development of categories in the *Logic* turns upon the progressive achievement of categories that explain themselves by being inclusive, and hence dealing with all that is implied by them.

Ultimately Hegel argues that a full, self-sufficient categorial explanation of reality must invoke categories that explain the character of conceptual explanation itself, which for Hegel is produced by categories of the Notion. The concrete representation of the Notion is the ego, the dynamic source of human, free thinking. But for Hegel a full explanation of reality must include categories that explain how the freedom of the infinite conceptual power of the ego underlies all reality. Hence the categories of the Idea exemplify the good infinite of developmental categorial thinking, in which the free self-development of thought itself is taken as pervading all categories. The Idea of Life takes reality as developing in a self-reproducing way, in which living organisms relate to one another and nature in ways that sustain the species. The death of the individual in the ongoing life of the species, however, points up deficiencies in this mode of being; the gap between the individual and the universal is palpable. The category of teleology is important in that Hegel recognises the deficiencies of an external teleology in which there is a gap between ends and means. He invokes the notion of an infinite teleology, expressing the circularity of a good infinite, in which the framing of ends and means are internal to the process of developing ways of thinking and being. The notion of an infinite teleology leads on to the Absolute Idea, which is seen by Hegel not as an absolute beyond what has gone before but a category that posits reality as a series of categories that successively capture its character as an infinitely self-related series of concepts. The Absolute Idea is absolute because it is reflexive and inclusive in its explanation of its own status as a category involved in all other categories. There is nothing external to it that limits its perspective; it registers difference, not as an unknowable, external barrier but as a series of distinct expressions of its own character.

Hegel's notion of the interrelated character of the finite and the infinite entails that his system as a whole does not privilege thought as the abstract but potent subject that Taylor and Michael Rosen have identified as the creative, Hegelian source of nature and the finite.[4] Hegel's dialectic is not the outcome of the externalisation of a preconstituted subject, but is the presuppositionless investigation of categories and concepts that progressively make sense out of experience.[5]

The worlds of nature and human life, on this reading of Hegel, are not to be taken as created by thought but as inextricably linked to categories of thought if those categories are to be genuinely infinite and inclusive. The general categories of the *Logic* imply and apply to the more concrete explorations of the natural and human worlds that Hegel undertakes. The categories of the *Logic* invoke modes of subjectivity and objectivity that maintain references to natural and human worlds, and hence the concrete investigations where Hegel develops these implications. Indeed the priority for Hegel resides with the concrete, for without an actual natural and human world in which human beings develop ways of acting and thinking that make possible the logical investigations, reality would not be knowable.

The essential interconnectedness of Hegel's philosophical system has two important implications for this study of Hegel and Marx. It means on the one hand that Hegel's important categorial notions of good and bad infinites inform his other more concrete works, and that Marx's *Grundrisse*, in following the *Logic*'s deployment of notions of good and bad infinites, also evokes other works of Hegel. Hence Hegel's discussion of utility or profitability in the *Phenomenology of Spirit* exemplifies an endless and bad process of infinity that resembles Marx's account of money. Likewise Hegel's discussion of needs and freedom in the *Philosophy of Right* has affinities on the one hand with the infinite and insatiable expansion of capital, and on the other with the infinite self-mediating character of social labour under communism.

Hegel's *Phenomenology of Spirit* represents an investigation into the conditions whereby consciousness can undertake a philosophical explanation of reality. Its end point is the standpoint of absolute knowledge, where the conscious knowing mind sees truth as integral to the object of its consciousness. For Hegel, this standpoint of the Absolute is depicted in a way that evokes the notion of the Good Infinite. 'It is the process of its own becoming, the circle which presupposes its end as its purpose, and has its end for its beginning; it becomes concrete and actual only by being carried out, and by the end it involves.'[6] The absolute of self-consciousness, as it is depicted in the *Phenomenology of Spirit*, consists in the absolute mediation of finite and infinite.

This meeting point of the finite and infinite is what lies behind the significance of the dialectic of recognition in the *Phenomenology of*

Spirit. The format of the *Phenomenology of Spirit* is for the most part synchronic in its evocation of forms of consciousness that claim to know truth, and during the course of the work Hegel follows the inadequacy of modes of consciousness that invoke richer modes of consciousness. The dialectic of recognition in its depiction of the struggle between the master and slave makes clear that consciousness and its claims must be social. An individual consciousness cannot know itself; its determinacy and finiteness only make sense in a wider setting of reciprocal social recognition and the process of social development set in train by the master–servant relationship. Hegel, in his discussion of the master–servant interaction, explicitly recognises that the master–servant struggle actually takes place in history, but in the *Phenomenology of Spirit* he reviews this struggle for recognition conceptually so as to show the necessarily social and developmental aspects of human experience. While the struggle for recognition shows that individual, finite minds are self-mediating the master–servant relationship sets up barriers between minds that must be overcome if finite spirits are to see themselves as infinitely self-related.

Thereafter Hegel proceeds to examine a series of historic modes of human interaction, such as stoicism, scepticism and the unhappy consciousness in which the universal is either affirmed or denied in abstraction from finite concrete phenomena. Hegel, in dealing with the estranged world of post-medieval Europe and the dislocation of history and experience expressed in the Enlightenment, sees estrangement in ways that anticipate Marx's focus upon economic and social life. He depicts alienation in terms of a conceptual world whose discordance registers a bad infinite. For instance state power and wealth are seen as vital aspects of the absolutist states of the early modern world, sucking all human endeavours into an infinite series of supposedly contrasting activities that in fact imply one another, and in turn generate a spiritual critique that admonishes against the vanity of such enterprises.[7] Again, in his discussion of the truth of the Enlightenment, Hegel fixes on the way the drive for pure insight in Enlightenment thought focuses upon utility, the idea of the useful and the profitable, which posits 'the shifting change...of the moments of being-in-itself.[8] The notion of utility or profitably thereby relates finite objects to the infinite process of insightful judgment, but the objects are merely reviewed in an endless process of infinite specification without reflecting on the infinite character of thought, 'Thinking this knowledge about finitude as the truth to be the highest knowledge attainable.'[9]

The logic of the *Logic*'s characterisation of thought as setting up good and bad processes of infinite progression also informs the *Philosophy of Right*. While resting upon historical developments that Hegel himself set out in his *Lectures on the Philosophy of History*, the argument of the *Philosophy of Right*, like that of Marx's *Grundrisse*, is presented synchronically, in which basic and simple categories of social and political life are seen as insufficient in themselves. They are shown to generate more inclusive, self-sustaining ones. The key foundational concept in the *Philosophy of Right* is the notion of the will, which is taken to be coterminous with freedom. The simple notion of freedom is recognised to be infinite, matching the logical category of the notion itself. The pure freedom of the will is exemplified by the will's infinite capacity to abstract from any particular determination. But this infinite potential of the will is abstract and only invokes a bad infinite of endless repetition in which the form of the will is forever external to particular contents.[10]

The dialectical drive of the argument in the *Philosophy of Right* is to provide an inclusive concept in which the infinite self-determining power of the ego will be incorporated within a concrete world of social content that expresses this infinity. For Hegel the ultimate answer is the development of a concrete world of social and political life consisting of family life, a range of 'private' activities in civil society and the overarching political laws of the state. Any standpoint short of this encompassing social and political perspective is defective for Hegel as the universality of the will is taken as requiring a concrete expression in a universal pattern of social life. The institutions of property and contract, for example, are only seen as viable when they are understood as moments of a social and political perspective that explains their logical emergence. In the *Grundrisse* Marx shows that he is aware of the systematic logic of Hegel's argument in relation to property.[11]

MARX, CONCEPTUAL DEVELOPMENT AND INFINITY

Marx's *Grundrisse*, since its emergence in 1953, has been seen as notable, amongst other things, for its explicit invocation of Hegel and Hegelian modes of argument to analyse economic life under capitalism.[12] A notable presentation of this argument is in Uchida's *Marx's Grundrisse and Hegel's Logic*.[13] Uchida quite rightly observes the dependence of the *Grundrisse* upon Hegel's *Logic*. But his work suffers from an insufficient recognition of the overall manner in which Hegel and Marx approach the task of conceptual explanation. A brief summary of Uchida's argument is that the *Grundrisse*'s chapters on money and capital mirror the chapters on Being and Essence in the *Logic*. This explanation is neat and tidy but in itself does not do justice to the overall, common dialectical form of argument in the two works.

The notion of infinity in its good and bad variants helps to explain the dynamics of dialectical development in both Hegel and Marx. Just as for Hegel a bad infinite of finite beings or utilitarian, profit-making calculations does not register the infinitely self-related and self-producing character of categories, so money and capital in distinct ways reduce aspects of social reality to the external (bad infinite) rhythms of their own circulation. Again, just as for Hegel, social and political freedom and a philosophical consciousness register the goals of a good infinite in their capacity fully to explain their own character, so capital, in its capacity to reproduce its own conditions and control all aspects of production, approaches a true infinity of self-mediated, self-production. Moreover beneath the surface of Marx's arguments about money and capital in the *Grundrisse* resides the notion of an explicitly ordered social organisation of social labour matching the requirements of true infinity.

In the Introduction to the *Grundrisse*, Marx makes some general comments on his approach to the study of political economy that make clear his general intellectual and methodological debt to Hegel. As Smith observes in *Dialectical Social Theory and Its Critics*, Marx is concerned to establish a methodological procedure that points in the direction of Hegel and allows a systematic conceptualisation of economic phenomena.[14] This procedure allows scope for Marx's self-conscious use of Hegelian notions of good and bad infinity to advance his subsequent arguments.

Marx observes that social reality is not a world of discrete things but is relational, which Ollman has justly noted to be foundational for the practice of dialectical argument.[15] The basis of the relational character, of reality for Marx lies in its social character, which he affirms in his critique of political economists. In the course of the *Grundrisse* Marx employs an argument against the notion of a private language to confirm conceptually the social, relational character of reality.[16] While in the Introduction Marx emphasises that his material reading of reality contrasts sharply with Hegel's idealist reading, at the same time he observes that relations 'can be expressed, of course, only in ideas'.[17] The conceptual expression of the thoroughly relational character of reality allows Marx, in the *Grundrisse*, to conceive of the capitalist political economy in terms of infinitely self-related categories.

Marx also affirms in the Introduction that the correct mode of theoretical analysis ascends from a small number of determinant abstract general relations. His rationale follows Hegel's line of reasoning. 'The concrete is the concrete because it is the concretion of many determinations, hence unity of the diverse.'[18] Marx's theoretical procedure assumes that a developed explanation will have the form of a self-mediated unity in diversity, which Hegel sees as the hallmark of the good infinite and Smith and Arthur identify as characterising the systematic mode of explanation in *Capital*.[19] Marx explicitly recognises the concordance of his theoretical method with that of Hegel. Marx invokes the *Philosophy of Right* to explain how more abstract categories should be tackled before more complex ones, thereby confirming the relevance of the *Philosophy of Right* for the *Grundrisse* and Marx's recognition of the intimate relationship between the argument of the *Philosophy of Right* and the *Logic*. Marx notes how, in the *Philosophy of Right*, possession is treated before the concepts of the family, clan or state even though the latter are historically prior to and conditional for possession. What Hegel has rightly alighted upon, for Marx, is an ordering of concepts whereby the more inclusive and explanatory succeed the relatively simpler ones.[20] The succeeding chapters on money and capital exemplify this methodological precept in that the concrete world of material production is developed out of simple general abstractions: money and capital.

Finally, the Introduction to the *Grundrisse* emphasises that a political economy is an interconnected world in which production, distribution, exchange and consumption must be seen as interrelated phenomena. Within this notion of an interconnected set of relations, Marx gives priority to production; the priority is a logical one in that the interrelated conditions of a political economy must be produced and reproduced by a given mode of production in history. The chapter on capital shows how a capitalist political economy can only be seen as a self-reproducing system within the context of capital determining the conditions of labour and production. It is capital's capacity to make its own conditions of production and also to determine the patterns of exchange and distribution and consumption that gives capital the form of a good, self-mediating infinite system in which all determinations function as internally related conditions, rather than external limits.[21] The interrelated conditions of a productive system are established at the outset of the *Grundrisse* by Marx's critique of Proudonist schemes for credit reform. These schemes are condemned as partial measures due to their abstraction from the totality of interrelated conditions comprising a system.

The introductory chapter of the *Grundrisse* sets out an Hegelian conceptual framework, which is subsequently exemplified in the chapters on money and capital. In making sense out of these discursive conceptual investigations, it is important to see the argumentative wood for the terminological trees. Uchida, in *Marx's Grundrisse and Hegel's Logic*, connects the two works by observing how particular concepts employed by Marx match those deployed in the *Logic*.[22] Overall, however, he does not show how the dynamics of the arguments of both Hegel and Marx display a common pattern. While there are many affinities between the terms and concepts used in the *Grundrisse* and the *Logic*, their shared conceptions of good and bad infinites are central in an explanation of the development and logic of their arguments. A concept or category such as money or quantity, capital or measure is at key points shown to require development when it specifies an endless series of instantiations that do not reflect back to explain their conditions. The resulting failure of explanation demands a new form of categorisation. Likewise in both works a concept is taken to be satisfactory insofar as it is truly infinite in explaining its own conditions and development.

One of the implications of a developmental argumentative procedure, as employed by Hegel and Marx, is that concepts and levels of argument are not external to one another. A Hegelian interpretation of reality is, as Smith has observed, 'overdetermined'.[23] Hence, while Hegel's *Logic* concludes by conceiving reality as a self-mediating series of thoughts, this standpoint continues to maintain that reality has the being designated in its opening category. Likewise Hegel's sophisticated conceptual understanding of a complex world of social and political practices does not exclude specific acts of freedom. Similarly Marx's conceptions of the circulation of money and the self-reproduction of capital contain simpler determinations of the conceptions of commodities and exchange value. The linkages that Uchida observes between the *Grundrisse*'s chapter on money and the *Logic*'s chapter on Being, and the *Grundrisse*'s chapter on capital and the *Logic*'s chapter on Essence obtain: money and commodities exist and capital appears in many guises. These connections, however, do not preclude an affinity between the overall dynamics of argument within the two works, which takes its bearings from the completely self-mediating, comprehensive categorial explanation exhibited by the good infinity of Hegel's absolute idea.

Marx's understanding of a commodity, whereby a commodity's identity is bound up with its determinate relation to another commodity, recalls Hegel's notion of determinate being in the *Logic*. Commodities are distinguished from one another by endless discrete qualitative use values. Money is an endless quantitative measure of exchange value, and exchange value is expressed phenomenally in the 'becoming' of monetary transactions. Again, Marx's account of circulation, in which the identity of objects turns upon a rhythm of change, is allied to Hegel's account of becoming in the chapter on Being in his *Logic*.

Marx's account of capital in the *Grundrisse* also evokes Hegel's account of semblance and appearance as categories of Essence. In the simple circulation of commodities and money, the determination of the distinct phenomenal forms in which they appear is not explained. Uchida is right to see within Marx's explanation of the increasingly self-reproducing nature of capital intimations of the logic of Hegel's account of essence.[24] The form of capital lies behind its various appearances and acts as their ground. The capitalist political economy in a developed capitalist world expresses the logic of essence in that it constitutes a unified whole composed of distinguishable parts, which act upon one another reciprocally.[25]

Central to the dynamics of Marx's explanation of money and capital in the *Grundrisse*, however, are the contradictory natures of the bad infinite constituted by the circulation of money and the quasi good but ultimately flawed infinite described by capital as a self-reproducing system. Insofar as capital and money in one of its circuits exhibit the self-reproducing character of Hegel's category of the Notion, then Uchida's understanding of the *Grundrisse* as exhibiting the Hegelian logical categories of Being and Essence is partial.[26]

In the *Grundrisse* the circulation of money comes up against the 'bad infinity' of limits acting as barriers to its own continued production. Marx observes that 'The circulation of money, like that of commodities, begins at an infinity of different points, and to an infinity of different points it returns.'[27] Marx highlights the way in which the circulation is infinite in the sense of being endless, but also notes that this endless process does not explain the conversion of money into and from commodity form. 'At first sight, circulation appears as a simply infinite process. The commodity is exchanged for money, money is exchanged for the commodity, and this is repeated endlessly.'[28] This circuit (CMMC) appears endless and neither produces nor explains its own conditions. Likewise the reverse circulation, where money is translated into a commodity and commodity translated into money (MCCM), inserts break points in the circle of motion where money might be expended. But when money is deployed to make money through the purchase and sale of commodities, thereby generating more money to acquire commodities so as to make money a continuous process, then, for Marx, the logical basis of capitalism has arrived.[29]

Insofar as money in circulation generates its own conditions for circulation, then it assumes the aspect of a good infinite, but it has not established a rhythmic control of the productive process. Capital expresses the self-mediating character of the good infinite more adequately by acquiring in commodity form fixed and variable capital, which it deploys to generate the conditions of its own production. 'The immortality which money strove to achieve by setting itself negatively against circulation, by withdrawing from it, is achieved by capital which preserves itself precisely by abandoning itself to circulation.'[30]

But while capital has features of the good infinite, it is nonetheless beset by contradictions that undermine its claims to be a good infinite. Whereas the trajectory of the self-reproducing process of capital constantly promotes the build-up of fixed capital, surplus value depends upon the use value of labour power. The logic of the process of capitalism thereby undermines its own process of reproduction, and a token of this internal failing is the tendency for the rate of profit to fall. The tendency for capital to be infinitely self-reproducing is thereby undermined. Additionally, the kind of infinite self-reproducing system to which capitalism aspires is also one in which the generative, creative conditions of its production and reproduction are distorted rather than affirmed. The creative power of social labour, which the infinite self-reproducing power of capital trades upon, is expressed in an alienated form. 'The creative power of his [proletarian] labour establishes itself as an alien power confronting him'.[31] In the *Grundrisse* Marx refers to the master–servant dialectic of intersubjective misrecognition in Hegel's *Phenomenology of Spirit* in expressing this alienated, limited aspect of capitalism. 'It [the master–servant relation] is represented – in mediated form – in capital, and thus likewise forms a ferment of its dissolution and is an emblem of its limitation.'[32]

The 'bad' limits of the infinity of capital are also exhibited in the denial of the social and creative power of labour, whereby capital is driven constantly to seek more quantitative profit, and in so doing maintains an endless and sterile bad infinite. Marx observes that capital functions as Hegel's bad quantitative infinite. 'Fixed as wealth, as the general form of wealth, as value which counts as value, it [capital] is therefore the constant drive to go beyond its quantitative limit, an endless process.'[33] Hegel, in his lectures on the themes of the *Philosophy of Right*, likewise concludes that the multiplication of needs under the spell of those hoping to make a profit exemplified a bad infinite. 'What the English call "comfort" is inexhaustible and illimitable.'[34]

Capital, for Marx, contains the seeds of its own destruction in terms of the kind of self-reproducing infinite system it generates. It will be superseded by a form of social organisation that exemplifies the self-limiting ideal of ethical life that the Greeks recognised.[35] Social labour under communism will generate the conditions for social individuals to find fulfilment in productive activity and leisure consequent on a rational organisation of social labour. The social and creative conditions of production will be enhanced and recognised in social development.

The self-sustaining 'infinite' logic of communism is highlighted in Marx's early writings. In the *Economic and Philosophical Manuscripts*, species-being is portrayed in ways that evoke Hegel's good infinite. The species character of man's being resides in a person's universal character; he can produce freely and universally, and under communism the free universal character of the individual will be expressed in a productive system in which the individuals mark thier universal character by developing a range of powers and needs. The 'infinite' character of species life, whereby the species and individual are internally self-related, is exhibited in the following quotation: 'Man's individual and species-life are not two *distinct things*, however much – and this is necessarily so – the mode of existence of individual life is a more *particular* or a more *general* mode of the species-life, or a species-life a more *particular* or more *general* individual life.'[36] Marx, in the *Economic and Philosophical Manuscripts*, shows his awareness of Hegel's notion of a good infinite by characterising the relationship between the three parts of Hegel's mature system as an illicit portrayal of a movement from the infinite to the finite and back.[37] Marx's appreciation of self-determining explanations in which arguments are 'infinitely' self-related is exemplified in his ranking of Epicurean atomism above Democritean in his doctoral dissertation.[38]

The continuity of Marx's interest in and employment of the argumentative logic of Hegel's notion of infinity is also exemplified in *The German Ideology*. In the preceding chapter Marx and Engels were shown to invoke Hegel's notion of a good infinite in its section on Stirner, in framing an understanding of the universality of the social individual so as to criticise Stirner's idea of the unique, particular individual.[39] In a discussion of Marx and the finite, Smith urges that Marx's conception and support for the Paris Commune is derived from its purported achievement of a rational unity of the universal (or infinite) and the individual.[40]

In a breezy, short, critical review of Marx's thought, Elster has specifically castigated the Hegelian conceptual dialectic of the *Grundrisse*. He urges, 'Although some of the transitions make sense when seen as historical developments, the purported dialectical connection is unintelligible. Concepts have no "logic of development" independently of the actions that men undertake for purposes of their own.'[41] This chapter has been concerned to make Marx's *Grundrisse* intelligible in terms of its use of an Hegelian mode of argument. Moreover, while Elster is right to point to the fact that concepts are not independent of the actions of men, it is also true that individual actions are related to a world of social meanings. Hegel's *Logic*, on my reading, is concerned with the interrelations of concepts involved in man's contact with the world and one another and remains a plausible project. Marx's *Grundrisse* founds its conceptual investigations on the basis of the social nature of men and women. Human activities are seen as social and interrelated and the only way of expressing and understanding these relations is through ideas. The exploration of the interrelation of ideas in a political economy is intelligible and does not exclude, rather it demands accompanying human activities. Smith has observed that Marx and Hegel entertained the reciprocity between the individual and the social in undertaking categorial explanations. 'It is not generally appreciated how social theorists such as Marx and Hegel sought microfoundations when motivating categorial transitions.'[42] The notion of the good infinite in both Hegel and Marx turns upon a recognition that the activities of men and women are interrelated and that if human beings are to be free, then a way of grasping and structuring these relations must be found. This is a distinct view of freedom, but it is not a nonsensical one.

8 New Leviathans for Old: Collingwood's Hobbes and the Spirit of Hegel

INTRODUCTION

In the Preface to the first edition of *The New Leviathan*, Collingwood states that 'A reader may take the title of this book in whichever way he pleases.'[1] In contrast the title of this chapter is designed to impose constraints on how the title and the contents of *The New Leviathan* should be interpreted. The title 'New Leviathans for Old: Collingwood's Hobbes and the Spirit of Hegel' is framed so as to highlight how Collingwood's critical, revisionary reading of Hobbes's *Leviathan* is inspired by the spirit of Hegel's understanding of intellectual history, mind and culture.

The transformation of the old *Leviathan* into *The New Leviathan* reflects Collingwood's adherence to an Hegelian form of historicism. Investigation into the nature of mind and civilisation in *The New Leviathan* is undertaken by reviewing the history of the development of mind and civilisation in theory and practice. The very title of *The New Leviathan* intimates its defining links with the past. In *The New Leviathan* Collingwood sees mind and civilisation as historical achievements, lacking fixed extra-historical identities, which are only to be understood through historical enquiry. These assumptions render Collingwood's approach historicist. Collingwood's historicism reflects Hegel's recognition that Spirit, the capacity for meaning exhibited in human activities, is to be known through its actual historical development.[2] Collingwood's commitment to the significance of history in human affairs neither entails adherence to a version of historicism that has been castigated by Popper for its presumption that there are general laws of historical development, nor involves the thorough going relativism that has been attributed to his later works.[3]

Collingwood, in *The New Leviathan*, adheres to Hegel's conception of intellectual history, as exemplified in the *Lectures on the History of Philosophy*. For Hegel, progress in philosophy is a process of continuous historical engagement with preceding philosophies that distils the key principles of prevailing cultures. 'Every philosophy has been and still is necessary. The principles are retained; the most recent philosophy being the result of all preceding and hence no philosophy has ever been refuted.'[4] In *The New Leviathan* Collingwood's critical reading of Hobbes aims to fulfil the Hegelian agenda of resuming and improving upon the standpoint of a theoretical predecessor within the context of a subsequent intellectual and cultural context. This affinity between Hegel and Collingwood is remarked upon by Boucher, and doubtless arises out of Collingwood's subtle appreciation of Hegel's *Lectures on the History of Philosophy*, which is recorded in *The Idea of History*.[5]

For Collingwood, the transformation of the old *Leviathan* into *The New Leviathan* represents progress.[6] Progress, however, is not seen as a mere repudiation of a preceding standpoint but as a new substantive account of mind and civilisation that is developed out of reflection on and criticism of its historical predecessor. This Hegelian notion of intellectual progress reflects and supports the standpoint set out in Collingwood's essay 'Progress as Created by Historical Thinking'.[7] In this essay, Collingwood argues that a new intellectual achievement, if it is to count as progress, must be authenticated by invoking an historical perspective, in the form of past achievements and standards. 'The reason for this [the role of historical thinking in intellectual progress] is that progress in those cases (common or rare) when it happens, happens only in one way; by the retention in the mind at one phase, of what was achieved in the preceding phase.'[8]

Collingwood's views on progress in moral philosophy are declared in his 'Lectures on Moral Philosophy for Michaelmas Term, 1921'. In these lectures the possibility of progress in moral philosophy is seen as arising out of combining ancient ethical objectivism with a modern recognition of morality as being tied to the freedom of human agency. The general conditions for this achievement are taken as depending upon the historical development of modern forms of freedom. The successors of Kant, who aimed to unite modern subjectivity with ancient objectivity, are identified as laying the intellectual foundations of moral progress. In the lectures Collingwood refers positively to 'The kind of view which Kant and his successors have been gradually building upon as a synthesis of the ancient objectivism with the modern subjectivism.'[9]

Insofar as Hegel represents the key successor to Kant, self-consciously aiming to synthesise ancient and modern forms of idealism, then Collingwood looks to Hegel as playing a crucial role in the formulation of an ethical standpoint superseding earlier historic accounts. On the one hand Hegel inspires Collingwood's enterprise of constructing a progressive moral theory on the basis of a critical reading of past theory and practice. On the other hand Collingwood, in reworking ancient and modern standpoints, looks to Hegel's substantive account of ethics in which Hegel is self-consciously aiming to combine an objectivist account of ethics with a recognition of the freedom and subjectivity of individuals.[10]

The notion of intellectual progress advanced above is exemplified in *The New Leviathan*. In this work, Collingwood develops an historical understanding of the development of mind and civilisation. Central to this undertaking is its specification of the conditions of a political community that expresses the freedom of its members and thereby furnishes the conditions for civilised interaction between human beings. Collingwood recognises that a free political community and the ideal of civilisation are historic achievements. He also understands their intellectual identification to be the product of successive historical endeavours. In advancing his account of a free political community and the ideal of civilisation, Collingwood incorporates the Hegelian notions of historical development and political association as a synthesis of free, individual agency and the sustaining 'educative' practices and institutions of the community.

Given the affinities between Hegel and Collingwood on history, politics and culture it is ironic that Collingwood, in *The New Leviathan*, disparages Hegel's political thought and sense of historical development.[11] The oddity of this disparagement has been remarked upon in recent discussions of *The New Leviathan* by Nicholson and Vincent.[12] Nicholson, in his paper 'Collingwood's *New Leviathan*: Then and Now', constructs his reading of *The New Leviathan* around the solution of the following double puzzle: 'why does he [Collingwood] make so much of Hobbes and so little of Hegel?'[13] Nicholson diagnoses this double puzzle as arising out of *The New Leviathan*'s affinity with Hegel's political thought and its sharp divergence from that of Hobbes. Nicholson cites the cleavage between rulers and ruled and the lack of concern for the need to prepare individuals for citizenship in the old *Leviathan* as distinguishing it sharply from Collingwood's preoccupations in *The New Leviathan*. He also recognises how Hegel's identification of the dependence of political institutions upon a range of social practices and promotion of an ideal of citizenship anticipate the overriding concerns of Collingwood in *The New Leviathan*.[14]

Nicholson contrives to resolve the puzzle by pointing to the contingent circumstances in which *The New Leviathan* was written. Collingwood wrote *The New Leviathan* when England was pitched in battle against Germany. In this war, England could be seen with some plausibility as a standard bearer for civilisation against the forces of barbarism unleashed by Nazi Germany. Nicholson urges that the circumstances of the war induced Collingwood to deny the intellectual kinship of a leading German political philosopher, Hegel, and to overplay the significance of Hobbes, whom he regarded as a most English philosopher.[15]

Nicholson's views on Collingwood's reading of the relative importance of Hobbes and Hegel for the argument of *The New Leviathan* is supported by research by other commentators.[16] While Nicholson's interpretation of and solution to the paradoxes involved in the readings of Hobbes and Hegel in *The New Leviathan* is generally persuasive, Collingwood's conceptions of Hobbes and Hegel may be explored further. The irony of Collingwood's praise of Hobbes and disparagement of Hegel, for example, is heightened by recognising the Hegelian inspiration for the notion of intellectual history underpinning Collingwood's positive reading of Hobbes's *Leviathan*. Again, on the Hegelian assumption of the critical and progressive character of intellectual history, Collingwood's positive reading of Hobbes is more intelligible. Moreover, while the negative and one-sided reading of Hegel in *The New Leviathan* was doubtless provoked by the exigencies of war, Collingwood's criticisms are consonant with remarks he makes elsewhere. Collingwood, in maintaining that Hegel does not allow for the freedom of citizens, invokes a reading of authoritarian German political practice as disallowing its intellectual comprehension. While this reading of German politics is partial and summary, the standpoint does reflect Collingwood's belief in the dependence of theory on practice. Collingwood's general critique of Hegel's philosophy is questionable, and jars with his sympathetic and close reading of Hegel in *The Idea of History* and elsewhere.[17] Indeed my own review of Collingwood's published and unpublished writings on cosmology and nature highlights how Collingwood draws upon Hegel's natural philosophy.[18] On the other hand, the critique of Hegel's idealism in *The New Leviathan* on the ground of its illicit imposition of a preformulated rational scheme upon nature and history, rehearses a standpoint evident in other published and unpublished works by Collingwood.[19]

MIND, SOCIETY, CIVILISATION AND BARBARISM

Mind

Collingwood's *The New Leviathan* is a systematic study of the nature of civilisation and the character of the contemporary revolt against it. Central questions concerning civilisation are taken as presupposing subordinate ones and the series of answers are seen as forming inter-related categories of mind and forms of social experience. This systematic elaboration of the conditions of man and society that underpin civilisation links Collingwood to both Hobbes and Hegel. Hobbes and Hegel are political philosophers who undertake a systematic exploration of man and his political activities. Where *The New Leviathan* approximates to Hegel rather than Hobbes, however, is in its emphasis on the historical character of mind and society.

In *The New Leviathan* mind and society, the bases of civilisation, are seen as historical achievements and objects of historical study. For Collingwood, the character of mind and the way it is to be studied are dialectically linked in that historical study itself is seen as a product of modern history and is of a piece with the notion of duty, the highest sphere of practical reason, which likewise is an achievement of modern times. The dialectical relationship between the character of mind and its comprehension maintained in *The New Leviathan* rehearses Hegel's dialectical notion of mind. *The Phenomenology of Spirit*, Hegel's study of consciousness and self-consciousness, is organised so as to express the way the mind, in being conscious of a mind-affected reality, is exploring its own self-conscious character.[20] Its review of forms of consciousness invokes historical, social modes of consciousness such as ancient stoicism and scepticism, for consciousness is shown to be inherently social and historical. At the outset of *The Phenomenology of Spirit* Hegel observes, 'Of the Absolute it must be said that it is essentially a result, that only at the end is it what it is in very truth; and just in that consists its nature, which is to be actual, subject, or self-becoming, self-development.'[21] Hegel's historical, developmental view of Spirit culminates in his own philosophical understanding of the spiritual or mind-affected nature of reality, just as Collingwood's study of mind in *The New Leviathan* culminates in the study of history, which is presented as the means of apprehending the developmental nature of mind.

The New Leviathan and *The Phenomenology of Spirit* are at one in seeing the mind as inherently free, and in taking this essential freedom as being developed in a series of stages. Hobbes, as I have observed in a previous chapter, does not see the mind as susceptible to develop-ment.[22] In the *Leviathan* the behaviour of human beings is seen as mechanistic and determined. Men, for Hobbes, are free if their choices are not constrained by other human beings. Freedom is not taken to imply that human beings supersede the causal determination of their desires.[23] Hobbes does not allow for the self to discriminate its motivations and character.[24]

Collingwood's account of the mind in *The New Leviathan*, however, appears to diverge from Hegel in its adherence to an historical rather than philosophical method of enquiry. Collingwood claims to employ 'Locke's historical plain method'.[25] Whereas Hegel, in his *Phenomen-ology of Spirit*, combines synchronic with diachronic investigation, Col-lingwood purports to undertake a thoroughly historical study. Sense certainty, for instance, is taken by Hegel to be a ubiquitous feature of human experience, whereas he reviews the Enlightenment as a specific historical phenomenon.[26] For Collingwood the entire project of study-ing the mind, including appetites and feelings, is an historical study.

Collingwood's conception of his method in *The New Leviathan* as historical is problematic not least because it does not fit neatly with his account in *The Idea of History* of the nature of historical understanding as the reenactment of past thoughts.[27] His examination of cultural conventions such as marriage and the presuppositions of practices such as science can only be seen as consonant with the reenactment doctrine if, as Van Der Dussen has observed, they are construed as applicable to thoughts implicit in institutions and customs.[28] What is frankly puzzling in Collingwood's account of mind in *The New Leviathan*, however, is his avowedly 'historical' treatment of precon-scious and low-grade forms of consciousness. Historical reenactment in *The Idea of History* relates only to purposive behaviour that expresses rational thought. Resolution of the problems posed by Col-lingwood's depiction of the entire project of *The New Leviathan* as historical can only be conjectural. Perhaps Collingwood takes the whole of *The New Leviathan* as being susceptible to historical treat-ment insofar as low-grade forms of consciousness are understood as leading to the higher grades of consciousness that do develop historic-ally and can be apprehended by historical reenactment. Consequently the entire project of mapping the nature of mind assumes an historical aspect as an act of thinking by a representative of modern European civilisation. This admittedly conjectural construal of the historical character of *The New Leviathan* implies a mix of synchronic and diachronic perspectives reminiscent of Hegel's *Phenomenology of Spirit*.

The functions of the mind catalogued in *The New Leviathan* exhibit a progressively developing degree of freedom and understanding. The highest reaches of the mind are declared to be duty, the apogee of practical reason and theoretical reason. Duty is designated as superior to the preceding forms of practical reason, right and utility on account of the insufficiently rational deliberation of ends and means undertaken by the self in these forms in determining its choices.[29] The superiority of duty to utility represents an implicit critique of Hobbes in that practical human action is characterised in utilitarian terms in the *Leviathan*. An analogue of Collingwood's notion of duty is Hegel's conception of Forgiveness (*Verzeihung*) in *The Phenomenology of Spirit*, which harmonises the individual's moral standpoint with his or her social world and hence supersedes the unworldly self-righteousness of the Beautiful Soul and the all too worldly cynicism of the Man of Action.[30]

Dutiful action, for Collingwood, eliminates all caprice and externality from action, an achievement that reflects the judgement on mind and reality in his lecture 'Method and Metaphysics' (1935), where 'the more real is the more self-dependent'.[31] Collingwood links the modern development of duty to the emergence of historical thinking as the characteristic theoretical perspective of the modern age. In his discussion of theoretical reason, Collingwood observes that the specifically historical perspective has superseded the previous dominance of regularian and utilitarian perspectives. The exalted status of historical study contrasts starkly with Hobbes's endorsement of the geometrical method. It also differs from Hegel's assessment of the supreme status of speculative philosophy, even if philosophy, for Hegel, is predicated upon history and historical understanding.

Society, Civilisation and Barbarism

The rationale for the elaboration of a theory of mind in the first part of *The New Leviathan* is to provide a basis for a discussion of society and civilisation, because society and civilisation are assumed and shown to be things of the mind. The other side of this coin, however, is the dependence of mind upon social life. Collingwood's conception of man as a social being is intimated in his discussion of the role of language in allowing for consciousness of feeling. Hobbes is praised for his recognition of the indispensability of language in furnishing the basis of knowledge, but Collingwood anticipates more contemporary theories of language, as in his unpublished 'Observations on Language', where the lexicographer's determination of meaning is dependent on 'correct usage as existing'.[32] The dependence of the individual on his or her social setting assumed in this notion of language is rehearsed in the discussion of will in *The New Leviathan*: 'The idea of oneself as having a will is correlative, therefore, to the idea of something other than oneself as having a will.'[33]

Collingwood's notion of the mutual recognition of wills recalls Hegel's accounts of recognition, the most notable of which are in *The Phenomenology of Spirit* and *The Philosophy of Right*. In *The Phenomenology of Spirit* Hegel depicts the struggle for recognition as an inescapable feature of self-consciousness. It is taken to involve a life-and-death struggle and the subordination of one will to another in a master–slave relationship. Its resolution is seen as residing in the mutual recognition of self-conscious, social subjects. Haddock has rightly observed how this theme is rehearsed in *The Philosophy of Right*'s account of property and contract.[34] Collingwood's understanding of the reciprocity of mind and society, then, is reminiscent of Hegel and he articulates the individual's dependence upon society more explicitly than Hobbes. Indeed this accenting of the social nature of the individual is an example of the process of transformation of the old *Leviathan* into *The New Leviathan*. In his unpublished 'Lectures on Moral Philosophy' (1921), Collingwood highlights this 'social' dimension of human beings by emphasising that man was never the solitary creature assumed in 'state of nature' theories, such as Hobbes articulated.[35]

Central to the account of social life that Collingwood presents in *The New Leviathan* is the distinction between a community and a society. A community is taken to be a set of people operating within a given territory and maintaining a division of functions, held together by external rule rather than the free will of its members. A society is taken to represent a joint enterprise of mutually recognising free wills. Command and obedience in a society are seen by Collingwood as being exercised by the joint free will of its members, whereas in a community what passes for authority is, in effect, a force resting on the strength of those who exert power. Societies, according to Collingwood, can degenerate into communities when the will of its members crack, a danger that can be guarded against by conferring authority on those most suited to rule, and by maintaining a criminal law to deal with socially delinquent behaviour.

Collingwood sees societies and communities developing historically. He observes how in Roman law *societas* was understood as a relationship between *personae* (adult free men capable of suing and being sued, Roman citizens and heads of families), who join together in a partnership based on consensual agreement, signified through a social contract. Recognising the historical character of societies, Collingwood revises this ancient formulation by theorising a society as a partnership of persons, that is, agents of either sex possessed of and exercising free will.[36] Collingwood's recognition of this historical nature of social life is aligned with Hegel's appreciation of the historicity of political cultures and contrasts with the purported analysis of the universal, non-changing features of social and political life undertaken in the *Leviathan*.[37]

Collingwood recognises a synchronic and diachronic diversity of types of society. He identifies the family, a mixed community, partly social and partly non-social, as integrally linked to political life. Collingwood conceives of the family as a hybrid community, the marriage partners in modern Europe exercising immanent, self-rule over their society, and the parents exercising transeunt (i.e. external) rule over the children, whom they educate to exercise subsequent responsibilities as free social agents.[38] The family therefore plays a key role in preparing individuals to be free citizens.

The family's character as a mixed community is replicated, according to Collingwood, in the nature of the body politic. Characteristically Collingwood explores the nature of the body politic through an historical examination. Collingwood reviews the changing and interrelated practice and theory of past forms of political life. His developmental reading of political identity departs from Hobbes's naturalistic standpoint, but it does not replicate Hegel's teleological notion of the development of political freedom.[39]

Collingwood identifies the political community in Ancient Greece and Rome to be a social one, composed of citizens, demarcated from a range of other inhabitants such as wives, slaves and foreigners. Thereafter Collingwood sees the medieval world as witnessing a transformation, whereby the body politic is regarded as being composed of a collection of humans rather than a society of agents. The non-social political community of the medieval world, subject to transeunt (i.e. external) rule, is seen by Collingwood as spawning an irregular series of societies and estates that enjoy rights and liberties. Machiavelli is taken as reasserting the power of the body politic in reaction to the political instability generated by the granting of such liberties and rights. Hobbes is seen by Collingwood as theorising the conditions of a specifically modern notion of the political community. In this modern perspective the political community is seen as poised between the social and the non-social, for the body politic is viewed as being engaged in converting a natural, non-social community into a political, social association.

Collingwood aligns Hobbes with Locke and Rousseau in elaborating the classical theoretical exploration of the terms of a modern notion of political association. The device of the social contract is seen as highlighting the consensual basis of free, social obligations and the work of transformation from nature to society to be undertaken by a body politic. What Collingwood highlights in Hobbes is the latter's appreciation of the artificiality of the state and the dependence of sovereign power upon the will of social subjects, against a background of the non-social basis of family life and international relations.[40]

Collingwood, however, is far from attributing to Hobbes the final word on politics. He subjects the Hobbesian standpoint politics to a profound transformation. Rather than depicting political life as arising out of an express contract between specific agents emerging from a non-social condition, Collingwood sees the body politic as a permanent society engaged in perpetual expansion into a non-social community. This perpetual process of transformation, whereby members of the non-social community are converted into members of society, is held to involve three laws of politics. These laws of the ongoing practice of politics highlight the radicalism of Collingwood's transformation of Hobbes's political thought.

The laws of politics, for Collingwood, consist in the inexorable division between rulers and ruled, ensurance that the barrier between rulers and ruled is permeable in an upward sense, and the maintenance of a correspondence between rulers and ruled in their recognition of and adaption to one another's character. Collingwood's designated ongoing interaction between rulers and ruled diverges sharply from the separation of the sovereign from the making and terms of the covenant in Hobbes's *Leviathan*. Likewise Collingwood sets out a theory of the ongoing practice of politics that calls upon extensive and disinterested political participation, which contrasts with Hobbes' concentration of political decision making in the hands of a sovereign. Collingwood also departs from Hobbes in his celebration of the ideal of political action as being the practice of dialectic. Collingwood holds that the achievement of a joint political will on the part of the political association presupposes a spirit of openness in debate and a commitment to reconciling differences.[41] This ideal of a balanced harmony between individual and community is epitomised by Collingwood's notion of duty as the highest political action. In dutiful political action the citizen undertakes the concrete political actions demanded by an honest review of his or her situation. For Collingwood it is evoked by historical political thinking that undertakes to explain the performance of concrete individual political acts.[42]

Collingwood's understanding of how the ethical life of the family prepares individuals for life in a political community rehearses the standpoint of Hegel in the *Philosophy of Right*. Hegel, like Collingwood, recognises that individuals are not to be conceived outside social contexts. A political association, for Hegel, does not rest simply upon individual volition; a political community is integrally related to a variety of social practices, such as the family. Hegel's conception of politics is also linked to Collingwood's insofar as he maintains the political ideal of achieving a balance between individualism and community. Hegel considers that individual rights of the person and institutions allowing for individualism are required to promote a free political community. On the other hand Hegel urges that individuals cannot realise their freedom unless they recognise their ties with fellow citizens.

Notwithstanding the affinities between the form and content of Hegel's and Collingwood's political thought highlighted above, in *The New Leviathan* Collingwood is highly critical of Hegel's political philosophy. Collingwood disparages Hegel for failing to appreciate the main thrust of the social contract theorists' conception of politics, namely that political association is founded upon the free joint will of its members.[43] For Collingwood, Hegel assimilates the dialectic of things to the dialectic of words in conjuring the concrete world of nature out of abstract logical thought and conceiving of historical and political development in objective terms that preclude the creative freedom of human agency.[44]

Collingwood's disparagement of Hegel is part of a wider critique of German political thought and practice, which in turn reflects Collingwood's views on the dependence of theory upon practice. According to Collingwood, in the absence of free, political association in Germany, German theorists misconstrue political life in non-social terms. Hence Kant and Marx as well as Hegel are condemned for failing to identify political activity in terms of free, human agency.

Collingwood's account of German social and political theory is linked to his understanding of what he terms the new barbarism's contemporary attack on civilisation. The new barbarism of Nazism is seen by Collingwood as arising out of an historical national context in which there has been no experience of political society and the cultivation of civilisation. Civilisation is understood by Collingwood as a process promoting the ideal of civility in human conduct, which he takes to be men and women showing a reciprocal respect for one another as free rational agents and displaying a spirit of intelligent exploitation towards the natural world.

CONCLUSION

Collingwood's critique of Hegel in *The New Leviathan* is at odds with the profound affinities between Hegel's and Collingwood's notions of mind, politics and culture. Collingwood's developmental, historical conception of mind and culture reflects the spirit of Hegel rather than that of Hobbes. Collingwood's invocation of Hobbes notwithstanding, his departure from Hobbes on a number of key issues, however, cannot be entirely explained by a wartime cultural nationalism. Collingwood, in the spirit of Hegel, understands intellectual history as a necessarily critical activity in which past theoretical projects do not function merely as museum pieces, but are to be invoked and criticised in the present. Hence Collingwood's deep-seated criticism of Hobbes's political theory does not render meaningless his claim to base a new political theory upon Hobbes's conception of free political association.

Collingwood's elliptical, fierce critique of Hegel jars with the profound affinities between the form and substance of Hegel's notion of mind and society and his own notion. Nonetheless Collingwood's criticism of Hegel's philosophical standpoint is voiced elsewhere and is generated by more than the mere exigencies of war. Moreover Collingwood's ideal of citizenship and civility as involving a commitment on the part of citizens to engage openly with others in debate and to seek to resolve differences actively and dialectically differs from Hegel's more passive notion of citizenship. Hegel's teleological conception of history tends to envisage the achievement of a balanced, harmonious political community as the unintended product of historical development. Collingwood, in contrast, sees the achievement of a balanced community as the product of intensive and extensive civic activity on the part of the citizenry. In this sense Collingwood's political philosophy maintains a more open and participative conception of politics than that of Hegel, a difference that is consonant with his elliptical critique of Hegel.

9 Lyotard's Hegel and the Dialectic of Modernity

Hegel is a central figure in the development of Lyotard's philosophical and political standpoints. From the outset of his career, Hegel's idealism epitomised what Lyotard consistently takes to be the 'other' of his own fast-moving thought. Hegel's otherness is seen to be his rationalist essentialism against which Lyotard's anti-essentialist and contrary standpoint is defined. Hegel's philosophy is presumed by Lyotard to consist in the reflective imperialism of establishing understanding and mastery of the world. Lyotard's goal as a philosopher and social theorist is to explode the imperial pretensions of rationalism. Throughout his career Lyotard worked at highlighting aspects of reality that resist the closure of explanation and thereby fail to be comprehended in the Hegelian network of concepts. In so doing, however, he displays a close knowledge of Hegel in that he purports to show how Hegel's dialectic betrays its aim of explaining how different aspects of the whole lead inexorably to a single route of explanation by imposing an external methodology upon reality.

Notwithstanding the closeness of his reading of Hegel, Lyotard's rejection of Hegel is taken in this chapter to point to limitations within his thought as well as well-grounded suspicions of purportedly comprehensive and absolute philosophical explanations. Lyotard is insightful in highlighting the tendency of Hegel and other 'modern' philosophers to downplay differences and inventiveness in the construction of unified ethical and theoretical frameworks. However, Hegel's concern to theorise difference so that the interrelations of distinct standpoints are realised remains salutary. Difference is never absolute. Hegel, in his political philosophy, traces the tensions and ties between different aspects of society. Moreover the Hegelian concern to establish a general framework of social ethics whereby the rights of various aspects of the social whole can be adjudicated responds to a deep human concern to establish justice, which is not to be overridden easily in the pursuit of the new and different.

Lyotard's *Phenomenology* (1954) was directed specifically against the pretensions of phenomenology to deal with prelinguistic experience by invoking the sophisticated language of intentionality.[1] While contemporary French phenomenologists were in the frame of

Lyotard's vision, the enemy lurking behind the front line of attack was Hegel, whose *Phenomenology of Mind* is taken as the inspiration for subsequent phenomenological explorations. Hegel's phenomenological project is indicted for its pervasive rationalism. Hegel is condemned for liquidating otherness in a determination to read reality as systematically and progressively identifiable with the ideal or rational. In *Phenomenology* and thereafter, Lyotard opposes intellectual imperialism. For Lyotard, reason cannot explain reality. There is always a *figural* resistance.

Lyotard highlights the opacity of reality, presented in the sheer, unanalysable *moment* of the event, the presentiment of desire and the practice of justice without rules, and in so doing sets his thought against Hegel. This antagonism to Hegel takes centre stage in his obituary for modernity and its grand narratives, which he sketches in *The Postmodern Condition – A Report on Knowledge*. In his 'Apostil on Narratives', a letter he wrote to Samuel Cassin in 1984, Lyotard emphasises his antagonism to Hegel in his repudiation of the grand narratives of modernity: 'Hegel's philosophy totalises all of these narratives and, in this sense, is a distillation of speculative modernity.'[2] Even after his thought moves on and his predeliction for seeing knowledge in terms of narrative wanes, Lyotard remains implacable in his hostility to Hegel. In *The Differend*, the ineluctable variety of phrase regimes, the sheer unredeemability of the holocaust are taken as opposing the monolithic explanatory world of Hegel's system. All the while, however, the sense of Hegel's importance for Lyotard remains. The constancy of Lyotard's citation of Hegel's name, the sharpness of his opposition to Hegel's words and his familiarity with a range of Hegel's writings, combine to confirm the importance of Hegel's role in Lyotard's thought. Hegel is a significant 'other' for Lyotard.

Hegel's name invokes the philosophical trademark of attempting an explanation of the whole without remainder and without external guides. Lyotard is both attracted and repelled by this Hegelian project. The very idea of an explanation of the whole, presupposing a unity of reason and a cosmic harmony by which all modes of meaning and ways of being can be understood transparently by a presuppositionless form of philosophical knowledge, repels Lyotard. Indeed his philosophy and politics at all stages represent so many ways of repudiating this idea. What may be said to inform Lyotard's work, though, is an Hegelian concern to work with and manipulate difference dialectically. In a sense, Lyotard rejects Hegel's philosophical standpoint for its failure to achieve its proclaimed goal, namely a philosophy that works through so many shapes of reality without presuppositions. Lyotard takes his own philosophical standpoint, explicitly articulated in *The Differend*, to be a phrase regime that invents its own practice as it goes along. For Lyotard, philosophy must justify its own project and practice by means that are generated internally. This indeed forms the basis of Hegel's own understanding of a 'notional' dialectical logic. Moreover, in his focused critiques of Hegel, Lyotard indicts Hegel for failing to deliver on his own philosophical claims and so the move to an anti-Hegelian position is generated by the dynamics of a critique of Hegel.

Hegel is important for understanding Lyotard insofar as Hegel represents the 'ideal' antagonist whose holistic idealism forms the grand cage that Lyotard strives to unlock by unpicking carefully the logic of the cage's construction. But reflection upon Hegel's grand narrative is instructive for understanding Lyotard in other ways. For one thing, Hegel's philosophy definitely does exhibit grand claims—epistemological and normative–and the meaning and force of Lyotard's challenge to the Western tradition of political philosophy is revealed by a close review of Lyotard's critique of Hegel. In this chapter Lyotard will be acknowledged as right in his questioning both of Hegel and the tradition of grand narratives. The extravagant claims made by a classic political philosopher such as Hegel to read the development of the modern world and signal the conditions of a truly 'rational' political practice are indeed questionable. On the other hand, Hegel will shown to be a more elusive target of criticism than is acknowledged by Lyotard. Hegel's determination to see things holistically, for instance, is seen to pay dividends in that the world is not made up of discrete practices unconnected with one another, and his political philosophy is seen as testifying to the strong normative claims to community and shared identity that motivate and empower political actors.

Hegel's sensitivity to actual forms of sociological and historical difference is also recognised as powerful, even though it is overridden in the last instance by his equally powerful urge to provide a single overall narrative storyline to his understanding of the human condition. In contrast to the depth of Hegel's historical understanding, Lyotard is seen to freeze his account of difference to that of the sheer recognition of incommensurability. The dynamism of distinct standpoints, albeit incommensurable, acting and interacting with one another over time is not explored by Lyotard, so that Hegel's ultimately untenable account of the historicity of mankind appears richer than Lyotard's philosophising.

HEGEL: THE GRAND NARRATOR

In *The Postmodern Condition: A Report on Knowledge*, Lyotard provides a focused critique of Hegel as the exemplary author of the grand narratives that define modernity. The book assumes a self-consciously postmodern standpoint and the postmodern is taken by Lyotard as implying 'incredulity to metanarratives'.[3] What is at stake between modern and postmodern perspectives is highlighted in Lyotard's repudiation of any attempt to ground or justify science in an overall summative story of knowledge and human development. The two grand narratives of modernity that Lyotard discusses in *The Postmodern Condition* are, on the one hand, the metanarrative strategy of legitimating scientific research in terms of its role in assisting the liberation of mankind, and on the other hand, seeing scientific knowledge as forming a part of the speculative unity of knowledge. The latter metanarrative is taken by Lyotard as being epitomised by Hegel's system.

Lyotard sees the Hegelian project as unifying and justifying the activities of science by linking them to the life history of a grand subject, Spirit. This subject, in narrating a totalising story, represents a metasubject, and for Lyotard is divorced from the actual phenomena it relates.[4] For Lyotard a totalising perspective is unable to do justice to the variety and heterogeneity of language games in which selves are located, and it violates untranslatable differences between activities and utterances. Lyotard conceives of the self in postmodern terms, which conflict pointedly with the universal, absolute meta-self he sees as unifying the Hegelian grand narrative. In *The Postmodern Condition* he observes:

> A self does not amount to very much but no self is an island; each exists in a fabric of relations that is now more complex and mobile than ever before. Young or old, man or woman, rich or poor, a person is always located at 'nodal points' of specific communication circuits however tiny these may be.[5]

Lyotard's antagonism towards Hegel informs the politics of *The Postmodern Condition*. Lyotard's postmodern acceptance of difference entails rejection of a universal formula for justice in favour of local, provisionally agreed rules of conduct that allow the improvisation of new rules and activities. This repudiation of the universalist aspirations of reason contrasts with Hegel, and the force of the contrast is not lost on Jameson, who, in his Foreword to the English translation of *The*

Postmodern Condition, endorses Lyotard's dismissal of the Hegelian project. He observes, 'the rhetoric of totality and totalization that derived from what I have called the Germanic or Hegelian tradition is the object of a kind of instinctive or automatic denunciation by just about everybody'.[6]

Lyotard's engagement with Hegel is evident in a number of his writings besides *The Postmodern Condition*. Indeed more focused critiques of Hegel confirm that his project for a postmodern philosophy emerges out of a critique of the Hegelian project. While Lyotard's philosophy is linked to predecessors such as Kant, Wittgenstein and Aristotle, whose works are invoked as positive reference points, Lyotard's long-standing and considered criticisms of Hegel's method and system signpost a conception of philosophy in their supposed supersession of Hegel's standpoint. Lyotard, in his 1986 paper 'Rewriting Modernity', has made clear that the postmodern is not a state of affairs that should be set apart from the modern. Rather, 'Modernity is constitutionally and ceaselessly pregnant with its postmodernity.'[7] In his essay 'Answering the Question: What is Postmodernism?' Lyotard takes the postmodern to be a modulation of the modern. The postmodern is held to be the search for the unpresentable, entertained by the modernist avant-garde.[8] Just as the postmodern, for Lyotard, is a development of the modern, so his postmodern philosophical standpoint emerges out of a critique of Hegel's philosophy. In Lyotard's essay 'Analysing Speculative Discourse as Language Game', Hegel's philosophy is not merely rejected; the language game of speculative idealism is held to be out of step with itself and exposure of its contradictions points in the direction of postmodernism.

Hegelianism is a prime example of one of the master narratives of the modern world, a world in which the metanarratives invoked to justify science and justice are held to be immanent in the narratives of human conduct and science. Hegel's speculative system purports to be immanent within the thought and action of the natural, experiential world. Lyotard attends to the 'logic' of *The Phenomenology of Spirit* and *The Logic*, which portray the internal contradictions and resolutions of, on the one hand, consciousness and self-consciousness, and on the other hand the general categories of reason. Lyotard's strategy is to reveal how the manoeuvres of Hegel's dialectical procedure obey the formula of a metalanguage, specifying the opposition of designated terms, their mutual implication and their resulting generation of a new term. The very abstractness of this dialectical procedure is taken by Lyotard to signal an *external* teleology that subverts the professed immanence of Hegel's dialectical, conceptual enquiry.[9] Following his formal critique of Hegel's enterprise, Lyotard develops his own understanding of language games and unsublatable difference, which is resumed in the guise of phrase regimes and differends in *The Differend: Phrases in Dispute*.

In the account of language developed in 'Analysing Speculative Discourse as Language Game', Lyotard takes a statement as copresenting a number of universes, one of which is actualised by a contingent follow-up statement. The looseness of contingent linking is lost or distorted, according to Lyotard, by the speculative language game, which imposes its version of necessary development upon language. Language, for Lyotard, wants itself; it wants the infinite, which is to be achieved by the inadvertency of 'moves'. The inadvertency of moves in and between language games is a pointed but developmental contrast to Hegel's notion of the good infinite, in which the snake of self-consciousness constantly returns to itself and in the absolute finds itself in the entire universe of thought and being.[10] Lyotard's concluding comments in this essay suggest that the formless, uncategorisable experimentation he identifies as the postmodern redeems the promise of a purely immanent account of thought and action purportedly offered by the Hegelian dialectic. The divergencies, creativity and incompatibilities of language in this view can neither be tamed nor subordinated to a general rational pattern; they can only be gestured at in a language that follows their trails but does not 'explain' them.

A similarly thoughtful confrontation with Hegel is offered by Lyotard in his essay 'Discussions, or Phrasing "After Auschwitz"'.[11] The phrase 'after Auschwitz' is invoked to register the bankruptcy of the totalising discourse of the dialectic when confronted with forms of suffering and experience that resist assimilation into traditional patterns. Any continuation of speculative discourse after Auschwitz assumes that Auschwitz can be seen as part of a learning curve for a 'we', the common subject of history. For Lyotard, the name Auschwitz stands for the sheer distinctness of phrases and the mutual incommensurability of phrase regimens. Lyotard draws upon the absolute otherness of Auschwitz to highlight his own postmodern standpoint. For Lyotard there is no metalanguage or scheme to establish a common measure between phrases. Speculative reason, which purports to trace a pattern from the momentum of self-moving thoughts, is diagnosed as reducing the flow and otherness of phrases by imposing upon them an external rhythm. Selves for Lyotard are located in a fragmentary, mobile universe of diverse phrases and phrase regimes for which there is no common language.[12]

The Differend sets out Lyotard's conception of philosophy as saving the honour of thinking by seeking to testify to the *differend*, the inexpressible difference between phrases. Lyotard denies that philosophy can resolve the incompatibility between one phrase regime and another.[13] In *The Differend*, Lyotard identifies Hegel's speculative discourse as representing sterility and closure. 'But this presupposition of the same (made by speculative discourse) is not falsifiable. It is a rule that governs metaphysical discourse as its closure.'[14] In pointed contrast, Lyotard offers his own conception of philosophical discourse: 'The stakes of philosophical discourse are in a rule (or rules) which remains to be sought, and to which the discourse cannot be made to conform before the rule has been found. The links from phrase to phrase are not ruled by a rule but by the quest for a rule.'[15] Lyotard aims to resist closure, unity and finality; he invokes inventiveness and difference to subvert notions of sameness. Whereas Hegel sees infinity in the self seeing itself in all expressions of thought, Lyotard denies the sameness of the I in distinct phrases. It is this fragmentation of the ego which explains his rejection of humanism and Cartesianism.[16]

Lyotard's reading of Hegel, like his general reading of modernity, is in many ways persuasive. Hegel presumed his thought and system to be necessary and absolute. In *The Philosophy of Right* he distinguishes his absolute philosophical standpoint from the contemporary historical treatment of law. For Hegel, ethics, right and the law are more than contingent and local devices.[17] The trail of the dialectic, whether following the travails of consciousness or the movement of logical categories, is taken to be a necessary one. This necessity is decidedly questionable. *The Phenomenology of Spirit* purports to follow the various shapes of consciousness that are necessary for the eventual resolution of the contradictions between the object and subject of consciousness. The pathway of *The Phenomenology of Spirit* is an insightful 'highway' of despair but its dialectical development encompasses a multitude of specific, historic episodes, which can be categorised and organised in a variety of ways but hardly a 'necessary' sequence. For instance the life and death struggle and the succeeding master–slave relationship point to significant, if disquieting, features of the human condition, but their evocation of stoicism in *The Phenomenology of Spirit* is a plausible but not a necessary interpretation of their meaning.

Stoicism's recognition of the self as inherently free in thought is plausibly taken by Hegel to imply the negativity of scepticism.[18] This reading of the meaning of scepticism in relation to the object and subject of consciousness testifies to Hegel's powers of interpreting cultural and epistemological standpoints, but Hegel offers no convincing rationale of a specific route of conscious exploration such that stoicism, for instance, must precede scepticism. How is it to be decided how many incomplete stages are to be included in the pathway of consciousness? The ethical absolutism underpinning Hegel's political philosophy is likewise questionable. A constitutional monarchy supported by an interventionist bureaucracy overseeing a civil society incorporating an underclass immersed in poverty and an explicitly gendered division of the public from the private might be historically defensible regime but is not to be seen as a high-water mark of human development.[19]

Lyotard's postmodern alternative to Hegel's absolutism is instructive. His emphasis on inventiveness and difference asks challenging questions of Hegel's system. The self, for Hegel, is the free, dynamic universality intrinsic to thought and action. Ultimately the notion of meaning itself is seen as isomorphic with the pure form of the self. The point of Hegel's system is to systemise this relation of the self and the notion of meaning so that the self recognises itself in the forms of unifying, integrating structures that render experience a meaningful whole. The danger in such a strategy is that unity is privileged, while play, dissidence and difference are subjugated. Hegel's treatment of the state tends to overplay unity at the expense of difference. While he self-consciously allows for individualism and a vibrant civil society, women are restricted to a domestic role and he sees the collective commitment to war as a necessary reminder of ethical ties. Again, Hegel takes the directionality of world history as a unilear indicator of meaning, in that the teleological goal of Northern European political culture is presumed to be the rational standpoint in which previous cultural formations and contemporary divergent cultures are superseded. Hegel's tracing of a single path through historical and social forms of experience undercuts the sensitivity Lyotard displays to the diversity of experience. The notion of the *differend* itself is an inventive evocation of the irreducible diversity of differing perspectives; the ageing ex-apparatchik, the aspiring capitalist and the fervent nationalist in the former Soviet Union do not share a common language.

Hegel's system, then, is vulnerable to the postmodern critique of Lyotard to the extent that its absolutism and ethical objectivism overrides recognition of inventiveness, contingency and difference. But if the absolutism and unity in Hegel's thought can be pronounced as dead as its endism, its critical assimilation of a range of social and intellectual forces renders its spirit endlessly productive. Dallmayr has remarked upon Hegel as acting as both instigator and critic of the discourse of modernity.[20] From his earliest writings Hegel displayed a critical sensitivity to the crucial 'modern' forces of particularism and individualism; the mature Hegel develops an inclusive political philosophy, admitting variety and individual creativity, while allowing a role for the sense of community supportive of the integrity and social side of the individual. While Hegel's narrative of social and political life might not be grand, it is nonetheless perceptive and can be deployed to signal deficiencies in Lyotard's postmodern perspective.

Hegel's dialectical procedure may at times appear external to the practices it examines, but it also exhibits tensions within standpoints and practices and reveals connections between them. In *The Philosophy of Right*, for instance, Hegel highlights tensions within the discourses and practices of rights, contracts, individualistic moralities and market behaviour. The mere assertion of rights cannot guarantee their application, contracts presuppose political conventions governing their use, moral individualism cannot resist slippage into evil and the market threatens to unravel social ties by its celebration of particularism. Hegel's dialectical exploration of these activities signposts cross-cutting ties and signals their dependence upon a political setting in which rules are publicly established and a sense of community can be achieved. Lyotard's characteristic emphasis upon dissensus, agonistic jousting between phrases and celebration of sheer difference appears to preclude the maintenance of a stable public sphere. Connections between practices and the value of community and cooperative social action are underrated in Lyotard's thought. As Haber intimates in *Beyond Postmodern Politics*, the espousal of sheer difference threatens to disrespect difference in its undifferentiated respect for different language games/phrase regimes.[21] At the close of *The Differend* Lyotard opposes to the hegemony of the economic genre 'the heterogeneity of phrase regimes and of genres of discourse'.[22] But this emphasis on heterogeneity threatens to undermine the prospect of shared undertakings. Drolet, in his paper 'The Wild and the Sublime: Lyotard's Post-Modern Politics', diagnoses Lyotard's commitment to respect incommensurability as an abandonment of the notion of a shared discourse.[23]

CRITICISING A POSTMODERN CRITIQUE

The dialectical interplay between Lyotard and Hegel described in this chapter shows how the identities and possibilities of two characteristically modern and postmodern perspectives can be clarified by a process of cross-interrogation. Lyotard's commitment to indeterminate invention, respecting and celebrating dissensus and difference, can be seen as emerging out of a critique of Hegel's practice of 'immanent dialectic'. Lyotard's respect for difference and incommensurability subverts the endism and absolutism of the Hegelian system. But his close reading of Hegel and his immanent but productive philosophical critique highlights the one-sidedness of Readings's depiction of Lyotard in *Jean-François Lyotard: Political Writings* as 'this least Hegelian of thinkers'.[24] Lyotard's critique of Hegel is conducted as an internal critique and thereby shows an affinity with the ideal of the Hegelian dialectic. Moreover the links between his own philosophical practice and speculative idealism exemplify the connections between apparently diverse phrase regimes and undercuts Lyotard's emphasis on sheer difference. Lyotard himself in his revisionary formulation of Marxism attests to connections and distinctions between genres of discourse as testifying to the peculiar imperialism of the economic genre of discourse.[25]

Hegel is committed to community as well as difference. His endorsement of the possibility of shared values and cooperative ventures challenges the indeterminacy and social fragmentation apparently entertained by Lyotard's espousal of difference. Lyotard's critique of Hegel's grand narrative is powerful, but Hegel's legacy is ambiguous; human babies should not be thrown out with the spiritual bathwater. Both Benhabib and Giddens, while recognising the social side of subjectivity, highlight the reflexive powers of human beings in stepping back from and evaluating social practices and in cooperating on matters of common concern.[26] Lyotard's model of the Aristotelian judge in *Just Gaming*, who judges indeterminately without reference to general prescriptive criteria, is an unconvincing figure given that he is imagined as operating without reference to an authoritative set of conventions such as those maintained by the ethos of the Greek *polis*.[27]

10 Rawls and Hegel: The Reasonable and the Rational in Theory and Practice

INTRODUCTION

Rawls's *A Theory of Justice*, on its publication in 1971, was interpreted as being starkly opposed to Hegel and the Hegelian tradition.[1] The work generated a wealth of critical commentary, including an Hegelianised communitarian critique of its supposedly individualistic and non-historical methodological and ontological assumptions.[2] The assimilation of Hegel to an anti-Rawlsian communitarian standpoint was afforded by Hegel's consistent and trenchant critique of contractualist political theories, from his early critique of natural law theory to his mature political philosophy.[3] Communitarians, as Gutmann notes, drew upon an Hegelian conception of man as an historical social being, in condemning what they designated a Rawlsian image of man as a rational individual, lacking defining social ties.[4]

Affinities between Hegel and Rawls have been recognised in recent critical commentary. Inspiration for closing the critical gap between Hegel and Rawls has been derived from a variety of quarters. A more liberal reading of Hegel's political philosophy has encouraged some Hegelian commentators, for example Plant and Hardimon, to connect Hegel with Rawlsian liberalism. Schwarzenbach and Benson have deflected attention away from Hegel's metaphysical claims in exhibiting parallels between Rawls's constructivist procedure in *A Theory of Justice* and the nature of the political community actually constructed in Hegel's *Philosophy of Right*.[5] The grounds for contrasting Rawls and Hegel have also been disturbed by Rawls's work subsequent to *A Theory of Justice*, notably *Political Liberalism*, in which Rawls aims to refine and clarify his account of justice. In this latter work Rawls takes care to signal that individuals cannot be supposed to exist outside of historical and social contexts. The focus upon the historical and social dimensions of human nature in Rawls's later work has led Rawls himself and the Rawlsian critics Kukathas and Pettit to recognise similarities between Hegel and Rawls.[6]

Rawls resembles Hegel insofar as he predicates his abstract theorising upon a reading of historical development and a recognition of the inescapably social condition of humanity. The historical and social mediation of individual identity relieves Rawls's contractualism of problems associated with the contractual method identified by Hegel. Rawls's enterprise as a political theorist, then, should not be assimilated straightforwardly into an individualist tradition starkly antagonistic to Hegel. Likewise Hegel's speculative metaphysics should not be taken as an otherworldly system of thought irrelevant to Rawls's concerns about the distribution of material resources and the freedom of individuals, just as his alleged illiberal statism is a misconception that should not be invoked to disconnect his political theory from Rawlsian liberalism.[7]

While Hegel's political philosophy is part of a general speculative enterprise, his conceptual understanding of human freedom does not proceed from a speculative leap beyond the bounds of what is involved in human thought and action. He understands freedom as being expressed and developed in concrete practices and institutions, rather than being generated by speculation severed from actual behaviour. While Hegel, like Rawls, assumes that a political philosopher must deal with a prevailing political culture, he also follows Rawls in framing an account of politics in non-historical, theoretical terms. Hegel's *Philosophy of Right* aims to demonstrate the rationality of a form of politics by a process of rational construction, in which structures of social and political life are constructed progressively out of an abstract specification of human agency.[8]

The affinities between Hegel and Rawls, however, do not establish an identity of standpoint. Rawls's *Political Liberalism* invokes history and sociology to highlight a key feature of the modern world, namely the prevalence of a plurality of conceptions of the good, admitting of no certain means of rational adjudication. The dilemmas arising out of potentially ineluctable controversy is diagnosed as presenting a central, historical challenge to political philosophy. The solution, developed in Rawls's elaboration of political liberalism, is for political philosophy to set out a publicly demonstrable formula of principles conditioning the basic structures of society, which derives from assumptions about individual freedom and equality characteristic of a modern liberal democratic political culture. Rawls takes individuals in modern society to be fundamentally divided on comprehensive ends, but he maintains that reasonable agreement on principles applying to a delimited political domain can be elicted from 'modern' individuals, abstractly conceived as entertaining and pursuing their own conceptions of the good. Individuals can thereby be seen as recognising shared political ends and exemplifying common political virtues.

Hegel, like Rawls, recognises the force of modern individualism and deep controversy over ends. Hegel, however, sees questions of politics as involving a more profound interdependence of individuals, social practices and political institutions. Hegel's political philosophy explains how a set of social and political practices can be seen as allowing for individual freedom, as well as promoting a concern for the public good among individual citizens. Rawls's project of devising a reasonable political formula between abstractly conceived rational agents applicable to basic social structures, runs counter to Hegel's recognition of the irreducible reciprocity of individuality and social context. Rawls conceives of a 'thin' notion of mutually accommodating rational individuals as generating a reasonable formula to guide a strictly demarcated political sphere. Hegel, in contrast, explores a complex set of social practices that sponsor individual autonomy while generating a commitment to the public good, exemplified in conscientious adherence to the laws of a state. Rawls assumes that the agents he imagines as agreeing to fair principles of justice are historical and social actors. But his 'abstract' specification of their reasonable and rational character absolves his theory of justice from considering practices and institutions in terms of their promotion of these characteristics as well as their exemplification of fairness. To consider how conditions allowing for rationality, reasonableness and justice are promoted problematises Rawls's determination to delimit the 'political' from the 'private' and invokes the style of comprehensive enquiry undertaken by Hegel.

In general, Hegel might be said to envisage reason as being in history and the social practices he examines, while Rawls sees history as posing insurmountable problems for the establishment of a publicly demonstrable and operational conception of the good. Rawls advocates settling for a reasonable theoretical formula to operate within a limited domain of the political. Hegel sees the political as inextricably interwoven with a variety of social practices and articulates a complex and comprehensive account of the rationality latent within these practices. For Hegel the rational is the actual and *vice versa*, whereas for Rawls the rational must give way to a reasonable agreement on fair terms of social cooperation.

Hegel's political philosophy aims to articulate an interdependent set of practices and institutions, including the family and civil society, which engender and allow mutual recognition between agents of their free, self-determining character. The public character of institutions is seen as being dialectically linked to the publicly responsible identity of private individuals, thereby precluding the Rawlsian conceptual manoeuvre of divorcing a political conception of justice from more comprehensive moral notions.

Hegel claims to provide an objectively incontrovertible explanation of a rational political community by logically constructing the social and political structures required by mutually recognising free persons from an initial notion of their free character. There remains, however, an unacknowledged indeterminacy between Hegel's general understanding of socially situated human agency and his constructive specification of a determinate and historic set of 'thick' social practices and institutions as engendering and embodying the concrete conditions of political freedom.

Hegel's theory faces a serious unresolved problem. His representation of the patriarchal family and corporatist institutions as supremely rational rather than contingently explicable, for instance, is not convincingly justified. The contrasting circumspection with which Rawls defends his account of justice, however, does not resolve problems of justification. Rawls's self-conscious circumscription of his account of justice to a specifically political domain runs counter to Hegel's powerful account of the reciprocity of notions of the public and private. Rawls himself acknowledges that the notion of the reasonable he invokes to justify this procedure 'needs a more thorough examination than *Political Liberalism* offers'.[9] The strict demarcation of a private sphere in which individuals pursue publicly disputed conceptions of the good from a public sphere regulated by limited but publicly demonstrable principles of justice is as questionable as Hegel's absolutism. A revisionary Hegelianism, which abandons Hegel's claims to articulate an absolutely rational political philosophy, might draw upon Rawls's notion of reflective equilibrium. A revised Hegelian review of the interconnections between modern social and political practices engendering freedom and public spiritedness might be represented as the contestable outcome of the criticism of conventions and principles within a society, which Rawls has referred to as reflective equilibrium.

CONSTRUCTIVISM IN RAWLS AND HEGEL

Rawls

Political Liberalism is a demanding work whose arguments and procedures of validation invoke a complex series of inter- and intratextual
references. Its principles of justice are those set out in *A Theory of
Justice*, namely the promotion of equal basic liberties and a subordinate concern to ensure that social and economic inequalities are
arranged so as to benefit the worst off and to be attached to offices
and positions under conditions of equal opportunity. In *Political Liberalism* Rawls stresses that his theory of justice is not to be conceived as
independent of social and historical development. In highlighting its
social basis Rawls thereby rehearses the fine print of *A Theory of
Justice*, whose principles of justice are seen as being invoked and
justified by a process of radical abstraction deriving from and applied
to the range of intuitions and principles maintained within a liberal
democratic political culture. The principles of justice as fairness are
seen to be upheld by their putative capacity to render coherent a range
of lower-level intuitions and principles. The actual process of generating and justifying the principles in relation to lower-range intuitions
and assumptions, however, is never demonstrated effectively by Rawls.
He concentrates upon showing the achievement of a wide sense of
reflective equilibrium by comparing the principles of justice maintained in justice as fairness with rival theoretical standpoints, notably
intuitionism and utilitarianism.[10]

Political Liberalism modifies and recasts the formulation of justice as
fairness in *A Theory of Justice*. The ostensible motivation for the
reformulation is a concern for the projected stability of a society
structured by the principles of justice as fairness. In *Political Liberalism*
Rawls restricts the scope of his regulatory principles of justice to the
political domain. This manoeuvre is seen as promoting their acceptance by individuals who maintain a variety of reasonable, comprehensive doctrines. The application of the principles of justice as fairness to
the political domain is taken to be compatible with a range of reasonable comprehensive doctrines due to their limited scope and reasonable, publicly justifiable, procedural construction. The limits of their
jurisdiction allow for the expression of incompatible viewpoints in
other spheres of social life, and the reasonableness of their construction permits a variety of comprehensive standpoints to accept them as
compatible with their distinct but reasonable comprehensive doctrines

(though Rawls acknowledges that the reasonableness of redistributive measures might be disputed and hence might have to be sacrificed).

The key assumptions maintained in Rawls's construction of the terms of political justice are the rationality and reasonableness of the representative agents who agree to the contractual conditions of justice as fairness. These qualities of the representatives mirror those of the members of a liberal democratic polity, who are held to be capable of undertaking rational actions to pursue freely chosen goals expressing diverse conceptions of the good, and who are prepared to act reasonably so that they respect the reciprocity involved in making and keeping to agreements on fair schemes of social cooperation. These representatives are envisaged as agreeing to the two principles of justice as fairness in an original position. Their deliberations are posited as taking place under a veil of ignorance, a device that screens out knowledge of particular attributes and qualities and so ensures that principles are decided solely by the morally relevant factors of the freedom and equality of the people represented. Principles of justice are thereby seen to be established in publicly justifiable terms consonant with the reasonableness presumed to allow for an overlapping consensus of reasonable comprehensive doctrines.

The contractual terms in which Rawls sets out his principles of justice are deliberately framed so as to avoid Hegel's critique of classic contractualist studies of politics, such as those conducted by Hobbes and Locke. Rawls agrees with Hegel that explanations of political association, analogous to a legal contract, presume the background conditions of social trust which they purport to explain.[11] A situation of trust, for both Rawls and Hegel, is only tenable on the basis of settled political conditions that it is the object of a social contract to explain. In deflecting Hegel's critique of contractualism from his own recourse to the language of contracts, Rawls maintains that the point of his metaphorical deployment of a contract is distinct from the quasi-historical language of his predecessors.

Rawls argues that the contractual formulation of his argument is neither designed to show how states come about nor to identify the logic of political association in terms of express agreement between individuals, envisaged as actors distinct from any informing social context. Rather the contract arising out of the original position is seen by Rawls as a formulation of the conditions of a just society by representatives of a democratic liberal culture, whose use of the contract mechanism is to model assumptions and principles maintained in liberal democratic culture.

Rawls's respect for Hegel's critique of classical contractualism is accompanied by an acknowledgement of Hegel's historical insight. In *Political Liberalism* Rawls takes a specifically *modern* political culture, comprehended in ways associated with Hegel, to be the object of his theorising. Rawls, like Hegel, understands modern political culture as being distinguished by its individualism and profound conflict over moral and religious ends. In citing Hegel's appreciation of the impact of religious pluralism unleashed by the Reformation, Rawls signals his assimilation of Hegel's historical conception of modernity.[12]

Rawls highlights the nature of a modern liberal democratic political culture by contrasting it with the culture of Homeric Greece. A modern accommodation of a plurality of reasonable comprehensive doctrines of the good is contrasted with the Homeric uniformity of outlook.[13] Modern pluralism is taken by Rawls to reflect a complex set of events, but he picks out the unrelenting clash of religious doctrine in the Post Reformation world as generating the political impetus for accommodating opposing, reasonable standpoints. For Rawls the practical emergence of pluralism sets the agenda for a specifically modern form of political philosophy, namely one concerned with the specification of the terms of fair social cooperation for members of a political culture embracing liberty and equality, but divided by a plurality of reasonable but incompatible doctrines.

The explanatory status of the account of justice in *Political Liberalism* turns crucially upon the notion of reasonableness with which it operates. A variety of reasonable actors maintaining distinct comprehensive standpoints are taken to be able to support a political notion of justice that makes no unreasonable assumptions. It is unfortunate, as Mulhall and Swift, Caney and others have noted, that the notion of the reasonable is ambiguous in *Political Liberalism*.[14]

On the one hand the reasonable is specified in epistemological terms, whose generality is at odds with the Rawlsian notion of justice as reflecting the reflective equilibrium of the moral and intellectual resources of a particular political culture. On this view, reasonable pluralism is held to emerge from the burdens of judgement to which reasoning on comprehensive doctrines is subject. These burdens are taken to include the vagueness of concepts, the complexity of forms of evidence and the experiential dimension of judgements. They are seen as ruling out agreement on a comprehensive account of justice and as favouring a publicly justifiable construction of a specifically political account of justice. This epistemological specification of the reasonable jars with the idea, which is assumed in *Political Liberalism* and *A Theory of Justice*, that a theory of justice represents equilibrated reflection on an interplay of principles and intuitions maintained within a society, rather than an exercise in suprasocietal reasoning. As well as running counter to another feature of his thinking, Rawls's conception of the burdens of judgement is highly contestable in that the isolation of a specifically political form of justice is surely as susceptible to the designated burdens of judgement as the formulation of comprehensive doctrines.[15]

On the other hand, Rawls also appears to define the reasonable at the outset of *Political Liberalism* directly in terms of the assumptions underpinning his construction of justice as fairness, namely the commitment of free and equal individuals to establish and maintain fair terms of social cooperation. This characterisation appears circular and disqualifies the notion of the reasonable from playing an independent role in establishing justice as fairness. The two principles of justice as fairness provide the only substantial exhibition of what a commitment to establish fair terms of social cooperation might mean in practice.[16]

The 'reasonable' in Rawls's *Political Liberalism* emerges out of an historical recognition of a deep conflict over ends that are insusceptible to theoretical resolution. The grounds for fixing a particular understanding of the political, however, are questionable rather than reasonable. The entire project of halting discussion of what constitutes the political and divorcing the private from the public undermines the sense in which political activity expresses creative freedom. As Bellamy and Castiglione have noted, 'the proposed insulation of the political sphere from people's prime concerns is not only impossible but undesirable'.[17] There seems no compelling reason, for instance, why religious or radical environmental beliefs should be prohibited from the domain of public debate. To exclude comprehensive beliefs from entering public debate about abortion, as Rawls appears to do in a footnote in *Political Liberalism*, is a response to the incommensurable standpoints informing political thought and practice that is as unjustifiable as it is unlikely. The incommensurability of perspectives, which is highlighted in Lyotard's work on language and practice, is what makes politics problematic and challenging. Politics cannot be insulated from the conditions that shape its character. Even within a Rawlsian perspective, however, deciding between the various freedoms of the first principle of justice involves incommensurabilities.

Rawls, in *Political Liberalism*, is at pains to stress that his conception of the free rational individual presupposes a social context. His refinement of his theory of justice is inspired by a reading of modern history that highlights social and political conflicts generated by disputes over ends. In his elaboration of the social and historical dimensions of his theory, which disturbs a communitarian caricature of it as individualistic and universalistic, Rawls recognises an affinity with Hegel. Rawls and Hegel both recognise man's historical and social identity, but their theories of social and historical identity are not the same.

Hegel's understanding of politics is informed by a deep sensitivity to the reciprocity of individuality and social practices, which is distinct from Rawls's recognition that his abstract specification of reasonable, rational individuals pursuing distinct conceptions of the good reflects the conditionality of a liberal democratic culture. Hegel's reading of the social construction of individuality and the tensions involved in the social practices that harbour individualism is revealed in his understanding of the complexity of the modern historical context. He recognises that all experience is present experience, and that there is a gap between past and present that cannot be bridged by any modes of conceiving of history save that of a philosophical one that sees meaning and understanding as necessarily developmental. Hegel sees individual and social identity as intertwined with the development of political culture. He portrays the development of individuality as part of the progressive enactment of the freedom intrinsic to the human mind, which receives a full expression in modernity.[18] His reading of modernity is highlighted by the problematic contrast he draws in his early writings between the modern and the ancient worlds. Whereas the ancient *polis* is taken as a harmonious culture in which the energies and talents of a people are happily united, the modern world is diagnosed as alienated and fragmented. By his maturity, however, Hegel sees modernity as expressing human freedom, for the modern state is taken to exhibit a complex unity, admitting a plurality of comprehensive religious doctrines and a variety of ways for individuals to exercise freedom.

Insofar as Hegel emphasises the freedom of the individual to pursue self-chosen ends and the toleration of a plurality of comprehensive religious beliefs within the modern state, there is a distinct affinity between Hegel's and Rawls's conceptions of the historical context of modern political philosophy. Hegel's coupling of individual self-determination with the reciprocal development of modern social practices, however, entails a focus upon the analysis of 'thick' modern social practices that is absent from Rawlsian theory. In *Political Liberalism* Rawls envisages the abstractly conceived, free and equal individuals in the original position as being both rational and reasonable in their consideration of the principles of fair social organisation. Hegel is concerned to explore the social institutions and practices that allow for the emergence of rational and ethical individuals. Political morality, for Hegel, is not to be conceived as a fixed set of principles conforming to abstract notions of individuality, but as a social ethics dependent upon the organisation of social and political practices. While Rawls recognises the public good of developing and practising the political virtues consonant with maintaining the conditions of a just polity, he does not examine how they are conditioned, fostered and thwarted in a variety of practices.

Hegel

Hegel sees the rational state he outlines in the *Philosophy of Right* as historical. His Preface to that work observes that political philosophy reflects and reasons about actual practices. He sees the rational as embedded in the actual, contriving to read Plato as articulating the structure of the traditional Greek *polis*. While the rational depends on the actual, Hegel distinguishes his approach from a merely historical mode of explanation: 'When an historical justification confuses an origin in external factors with an origin in the concept, it unconsciously achieves the opposite of what it intended.'[19]

To underline the objective status of his account of politics, Hegel self-consciously develops his argument in the *Philosophy of Right* in suprahistorical terms. Benson has rightly observed Hegel's philosophical construction of the interconnected requirements of the conditions of right. Notwithstanding its provenance in history, Hegel undertakes a non-historical, conceptual articulation of the ethical framework for the social interaction involved in human agency and conduct.[20] Conducting a thought experiment, beginning from a general conceptual specification of human agency and practice, Hegel demonstrates the internal interdependencies of a variety of principles and practices within an ethical political community.

At the outset of the *Philosophy of Right* Hegel states that its starting point is the notion of freedom.[21] The initial specification of freedom is recognition of the self-determination of an individual and acknowledgement of the *indeterminacy* of this notion when seen as a mere abstract capacity of an individual. Hegel's understanding of freedom is progressively developed in the *Philosophy of Right* to show that individual freedom can only be expressed in social interaction. Its rational expression is shown to require reciprocal recognition among individuals and support for shared practices that allow the pursuit of individual ends. Hegel's starting assumption of individual agency corresponds to the notion of rational individuals forming and acting upon a variety of conceptions of the good in Rawls's original position.[22] While the original position resembles Hegel's initial designation of the human will in being a self-conscious abstraction from a modern political culture, Hegel differs from Rawls in subsequently highlighting the network of social institutions that render this starting point credible.

For Hegel, individuals' capacity to undertake free, meaningful actions entitles them to the Nozickean rights of life and private property.[23] In contrast to Nozick, though, Hegel does not see these abstract rights as absolute, undeveloped, side constraints on human action. For Hegel, rights of the person must be seen as operating with a host of other conventions, principles and practices. The logical grammar of possessive pronouns is held to imply a social perspective of comparison. There can be neither property nor a developed sense of personal identity without an informing social context. Recognition of the social context evokes the claims of contractual relations to organise relationships of property.[24] Contracts, however, as Rawls acknowledges, are rightly seen by Hegel to presuppose a background framework of trust to explain their functioning. Hegel proceeds to argue that conscientiousness is a necessary but insufficient condition for the generation of a clear, settled intersubjective framework of ethics. Neither moral athleticism nor theoretical ingenuity can enable individuals to create the conditions of reasonable social interaction. For Hegel, a rational and self-sufficient ethical life presupposes a range of concrete social practices. He invokes patriarchal family life, the practices of civil society and rationally organised political institutions as completing the conditions of a rational ethical world.

Hegel recognises that the modern demands of individualism are in tension with the value of community. He takes the experience of social ties in the practices of social life as sustaining the modern commitment to respect the moral rights of individuals. In Hegel's account of family life the pursuit of merely individual ends, notably the subjective concerns of women, is to be subordinated to the family unit. The family unit, though, is seen as nurturing individuals. Likewise the egoism generated by the universal pursuit of self-interest in civil society expresses individualism but should be mitigated by corporate associations promoting a sense of shared goals if a sense of community promoting respect for the public good is to be achieved. Again,

Hegel sees the inevitable generation of poverty amidst wealth in civil society as requiring intervention by the state to mitigate the alienation engendered in an underclass of the poor. For Hegel, however state intervention should be limited by the need to respect the 'private' space for individuality within civil society.

In the *Philosophy of Right* a variety of principles and theories such as a rights-based view of persons, Kantianism (in morality) and utilitarianism (in civil society) are shown to be accommodated but superseded by their integration within the internally differentiated practices of an ethical community. Rawls presents his theory of justice as fairness as the outcome of reflective equilibrium, revealing itself as an overarching theory in its putative superiority to other general theories. Hegel, however, presents his theory as the dialectical outcome of a process of construction, incorporating principles and practices that express differing aspects of individual and social self-determination. In so doing Hegel engages more directly than Rawls with social practices and develops a comprehensive explanation of politics. Hegel's theory of the state bears an affinity with that of Rawls in its determination to allow for both public and private virtues. But while the political virtues of Rawls arise out of an ongoing commitment to the conditions of a reasonable polity, they do not obtrude into consideration of the pursuit of individual conceptions of the good. For Hegel, the very idea of individuals possessing the attributes of rationality and reasonableness, which permit the entertaining of conceptions of the good and a moral recognition of the claims of others, presupposes a range of social practices and institutions that are comprehended in terms of a comprehensive account of what constitutes a good society.

Hegel's constructivist procedure purports to provide a comprehensive account of a rational political community by deriving its conditions from a general conceptual understanding of freedom. Within this account, however, there is a disguised indeterminacy operating between its invocation of a general notion of human agency and its concrete specification of social practices and institutions. Hegel's absolutism runs counter to the evident gap between his understanding of human freedom and the historically contingent forms of patriarchal family life, corporate political representation and constitutional monarchy, which he portrays as establishing a coherent self-sustaining world of freedom. The gap is evident throughout Hegel's comprehensive conception of spiritual freedom and it is not closed by Hegel's unconvincing account of contingent historical development as exhibiting a necessary telos towards the development of a rationally organised state. Hegel is perceptive in pointing to the dependence of human freedom on complexly interrelated social practices that allow the nurturing of individuals by an ethic of care, a sphere of civil freedom in which individuals conscientiously pursue a variety of conceptions of the good and a representative form of government that oversees and adjusts the conditions within and between practices to accord with reasonable notions of what is right. But the appropriate forms of these social practices and the judgements made about them are inherently contestable.

CONCLUSION

A common feature of the political philosophies of Rawls and Hegel is their shared recognition that their theorising rests upon the historical development of a distinct, modern form of political culture. Moreover their specifications of the identity of this culture highlight its recognition of human freedom and toleration of a plurality of comprehensive doctrines. Again, their political philosophies are justified by a process of construction designed to accommodate prevailing historical and social conditions without subscribing to relativism.

Notwithstanding similarities, the political philosophies of Rawls and Hegel model the individual's relation to social practices differently. Rawls takes his schematised, reasonable, rational individuals following distinct conceptions of the good to be social, historical creations. Nonetheless he understands the task of political philosophy to be the delivery of fair principles governing social interaction between these abstract, schematised individuals. *Political Liberalism* is not interested in probing the concrete social and political practices in which these schemata develop and express themselves. Hegel conceives of individuals as inextricably involved in the relationships maintained intentionally and unintentionally in concrete social practices. For Hegel, political philosophy is not to specify a set of fixed principles regulating the conduct of abstractly conceived individuals. Hegel theorises an interrelated set of practices that allow individuals to develop their individuality and a sense of ethical responsibility. In reviewing these practices Hegel recognises a number of values, including individual freedom, fairness and a sense of community amongst citizens. These values, however, are to be orchestrated and maintained in the ongoing life of a political community; they are not to be fixed by abstract thought.

Rawls also differs from Hegel in how he presents his standpoint as being demonstrably objective. In *Political Liberalism* the political indeterminacy of reasonable comprehensive doctrines is seen as allowing for an overlapping consensus around Rawls's construction of a non-comprehensive political conception of justice. This consensus, for Rawls, is not a mere *modus vivendi* but a reasonable framework of justice, given its compatibility with a range of reasonable comprehensive doctrines and its publicly convincing mode of construction.[25] The reasonableness of isolating a specifically political domain of justice, however, is not demonstrated convincingly. The juxtaposition of the condition of modern pluralism with the theoretical restraints demanded by the purported demands of epistemological reasonableness is a mere serendipity.[26]

Rawls's designation of a clearly distinguishable political domain to which a discrete, limited theory of justice can be applied runs counter to Hegel's persuasive account of the dialectical interdependence of the 'political' on 'non-political' social practices. Hegel's notion of a patriarchal family breeding and nurturing the individual agents who comprise a political association offends against sexual equality, but it highlights that the generation of the rational and reasonable individuals assumed in Rawls's account of political liberalism invites questions about how 'non-political' relationships of care can foster responsible, rational agents. Once the character of individual agents pursuing apolitical conceptions of the good is seen as turning upon social arrangements, susceptible to political influence in the guise of regulations concerning marriage and parenthood, the divorce between private and public goods is annulled. Contemporary developments confirm the contestable character of Rawls's 'liberal' reading of politics. Recognition of and debate over the 'public' construction of cultural and sexual identities and the dominance of political institutions by global market relations, as well as the emergence of a radical critique of human interaction with the natural world, problematise conventional readings of politics. Given the contestability of Rawls's designation of the political, the claim of his theory of justice to express a reflective equilibrium of principles and intuitions is not redeemed.

The limits of Rawls's liberalism aim are paradoxically revealed in the self-conscious broadening of his theory's reach to incorporate Hegel's political philosophy in 'The Law of Peoples'.[27] Hegel's rational state is taken as a well-ordered, non-liberal hierarchical regime to which an attenuated Rawlsian conception of justice can apply. Hegel is seen by Rawls as accommodating human rights but within a limiting hierarchical framework. Rawls's reading of Hegel's corporatism is questionable. Hegel's identification of the importance of corporations in civil society and his favouring of corporate political representation testify to his perception of the need to balance individualism with the promotion of a sense of public responsibility rather than his preference for hierarchy over liberal institutions. Corporatism does not override provisions for the rights of persons in *The Philosophy of Right*. Corporations are seen as free and representative institutions that foster social solidarity amidst the generally egoistic perspective maintained in market transactions.

Rawls's identification of the corporatist aspect of Hegel's political thought highlights one of the dated features that undermine its absolutist claims. An indeterminacy obtains between the general postulates of Hegel's political theory and the thicker social and political structures that are held to derive from them. Hegel is persuasive in signalling the practical necessity of institutional forms and practices that allow for individual freedom and a sense of community. The particular institutions and practices theorised in *The Philosophy of Right*, such as the patriarchal family, corporations and a hereditary monarchy, are implausibly characterised as objectively rational expressions of social and political freedom. Indeed Hegel's philosophical enterprise involves many contentious moves unwarranted by dialectical 'necessity'. Nonetheless his enterprise of relating politics to a comprehensive philosophical position seems unavoidable given the controversial nature of any specification of the political.

Stripped of its advertised absolutism, Hegel's political philosophy can be construed as articulating a political community that represents a reasonable but controversial distillation of key institutions, practices and principles within the political culture of modernity. This revisionary way of reading the Hegelian state allows it to be seen, therefore, as the contestable outcome of an achieved reflective equilibrium. The contestability of the actual Hegelian state and the 'unreasonableness' of insulating political from private practices are underlined by recognising that contemporary reflection upon social and political practices might accent disequilibrium rather than equilibrium. Relationships of care, such as the family that sustain and nurture individuals are evidently imperilled by the heightened individualism promoted by the extension and intensification of market activities. Likewise global market activity is often in tension with local forms of democracy as well as endangering the harmony between the natural and social worlds.

11 Conclusion: Politics, Philosophy and Critique

HEGEL IN HISTORICAL PERSPECTIVE

At the outset of this book, the interdependence of Hegel's conceptions of philosophy and history maintained in his history of political philosophy was explored. The succeeding chapters may be seen as demonstrations of an Hegelianised notion of the history of political philosophy. In surveying Hegel and a range of predecessors and successors, the essays contained in this volume show how political philosophy is not to be divorced from its history. Hegel's self-image as a 'modern' political philosopher, theorising the rational and historic practical realisation of freedom is examined in the chapters that consider Hegel's appraisal of ancient and modern political philosophy. Hegel's theory of the modern state is itself an intellectual event in modern history and its meaning unravels in subsequent development and criticism. The essays in this volume that relate Hegel to his successors track a diversity of ways in which Hegel's political philosophy has been taken, criticised and reformulated.

The aim of this chapter is to appraise Hegel's political philosophy. Its perceptiveness and blind spots are highlighted by considering the different aspects of Hegel's political philosophy discussed in the preceding chapters. Hence this chapter reviews what has been intimated previously. While its critical fire is concentrated upon Hegel's substantive political theory, the pros and cons of Hegel as an historian of political philosophy, discussed in the Introduction, are shown to bear upon Hegel's substantive notion of politics given the interdependence of philosophy and history in his thought.

Hegel's interpretation of Hobbes and Plato shows his awareness of the historicity of political philosophy. His readings of Plato and Hobbes are mutually related testimonies to his understanding of the modern world. Plato's political philosophy is taken by Hegel to presume that the objectively rational order of a community transcends its individual members. Hobbes is seen as explaining the logic of the state in terms of the self-determining powers of the individuals who comprise it. This contrast between the Hobbesian and Platonic conceptions of the ground of political authority is central to Hegel's notion of

modernity. Hobbes is seen as a modern theorist due to his identification of the state as an artificial product of free human activity, whereas
Plato's conception of rational political order is premodern insofar as
he disconnects it from actual human theory and practice.

   The 'modern' notion of the derivation of political order from human
thought and practice underpins the central role allocated to freedom in
Hegel's political philosophy. Political order is not to be conceived as
the imposition of a rational,'Platonic' form upon recalcitrant human
matter, but as the free expression of human identity.[1] While Hegel
recognises the creative role of human beings in fashioning their political identity, reflection upon the notion of freedom is taken to preclude the making of an arbitrary identity. For Hegel, a rational political
identity expresses the meaning and develops the possibilities of human
freedom.

   Hegel's conception of the non-arbitrary status of his own substantive
political philosophy is evidenced in his assessment of Hobbes. Hobbes
is criticised for reducing human conduct to the pursuit of arbitrary
individual desires. For Hegel, a contractual reading of political
association, insofar as it relegates the establishment of a settled framework of order to a means for the satisfaction of evanescent individual
desires, underplays the commitment to community requisite for
the realisation of freedom. Notwithstanding his critique of Plato's
political philosophy in terms of its prioritising of unity and neglect of
individual freedom, Hegel was nostalgic for the harmony and sense of
community he imagined as pervading the traditional Greek *polis*.
Hegel sees the disintegration of the unity of the Greek *polis* as precluding its modern revival, just as its reconstruction in Plato's *Republic*
cannot forestall its actual demise. Nonetheless his own political theory,
in contrast to that of Hobbes, undertakes to harmonise the self-determination of the individual with a renewed sense of communal political
identity.

   The pursuit of particular desires, for Hegel, is insufficient to establish human freedom. The recognition and development of human
freedom is taken to imply the determination of a shared, social world
of practices and institutions in the context of which individuals can
pursue their inclinations. In Hegel's philosophical vocabulary, self-
determination implies a measure of self-control, which in turn
presumes self-awareness. Self-awareness is to be achieved via the
reciprocity of mutual social recognition. The free, rational character
of the recognition of mutual rights and duties is taken by Hegel to be
constitutive of a 'modern' notion of community. For Hegel, human

beings are meaningful beings whose identity is constituted by their capacity for meaningful activity, a process he designates as Spirit.

Hegel's readings of Plato and Hobbes are interwoven with a philosophical conception of political rationality, which arises out of but supersedes an historical context. Hobbes and Plato are taken to be divided by historical developments separating the advent of the modern world from its classical past. The expression of individual freedom in modern political culture is invoked to explain the supersession of ancient political philosophies by a more rational standpoint. Modern freedom, however, must be comprehended by a theoretical perspective that can accommodate its complexity. Hobbes's theory is diagnosed as suffering from the inadequacy of its characterisation of political association. This diagnosis derives from Hegel's own philosophical conception of a rational political community. Hegel's transhistorical judgements on Plato and Hobbes reflect his notion of the mutual involvement of philosophy and history.[2]

In a paper entitled 'The Truth in Relativism', Williams recognises the case for justifying relativism in regard to significantly divergent and diachronically distinct ethical practices.[3] The argument turns upon the remoteness of culturally divergent standpoints from one another, which thereby undermines the sense of a confrontation or conflict obtaining between them.[4] Notwithstanding the remoteness of culturally distinct ethical standpoints from one another, Hegel makes a reasonable case for maintaining the rational superiority of modern freedom over the authoritarian order of Plato's *Republic*. Given that a political order is constituted by human beings without reference to an objectively demonstrable transcendent model, Hegel is right to recognise the freedom involved in the delivery of political order. His account of its social and developmental character is perceptive.

What is deeply problematic about Hegel's treatment of past theorists, however, is his profession of a demonstrably rational reading of past and present. His presumption of an absolutely valid interpretation of past standpoints is questionable, just as his claim to provide a definitive explanation of a modern state is problematic. The assumption that modern political culture may be uncontroversially interpreted in a single reading is matched by an unjustifiable presumption that a particular context fixes clear limits to what a theorist can imagine. Plato, for instance, on Hegel's reading, is taken as necessarily rehearsing an actual tradition of political life. The impact of the prevailing political culture on Plato is conceived as precluding his imaginative philosophical design of experimental political projects. It is, at the very least, highly questionable that Plato is simply embracing a political tradition.[5] There is no *a priori* reason for precluding an interpretation of Plato which takes him to be innovative. Innovation is a feature of human thought and action.[6] The plausibility of Hegel's reading of Hobbes as a humanistic theorist whose political theory highlights the artificial construction of political order, is confirmed by its development by subsequent scholars.[7] Nonetheless it is a contestable reading that runs counter to theistic interpretations of the *Leviathan*.[8]

Hegel's contestable claim to provide a definitive reading of the history of political philosophy is linked to the equally contestable claim of his substantive political philosophy to provide a conceptual map for an objectively rational political community. A more open reading of the past would allow a diversity of routes to the present, which would in turn engender a less closed understanding of the present. Macintyre's critical reading of modern theories of ethics rests upon his insight that questions of ethics cannot be reduced to one set of absolutised concepts. Macintyre's historicist conception of ethics disavows that its questions can be posed in narrowly naturalistic or subjectivist terms, and construes them in terms of a conversation between different ethical traditions. While Macintyre favours the Aristotelian tradition, he explicitly distances himself from Hegelian absolutism. In a postscript to the second edition of *After Virtue*, he observes that 'this kind of historicism unlike Hegel's involves a form of fallibilism; it is a kind of historicism which excludes all claims to absolute knowledge'.[9] Macintyre's communitarian Aristotelianism smacks of nostalgic conservatism, but his non-Hegelian fallibilism is reasonable given the lack of an undisputed object of ethical and political enquiry.[10]

Implicit in Hegel's reading of the past and present as exhibiting a teleological development is the notion of philosophical and political debate *ending*.[11] Running counter to this notion of historical 'endism', however, is Hegel's recognition that the unpredictable future development of thought and culture precludes a final, unrevisable statement of its character.[12] This sense of ongoing historical development is sharpened by an appreciation of the subsequent history of Hegelianism. The chapters in this book that deal with Hegel, Stirner and Marx demonstrate how Hegel was interpreted and challenged by succeeding thinkers. Stirner and Marx are only to be fully understood by recognising how their questions and styles emanate from an engagement with Hegel. Their polemical engagement with Hegel underscores the delicate and contestable ambiguity of Hegel's enterprise. Stirner, a Young Hegelian successor to Hegel, reacts against what he sees as the absorption of the individual in Hegelian spiritualised, social connections. Marx focuses on material relationships of production, in contrast to an exaggerated Young Hegelian celebration of critical thinking and individual self-creation, and in opposition to Hegel's comprehension of man in terms of the categories of thought.

The images of Hegel framed by Stirner and Marx are shaped by the contemporary context of Young Hegelian controversy. Marx's reaction to Hegel, for instance, is refracted through his confrontation with Stirner. Nonetheless Stirner and Marx highlight significant and contestable aspects of Hegel's thought in their unadvertised assimilation of an Hegelian style of theorising as well as in their reactions against Hegel. Marx subscribes to a holistic theoretical framework whereby men and women are understood within an historical and socially constructed network of relationships. Marx's interrogation of the dependencies between patterns of social and historical interaction evokes Hegel's understanding of history and society and defines Marx's enterprise as Hegelian. Similarly, Stirner's deconstruction of social and historical structures follows an historical and social pathway that is decidedly Hegelian in that it interprets frameworks of social interaction as representing an interconnected series of modes of repression.

The openness of political philosophy, its capacity for renewal and resistance to closure, and the protean ways in which Hegel himself can be portrayed in subsequent theorising is exemplified in the chapters of this book that compare Hegel with twentieth-century figures. Collingwood may be classified as a reluctant and recalcitrant Hegelian, given the harshness of his diatribe against Hegel in *The New Leviathan* together with his subscription to a decidedly Hegelian mode of theorising. Collingwood's commitment to an historical reading of man's unfurling identity, together with his holistic evaluation of the mind's activities and his revisionary presentation of a theory of the social contract in social and historical terms, renders his liberalism Hegelian.

Collingwood's Hegelian presentation of a modulated liberalism in which historical development and civilised creativity are not foreclosed by absolutism contrasts with his own image of Hegel and with the caricature of Hegel presented in Lyotard's account of modernity. The openness and creativity of postmodernity is defined by Lyotard in terms of a contrast with the closed, grand narratives of modernity supposedly epitomised by Hegel's system. Hegel is taken by Lyotard as disregarding difference and variety by assimilating all events and standpoints into a unitary account of history and society in which all developments promote the achievement of freedom. Lyotard's Hegel can be explained at least in part in terms of a reaction to Lyotard's own Marxist–Hegelian past and again in respect of its utility in presenting an unsightly 'modern' straw man to contrast with the wizardry of creative postmodernism. Hegel's system, in fact, can be read as allowing for internal differentiation and as maintaining unity only through diversity and contrariness. Nonetheless Lyotard's broadside captures the implausibility involved in Hegel's determination to read the gamut of meaningful experience from a single theoretical perspective. The possibilities of diverse readings of past and present resist their incorporation into one comprehensive standpoint.

Rawls's direct invocation of Hegel in the reformulation of his theory of justice in *Political Liberalism* is an acknowledgement of the relevance of Hegel for contemporary Anglo-Saxon analytical political philosophy. In responding to communitarian criticism of the alleged bogus universalism of *A Theory of Justice*, Rawls recognises the social and historical conditionality of political philosophy highlighted by Hegel. Rawls's Hegelian turn neatly demonstrates the Hegelian sense of the dependence of present standpoints on the preceding theories from which they emerge. Rawls's methodological defence of the social contract and his discussion of the explanatory force of his arguments are developed by drawing upon Hegelian arguments. Nonetheless there are important differences between Rawls and Hegel. Rawls himself observes illiberal, hierarchical aspects of Hegel's state that jar with Rawlsian liberalism. Again, Rawls's recognition of the social and historical conditionality of political philosophy is not reflected in an Hegelian interrogation of the inseparable ties between modes of individuality and social practices.

While Rawls conceives of his theorising as the product of considered reflection on principles and intuitions maintained in liberal democratic societies, its expression of a reflective equilibrium is presumed rather than demonstrated. The abstract assumptions concerning the reasonable and rational character of individuals with which Rawls operates in the original position are not explored by relating them to their provenance in actual practices. Notwithstanding its absolutist aspirations, the focus of Hegel's political philosophy is to show the interdependence of the modern notion of individuality and social and political practices that nurture and develop its character. Rawls, however, is right to characterise Hegel's rational state as illiberal in comparison with his own notion of a reasonable political order. In self-consciously extending the reach of his theory of justice to the international scene, Rawls depicts Hegel's rational state as a well-ordered but hierarchical regime.

In contrast to the thoroughgoing commitment to the promotion of individual liberty in Rawls's *Political Liberalism*, Hegel's support for an hereditary monarchy, the patriarchal family and virtual political representation through corporations renders his state hierarchial rather than democratic and liberal.

HEGEL REVISED

Hegel's political philosophy arises out of, but does not transcend, history. Its absolutist claims to establish the conditions of an objectively rational political community are questioned rather than redeemed when set against preceding and succeeding theories. Hegel's perspective on the past and present is insightful but not infallible. Hegel's reading of past political philosophies is contestable because its *a priori* assumptions about the necessary and specifiable relations between theory and practice are unsustainable. Hegel's substantive political philosophy is a plausible interpretation of a rational organisation of social and political practice. It combines the securing of individual freedom with the promotion of a commitment to the public good. The credentials of Hegel's rational state, though, have been disturbed by successors. The very project of aiming to resolve competing claims and standpoints within an inclusive, indisputable rational ethical framework ignores the incommensurability of differing perspectives highlighted by Lyotard. Likewise Collingwood identifies Hegel's general teleological conception of the state to be incompatible with the freedom of its members. Moreover the capacity of the particular institutions within *The Philosophy of Right* to promote the values of freedom and community is questionable in the light of issues raised by successors. Rawls observes hierarchical aspects of Hegel's state, and Marx and Stirner see the sense of community promoted by its institutions as masking the alienation of its members.

Given the evident contestability of Hegel's political philosophy in the light of its subsequent reception, a reformulation of its claims and procedures of justification and revisionary amendments to its substantive institutional provisions are required if its project of theorising an integrated political community allowing for crucial aspects of modernity is to be undertaken with any contemporary plausibility. Hegel's absolutism runs counter to its contestability. Postmodernism may be seen as emphasising the contestability of all such theoretical schemes. What is of persisting value in Hegel's approach, however, is his insight into the interconnections between actual institutions and practices in determining conditions for the expression of individual freedom and social responsibility. This insight justifies the revision, rather than rejection, of the Hegelian political project.

Hegel's review of the map of the social world can be reformulated so that it serves as a procedure undertaking what Rawls has referred to as the pursuit of reflective equilibrium between the various principles and intuitions maintained in a society. An admittedly revisionary form of Hegelian social and political philosophy can thereby be reconstrued as a process of examining the interconnected practices and institutions comprising modern society so as to comprehend how the principles and intuitions they exhibit can allow for their joint, coherent development as expressions of the key modern notion of freedom. The Hegelian dialectic, in turn, can thereby be presented as a plausible but contestable enterprise dedicated to establishing coherent internal relations between principles and practices in a society.[13] The procedure is best presented as contestable rather than necessary, for the kind of connection made by Hegel between a general conception of freedom and more particular sets of institutions is not deductive, but an interpretive judgement that rests upon reasons that may be questioned.[14]

In the light of subsequent criticism, the particular institutions Hegel sees as comprising a rational state must be amended if a revisionary form of the Hegelian state is to be advanced as a plausible and reasonable means of accommodating the most significant values and principles of modernity. The reasonableness of a revisionary Hegelianism, however, is not to be seen as deriving from a Rawlsian separation of politics and its comprehension from wider notions of the good. Its reasonableness, in contrast to the Rawlsian notion, emerges from the plausibility of the connections it discloses as existing between a variety of social practices. Indeed the enduring strength of an Hegelian perspective is that it connects rather than fragments the various aspects of the social world. Hegel appreciates that an individual in his or herself is no more than a mere abstraction, and that concrete modes of individuality require social practices that allow for the flourishing of individuals. Hegel sees individuality as only arising in a context of mutual recognition. He takes the social responsibilities that individuals assume in responding to the intersubjective context of recognition as expressing and developing the 'spiritual' identity of individuals. Hegel's perspective on politics supersedes a Rawlsian or contemporary liberal standpoint, because it explains how abstract assumptions about individuals' rationality and reasonableness are in fact inextricably linked to social practices whose character informs rather than reflects individuals' conceptions of the good.[15]

While Hegel rightly acknowledges the constitutive role of social institutions in framing the conditions of individuality and individual conceptions of the good, the way in which he perceives particular institutions as promoting the public good is problematic. Stirner's diatribe against the oppressiveness of Hegel's state is dictated by an unsustainable account of asocial individuality. Nonetheless Stirner's polemical perspective raises questions about the compatibility of social and political obligations and individual freedom. For instance Hegel's justification of the family as an essential component of a rational political community is questionable given the patriarchal aspect of his conception of the family. Women are taken by Hegel to be emotional carers in the family and are to forego the pursuit of individual ends in civil society. The dependent position of women is underlined by the designated male ownership of family property. Hegel's notion of the family, as Brod has observed, turns upon an unjustifiable view of women that denies women individuality.[16]

This critical account of Hegel's notion of the family is not to be taken as vindicating Stirner's notion that all commitments, such as family responsibilities, are subject to the vagaries of evanescent individual desires. Individuals are rightly seen by Hegel as incubated by social practices. Individuals do not make themselves. They are produced by a physical process of reproduction, and their subsequent survival and flourishing depends upon being nurtured in a caring social context, in which patterns of social, ethical behaviour are also learnt. An individual depends upon a caring social institution, such as the family, for his or her development, and the raising of children should limit the independence of parents. The obligations of parenthood, however, do not logically imply a patriarchal family, curtailing the freedom of women. A variety of arrangements, resting upon the free exercise of responsibilities by men and women, can provide effective nurture for children. A revisionary Hegelian account of the state demands that the nurture of children, within social practices expressing an ethic of care, is recognised as a necessary part of the social good but would not assume that responsibilities for child care should fall unilaterally upon women.

Stirner's denunciation of social obligations also challenges Hegel's view of the instrumentality of the state in realising human freedom. Hegel's recognition of the irreducibility of social ethics to the arbitrary choices of individuals is convincing, but his 'rational' state is insufficiently democratic to serve as a vehicle for the realisation of freedom. Collingwood, in *The New Leviathan*, envisages political freedom as the realisation of the spirit of dialectic, where all citizens engage in reasonable discussion on matters of disagreement. This ideal of widespread reasonable deliberation on the public good taps into the democratic spirit of modernity. Collingwood's recognition of the democratic aspect of the modern notion of freedom is reinforced by Rawls's identification of the illiberal, hierarchical aspect of Hegel's political theory. Rawls's presumption that the modern state coheres with abstract notions of equality and freedom may abstract unduly from the concrete conditionality of individuality, but it does provide a formula for highlighting the appropriateness of democratic decision making.

In *The Philosophy of Right*, political power is reserved for an executive of officials appointed by an hereditary monarch responsible to a merely advisory legislature, which is composed of members whose representation of a wider society is not established by democratic procedures.[17] This hierarchical state jars with the principles and practices expressing the equality and freedom so valued in modern societies. The institutional structures of Hegel's 'rational' state must be revised so as to ensure that the sense of community they express allows for democracy and widespread participation in the deliberation and execution of the public good. To establish a state according to procedures of reflection that take account of the notion of democracy, the executive should be responsible to a legislature composed of members elected by democratic principles and reflecting organised viewpoints, democratically determined in bodies such as political parties.

A distinguishing feature of Hegel's notion of the state is his exploration of the role of civil society in contributing to a framework of social ethics that allows individual freedom as well as civic virtue. Hegel's most famous critic, Marx, frames his conception of history and society in terms of a powerful critique of the subordinate, mediating role Hegel assigns to civil society in his general conception of social ethics. Civil society, for Hegel, consists of the social sphere in which individuals satisfy their own particular ends. While encompassing associational activity concerned with a variety of social phenomena, civil society is taken to be epitomised by market-related economic activity.

The individuality of actors in civil society is seen by Hegel as being nurtured by family arrangements. Hegel also sees the institutions of civil society as depending upon legal and ethical conventions overseen by the political state, and he takes the corporations within civil society and the civil service as acting to mitigate the selfish individualism of civil society. The significance of the notion of civil society has been trumpeted by liberal political theorists since the downfall of Soviet communism, for post-communist states are seen to require a functioning civil society to allow for the free development of ideas, associations and a sense of individuality requisite for the flourishing of liberal democratic states.[18] Hegel himself, however, was equivocal about the character of civil society, observing its propensity to promote an asocial egoism and its generation of poverty amidst affluence. Marx highlights these negative aspects of civil society in theorising modern society as dominated by the divisive and socially destructive pursuit of surplus value.

Marx, in his *Economic and Philosophical Manuscripts*, criticises what he takes to be Hegel's assumption that society fits with an integrated pattern of suprasocial reason.[19] For Marx, Hegel's approach is unacceptably idealistic and runs counter to the actual, observable phenomena of social life, in which the forces of production and the way they are organised are taken to have harboured discord in history and to exhibit discordant features in the prevailing capitalist mode of production. Marx's polemical reading of Hegel underrates the interdependence of theory and practice, and reason and sociality, maintained in Hegel's philosophy. In developing his own standpoint, however, as the preceding chapters on Marx and Hegel have revealed, Marx draws upon Hegel to provide a reading of capitalism that disturbs Hegel's own conception of the ultimately harmonious relations between civil society and the state. In *The Grundrisse* Marx conceives of capital in holistic, Hegelian terms as a self-reproducing system that locks social actors into roles demanded by the logic of the constant conversion of money into capital, and the deployment of labour power in ventures shaped by and promoting capital. The infinite process of capital's self-reproduction is taken as thwarting recognition of the character and power of social labour. In *The German Ideology* Marx and Engels employ a normative critique of the division of labour under capitalism, which is informed by a Hegelian conception of the interdependence of particular human beings and their activities.

Marx's recognition of the negative but powerful features of civil society, the sphere of economic relationships under capitalism, is not to be dismissed easily in a contemporary context in which the global power of capital and the commodification of activities such as education and welfare provision threaten to unravel non-economic political and social ties.[20] Hegel's ambivalence about civil society, however, is

more persuasive than Marx's radical critique. The particularity engendered and maintained by market relations in civil society is a defining
feature of modernity. Notwithstanding the alienation, inequality and
mindless insatiability of materialistic appetites endemic to the practices
of a distinctively modern civil society, which Hegel recognises and
Marx highlights, the self-expression of individuals in practices that
harbour and promote the pursuit of particular pleasures and needs is
not to be denied. The individualism of modernity is not to be transcended. Rather it demands the attenuation of its sharpest edges by the
recognition and fostering of social and political relations that engender
a balancing concern for social care and the public good. Hegel's
Philosophy of Right represents a flawed, outmoded but exemplary
model for this enterprise of establishing a realistic conception of a
modern community, which may achieve a reasonable balance between
individualism and more overtly social values.

Hegel's model of the political community requires institutional revision, however, if an effective balance between economic self-assertion
and political concern for the community's good is to be struck in
today's world. Hegel's easy assumptions about the integrity of the
nation state and the viability of corporations have been undermined
by the subsequent intensification of processes of marketisation. If
states are to act effectively nationally and internationally, then they
must relinquish absolutist aspirations to allow for interstate cooperation in monitoring and restraining the power of global capital. Hegel's
support for the undiluted sovereignty of nation states is as anachronistic today as his support for corporations within civil society. While
corporations have declined in the context of intensifying market activity, there is a continuing need to foster institutional means of balancing
the power of business and the divisiveness of an unrestrained
cultivation of individuality. Political institutions at a local and regional
level, in association with a range of voluntary associations, are now the
best means to achieve the sense of public spiritedness that Hegel
envisaged as being engendered by corporations. These institutions
may also serve as mechanisms to ensure that civil society allows
space and time for the effective nurturing of children.

The contemporary achievement of a balanced political community
harmonising individualism and civic virtue requires a vitalised, inclusive political community that allows for popular participation and the
widespread cultivation of what Collingwood has identified as the spirit
of dialectic. The prospect of achieving this political goal is rendered
problematic by the sheer power of civil society, and by the managerial

control of the political agenda by contemporary politicians and their influential supporters. The political agenda is amenable to management through the manipulation of a variety of media, which allows for the shaping of public debate and the disempowerment of ordinary members of the public. The problems complicating the contemporary task of achieving a harmonious political community expressing modern values endorse the pessimistic tone of Hegel's account of insoluble tensions afflicting the modern state. There is no guarantee that a reformulated Hegelian state can overcome modern social problems and reconcile all opposing tendencies.

In this final chapter a revisionary Hegelian state has been sketched and the absolutist claims exerted by Hegel on behalf of his political philosophy repudiated. What has been styled the Hegelian project of subjecting modern social practices and institutions, and associated ideals and principles to intensive scrutiny so as to develop a theoretical model of a political community allowing for the coherent expression of its most crucial values has been assumed to be a worthwhile project. In more particular terms, the Hegelian concern to articulate a community that allows for individual rights and the flourishing of reciprocal social and ethical ties has been recognised as perceptive, if in need of revision. Lyotard's postmodernism, however, casts doubt on the very project of establishing a coherent and settled account of the political good. Hegel's absolutism is vulnerable to Lyotard's scepticism towards grand narratives that affect to provide all-encompassing objective accounts of past and present. But Lyotard's scepticism embraces the very attempt to provide a general account of how social and political practices are to be organised. For the Lyotard of *Just Gaming* and *The Differend* the project of ordering practices according to a notion of justice or political reason runs counter to the sheer variety and incommensurability of practices and standpoints that should be celebrated rather than administered.

The thrust of Lyotard's postmodern savouring of difference and endless creativity over order and closure, is a reminder of the problems inherent in the enterprise of prescribing a pattern of social organisation. The foundations of prescription are contestable. To say that a prescriptive theory of politics is contestable, however, is not to say that it should not be undertaken. Human life is conducted in a social setting. The interrelated institutions and practices that comprise social life may be insusceptible to essentialist, uncontroversial definition, but the interactions between peoples and practices evoke an ethical concern for how they should be organised. The very gap between what is and what might be demands a response, just as it forecloses an uncontestable answer. Politics can be depicted as a practice that sets itself the goal of establishing a just and reasonable order of practices. It is a practice of contention precisely because its ethical concerns are contestable, but those concerns arise out of the unavoidable human enterprise of assuming responsibility for the ordering of a social world.

Hegel's account of a rational and ethical polity is a considered response to the questions posed by social ethics. It reflects the logical dependence of individuals upon social and historical conditions, and attends to how individuals are conditioned by and related to a variety of practices. Its working out of a broad framework of social and political institutions that allow for the flourishing of individuals freely engaging in social commitments and obligations attesting to their ethical, free character is an insightful and considered, if contestable and flawed, reading of the meaning of the key values involved in modern social life. The claims of Hegelianism need to be reformulated so as to respect the contestability of political prescriptions, and the substantive elements of Hegel's 'rational' state need revision to fit with subsequent developments and to answer subsequent criticisms. The claims of a revisionary Hegelian account of politics cannot be redeemed absolutely, they can only be sustained provisionally by their intersubjective recognition as plausible in the light of the nature of, and the principles maintained in, the modern world.

What a reformulated Hegelianism offers is a political theory that recognises the dependence of individuals upon social practices and institutions, so that it allows for an understanding of how a state incorporating individualism must at the same time attend to the provision of reasonable social practices. Gray is perceptive in recognising that even in its 'Hegelian or Deweyan mutation', Rawls's political theory, like most contemporary political philosophy, assumes an overly abstract notion of the individual.[21] Notwithstanding the assumption of much contemporary political theory, the 'right' of the individual does not trump everything else.[22] While Marx overstates the possibility of reasserting the community over the individual, Hegel does signpost a route by which individualism can be balanced by a countervailing sense of reciprocal social responsibility. It might be argued that the revision of Hegel suggested in this chapter is sufficiently substantial to be better understood as marking a clear departure from Hegel and the promulgation of a form of communitarianism. In its concern to accommodate individualism and civic virtue, however, Hegel remains a distinctive theorist who provides a guide to the present that supersedes a one-sided emphasis upon community. Moreover Hegel's political philosophy develops the sense of the interdependence of political philosophy and its history, so that even a substantial departure from Hegel can be seen as a means of its continuation.

Notes and References

1 INTRODUCTION

1 For an interesting collection of essays, incorporating interpretations of Hegel's political philosophy by a number commentators, see M. Riedel (ed.), *Materialen zu Hegels Rechtsphilosophie* (Frankfurt am Main: Suhrkamp, 1974–5).

2 For a thorough study of the Hegelian aftermath, see J. Toews, *Hegelianism: The Path Toward Dialectical Humanism, 1805–1841* (Cambridge: Cambridge University Press, 1980).

3 *PR: Werke 7*, p.27; G. W. F. Hegel, *Hegel's Philosophy of Right* (trans. T. M. Knox) (Oxford: Oxford University Press, 1967), p.13.

4 See for instance *VPRHN*, p.51. In these lectures of 1819 Hegel suggests that the actual will become rational.

5 *PR: Werke 7*, § 3R; Hegel, *Hegel's Philosophy of Right*, op. cit.

6 A balanced and thoughtful interpretation of Hegel's political philosophy that does not collapse it into either *a priori* rationalism or historicism is contained in M.Tunick, *Hegel's Political Philosophy – Interpreting the Practice of Legal Punishment* (Princeton, NJ: Princeton University Press, 1992).

7 See *PR: Werke 7*, p. 24, Hegel, *Hegel's Philosophy of Right*, op. cit., p. 10. For a more general discussion of the concept of actuality see Hegel's discussion in his *WL: Werke 6*, p. 186, G. W. F. Hegel, *Hegel's Science of Logic* (London: George Allen and Unwin, 1969), p. 541.

8 See, for instance the comments in the lecture series of 1818–19, 1821, 1822, 1822–3, 1824–5 and 1831 in *VPRG*, along with the introduction by Ilting, in which he argues persuasively that the variation in Hegel's assessment of monarchy is due to political expediency on Hegel's part.

9 *VPG: Werke 12*; G. W. F. Hegel, *The Philosophy of History* (New York: Dover Press, 1956).

10 *VGP: Werke 18*; G. W. F. Hegel, *Hegel's Lectures on the History of Philosophy* (New York: Humanities Press, 1968).

11 For a classic account and critique of this orthodoxy, see Q. Skinner, 'Meaning and Understanding in the History of Ideas', in J. Tully (ed.), *Meaning and Context – Quentin Skinner and his Critics* (Cambridge: Polity Press, 1988). See also J. Pocock, *Politics, Language and Time* (London: Methuen, 1971).

12 A. O. Lovejoy, *The Great Chain of Being: A Study of the History of an Idea* (Cambridge, Mass: Harvard University Press, 1936).

13 See Skinner, 'Meaning and Understanding', op. cit.

14 See Q. Skinner, 'Some Problems in the Analysis of Political Thought and Action', in Tully, *Meaning and Context*, op. cit.

15 Skinner, 'Meaning and Understanding', op. cit., p. 66.

16 R. Stern, 'Hegel and the New Historicism', *Bulletin of the Hegel Society of Great Britain*, nos 21–2, (1990).

158

17 Note Rawls's invocation of the social contract in J. Rawls, *A Theory of Justice* (Oxford: Oxford University Press, 1971), and Nozick's revival of the notion of the state of nature in R. Nozick, *Anarchy, State and Utopia* (Oxford: Basil Blackwell, 1974).

18 *PR: Werke 7*, Preface; *Hegel's Philosophy of Right*, op. cit.

19 For non-Hegelian interpretations of Marx, Collingwood and Stirner respectively, see the following: J. Elster, *Making Sense of Marx* (Cambridge: Cambridge University Press, 1985); R. Peters, 'Collingwood on Hegel's Dialectic', *Collingwood Studies*, vol. 2, 'Perspectives' (1995); K. Ferguson, 'Saint Max Revisited: A Reconsideration of Max Stirner', *Idealistic Studies*, vol. XII, no. 3 (1982).

20 See in particular *PR: Werke 7*, Preface, *Hegel's Philosophy of Right*, op. cit.; *VGP: Werke 19, Hegel's Lectures on the History of Philosophy*, vol. 2, op. cit.; *VPRW*, pp.126, 171; *VPRHN*, pp.47–8. In this latter lecture series of 1819–20 Hegel rehearses his notion of the *Republic* as revealing the actuality of Greek political life.

21 Contemporary individualist and communitarian essays in political philosophy are collected in S. Avineri and A. de-Shalit, *Communitarianism and Individualism* (Oxford: Oxford University Press, 1992).

22 For a classic interpretation of Hegel as an illiberal political philosopher see R. Haym, *Hegel und Seine Zeit* (Berlin: Egertner, 1857).

2 PLATO AND HEGEL: REASON, REDEMPTION AND POLITICAL CONSTRUCTION

1 Hegel's detailed consideration of Plato's *Republic* is contained in his *Lectures on the History of Philosophy*, in which he argues that the *Republic* reasserts the substantial form of traditional Greek political life: 'It is the Greek state life which constitutes the true content of the *Republic*.' *VGP: Werke 19*, p. 106; *Lectures on the History of Philosophy*, trans. E. S. Haldane and F. H. Simpson (London: Paul, Trench and Trubner, 1892), vol. 2, p. 96.

2 M. Inwood, 'Hegel,Plato and Greek "Sittlichkeit"', in Z. A. Pelzynski (ed.), *The State and Civil Society (Studies in Hegel's Political Philosophy)* (Cambridge: Cambridge University Press, 1984), p. 44.

3 In the account of the decline of the ideal state set out in books VIII–IX of the *Republic*, actual Greek states, for example Sparta, are explicitly criticised. Plato, *The Republic of Plato*, trans. F. M. Cornford (Oxford: Oxford University Press, 1945), pp. 266–320. Plato's critique of contemporary political practice is so trenchant that one notable commentator has concluded that Plato should be seen as a critic of politics rather than a political reformer or revolutionary. See L. Strauss, *The City and Man* (Chicago, Ill.: Chicago University Press, 1963), and L. Strauss, *The Argument and the Action of Plato's Laws* (Chicago and London: University of Chicago Press, 1975).

4 'Since the State is Spirit objectified it is only as one of its members that the individual himself has objectivity, genuine individuality and

an ethical life', *PR: Werke 7; Hegel's Philosophy of Right*, trans. T. M. Knox (Oxford: Oxford University Press, 1967), § 258R. (*Geist*, here, and in other passages drawn from this text, has been retranslated as Spirit.)

5   In developing an account of an individual's right to property, Hegel observes that property implies a relationship between one will and other wills: 'This relation of will to will is the true and proper ground in which freedom is existent.' Ibid., §71.

6   Ibid., §71.

7   Ibid., §185R. See also the various lecture courses given by Hegel in which he frequently refers to Plato's traditionalism, for example *VPRHN*, p. 48. 'Plato recognised the actuality of his world' (my translation).

8   M. B. Foster, *The Political Philosophies of Plato and Hegel* (Oxford: Clarendon Press, 1935).

9   R. Hall, 'Plato, Hegel and Subjectivism', *Polis*, vol. 13, nos 1–2 (1994).

10   The extent of Plato's authoritarianism is revealed in his observation on how the philosophical ruler would undertake the task of social reorganisation: 'He will take society and human character as his canvas, and begin by scraping it clean.' *Republic*, trans. Cornford, op. cit., book VI, 500, p. 209.

11   See *VGP: Werke 18–20, Lectures on the History of Philosophy*; K. R. Popper, *The Open Society and Its Enemies*, vol. I (London: Routledge, 1945).

12   Hall correctly observes that the discussion of justice in the *Republic* begins with the individual and the rationale for the analysis of politics is presented as being heuristic. Hall, though, fails to recognise the deep connections Plato holds as obtaining between the individual and the community. See Hall, 'Plato, Hegel and Subjectivism', op. cit.

13   'This individual is like a man fallen among wild beasts.' *Republic*, trans. Cornford, op. cit., book VI, 496, p. 204.

14   Ibid., book 11, 368, p. 55.

15   Plato, *Crito* (51A), trans. H. Treddennick, in E. Hamilton and H. Cairns (eds), *The Collected Dialogues of Plato* (Princeton, NJ: Princeton University Press, 1973), p. 36.

16   R. E. Cushman, *Therapeia* (Chapel Hill, NC: University of North Carolina Press, 1958), p. 141.

17   *Republic*, trans. Cornford, op. cit., book VII, 517, p. 231.

18   Ibid., book VII, 516, p. 230.

19   Ibid., book VI, 492, p. 200.

20   Cornford remarks upon this in a note to his translation of the *Republic*, ibid., p. 231.

21   Socrates is shown to be aware of the paradoxical, mould-breaking character of his recommendation: 'But I must state my paradox, even though the wave should break in laughter over my head.' Ibid., book V, 473, p. 178.

22   Plato, *Socrates' Defense (Apology)* (21A), in Hamilton and Cairns, *The Collected Dialogues of Plato*, op. cit., p. 7.

23   *Republic*, trans. Cornford, op. cit., book VI, 487–97, pp. 193–204.

24   R. M. Hare, *Plato* (Oxford: Oxford University Press, 1982), p. 58.

25 *Republic*, trans. Cornford, op.cit., book V, 473, p. 178.

26 Ibid., book VI, 501, p. 211.

27 Such a statesman's power, according to Plato, should not be limited by stipulating that he should rule by framing laws. Plato, *Statesman*, trans. J. B. Skemp, in Hamilton and Cairns, *The Collected Dialogues of Plato*, op. cit., pp. 1066–7.

28 'I mean, if our eyes, ears and hands seem to see, hear, act in the common service', Plato, *Laws*, book V, 739C, trans. A. E. Taylor, in Hamilton and Cairns, *The Collected Dialogues of Plato*, op. cit., p. 1324.

29 Morrow has also shown that the constitution outlined in the *Laws* is an amalgamation of elements drawn from the actual constitutions of Sparta, Crete and ancestral Athens. G. Morrow, *Plato's Cretan City* (Princeton, NJ: Princeton University Press, 1960).

30 See T. J. Saunders, 'Plato's Later Political Thought', in R. Kraut (ed.), *The Cambridge Companion to Plato* (Cambridge: Cambridge University Press, 1992).

31 *EG: Werke 9*, §384; *Hegel's Philosophy of Mind*, trans. William Wallace, op. cit., and the *Zusatze* from Boumann's text by A. Miller (Oxford: Oxford University Press, 1971).

32 Ibid., § 383R.

33 Ibid., § 431Z. 'I am only truly free when the other is also free and is recognised by me as free.'

34 P. Singer, *Hegel* (Oxford: Oxford University Press, 1983), pp. 74–5.

35 R. Plant, *Hegel* (London: George Allen and Unwin, 1973), p. 9.

36 G. W. F. Hegel, 'Religion ist Eine, "the Tubingen Essay of 1793"', trans. H. S. Harris, in H. S. Harris, *Hegel's Development Toward the Sunlight 1770–1801* (Oxford: Clarendon Press, 1972), p. 505.

37 R. Hardimon, *Hegel's Social Philosophy – The Project of Reconciliation* (Cambridge: Cambridge University Press, 1994).

38 'Finitude truly comprehended is, as we have said, contained in infinitude, limitation in the unlimited', *EG: Werke 9*, § 386Z; *Hegel's Philosophy of Mind*, trans. Wallace, op.cit.

39 *PR: Werke 7*, p. 26; *Hegel's Philosophy of Right*, trans. Knox, op. cit., p. 8.

40 *EG: Werke 3*, § 174Z; *Hegel's Philosophy of Mind*, trans. W. Wallace, op.cit.

41 See Hardimon, *Hegel's Social Philosophy*, op. cit.

42 *VPG: Werke 12*; G. W. F. Hegel, *Lectures on the Philosophy of World History. Introduction: Reason in History*, trans. H. B. Nisbet (Cambridge: Cambridge University Press, 1975).

43 Hegel believed that all human activities are shaped and sustained by the common character or 'spirit' that informs the community.

44 The basis of this type of state is freedom. 'The Germanic nations with the rise of Christianity were the first to realise that man is by nature free and that the freedom of the Spirit is his very essence.' *VPG: Werke 12*, p. 74; Hegel, *Lectures on the Philosophy of World History*, trans. Nisbet, op. cit., p. 54.

45 *PR: Werke 7*, p. 26; *Hegel's Philosophy of Right*, trans. Knox, op. cit., p. 11.

46 'By dint of obscuring the difference between the historical and the philosophical study of law, it becomes possible to shift the point of

view and slip over from the problem of the true justification of a thing to a justification by appeal to circumstances...' Ibid., § 3R.

47 'This is the unrestricted infinity of absolute abstraction or universality, the pure thought of oneself.' Ibid., § 4Z.

48 Ibid., § 185R. See also the similar comments that Hegel offers on Plato's *Republic* in his *Lectures on the History of Philosophy*. 'The *Republic* of Plato, the spirit of which really consists in the fact, that all aspects in which particularity as such has established its position, are dissolved in the universal – all men simply rank as men in general.' *VGP: Werke 19*, p. 119, Hegel, *Lectures on the History of Philosophy*, trans. Haldane and Simpson, op. cit., vol. 2, p. 109.

49 'It specially harmonises with this particular quality of excluding the principle of subjectivity that Plato in the first place does not allow individuals to choose their own class; this we demand as necessary to freedom.' Ibid. See also *PR: Werke 7*, § 206R; *Hegel's Philosophy of Right*, trans. Knox, op. cit.

50 Ibid., § 184Z.

51 Ibid., § 206R.

52 See Ilting's reading of Hegel's political thought. He urges that Hegel accommodated the political situation in Berlin, so that the explicit text of the *Philosophy of Right* is ambiguous given the need to conform to censorship decrees. K. H. Ilting, 'Der exoterische und der esoterische Hegel (1824–1831).' Introduction, *VPRG*: vol. 4. See also K. Ilting, 'Introduction' to *VPRG*: vol. 1, esp. p. 108.

53 The aspects of Hegel's state which, from a twentieth-century perspective, seem particularly contingent and susceptible to criticism are hereditary monarchy, corporate political representation, primogeniture for the agricultural class and patriarchal family relations. Hegel's view that the state can integrate individual freedom and social unity is well brought out in the following quotation: 'The principle of the modern state has prodigious strength and depth because it allows the principle of subjectivity to progress to its culmination in the extreme of self-subsistent particularity and yet at the same time brings it back to the substantive unity and so maintains this unity in the principle of subjectivity itself.' *PR:Werke 7*, § 260; *Hegel's Philosophy of Right*, trans. Knox, op. cit.

54 'War has the higher significance that by its agency, as I have remarked elsewhere, the "ethical health of peoples is preserved in their indifference to the stabilization of institutions..."', Ibid., § 324R.

55 D. Henrich,'Vernunft in Verwirklichung.' Introduction in *VPRHN*.

56 Avineri has highlighted Hegel's awareness of the social problems associated with modern poverty. 'Poverty, which for Smith is always marginal to his model, assumes another dimension in Hegel. For the latter, pauperization and the subsequent alienation from society are not incidental to the system but endemic to it.' S. Avineri, *Hegel's Theory of the Modern State* (Cambridge: Cambridge University Press, 1982), p. 148.

57 *PR: Werke 7*, § 184; *Hegel's Philosophy of Right*, trans. Knox, op. cit.

58 'Whatever [the age] we live in we can [immerse ourselves] as fully as we like in the life of Ancient Greece – which is congenial to us in many important respects – yet we will never be able to sympathise with the

Greeks and to share their feelings in the most important issues of all.'
VPG: Werke 12, p. 13; Hegel, *Lectures on the Philosophy of World History*,
trans. Nisbet, op. cit., pp. 17–18.

59 *PhG: Werke 3*, p. 39, 'The Preface to the Phenomenology', trans.
W. Kaufmann in W. Kaufmann, *Hegel: Reinterpretation, Texts and Commentary* (New York: Doubleday, 1966), p. 378.

60 *Republic*, trans. Cornford, op. cit., p. 179.

61 *PR: Werke 7*, p. 24; *Hegel's Philosophy of Right*, trans. Knox, op. cit., p. 10.

62 *VGP: Werke 19*, p. 119; Hegel, *Lectures on the History of Philosophy*,
trans. Haldane and Simpson, op. cit. vol. 2, p. 109.

63 Ibid., pp. 109, 99.

64 *PR: Werke 7*, pp. 27–8; *Hegel's Philosophy of Right*, trans. Knox, op. cit.,
p. 10.

65 Inwood has noted that, 'The main reason for Hegel's failure to criticize
Plato's state effectively was perhaps his reluctance to concede that Plato
was an innovator, proposing an ideal which was not put into practice.'
Inwood, 'Hegel, Plato and Greek "Sittlichkeit" ', in Z.A.Pelczynski (ed.)
Hegel and Civil Society (Cambridge: Cambridge University Press, 1984).

66 *Republic*, book VIII, pp. 544, 267, 560. See p. 285 for an implicit
reference to Athens in the critique of democracy.

67 Ibid., p. 18.

68 R. Kraut, 'The Defense of Justice in Plato's *Republic*', in R. Kraut (ed.),
The Cambridge Companion to Plato (Cambridge: Cambridge University
Press, 1992).

69 *Werke 6*, p. 273; *Hegel's Science of Logic*, trans. A. V. Miller (London and
New York: George Allen and Unwin, 1969)

70 S. Rosen, 'Self-Consciousness and Self-Knowledge in Plato and Hegel',
Hegel Studien, band 9 (1974), p. 126.

71 *PR: Werke 7*, p. 26; Hegel, *Hegel's Philosophy of Right*, trans. Knox,
op. cit., p. 12.

72 Hall, 'Plato, Hegel and Subjectivism', op. cit.

73 *PR: Werke 7*, p. 26; Hegel, *Hegel's Philosophy of Right*, trans. Knox,
op.cit., p. 12.

74 T. Saunders, *Plato's Penal Code* (Oxford: Clarendon Press, 1991);
L. Strauss, *The Argument and the Action of Plato's Laws*, op. cit.

75 Hardimon, *Hegel's Social Philosophy* op. cit., p. 58.

76 Among many other philosophers and social theorists, see L. Wittgenstein, *Philosophical Investigations*, trans. G. Anscombe (Oxford: Oxford
University Press, 1976).

77 W. Walsh, *Hegelian Ethics* (London: Macmillan, 1969), p. 11.

78 H. Brod, *Hegel's Philosophy of Politics* (Oxford: Westview Press,
1992); R. Tunick, *Hegel's Political Philosophy – Interpreting the Practice
of Legal Punishment* (Princeton, NJ: Princeton University Press,
1992).

79 *VGP: Werke 18*, p. 83, Hegel, *Lectures on the History of Philosophy*,
op. cit., vol. 1, p. 63.

80 See A. Shanks, *Civil Society and Civil Religion* (Oxford: Blackwell, 1995)
for an interesting consideration of the basis and power of Hegel's
religious thought.

## 3	HEGEL'S PLATO: THE OWL OF MINERVA, POLITICAL PHILOSOPHY AND HISTORY

1	Hegel considers both the perfect expression and the seeds of destruction of this Greek political tradition (identified as lasting from the Archaic period of 7800–500 BC to the advent of Alexander's empire) as lying within the fifth century BC. 'The perfect bloom of Greek life lasted only about sixty years – from the Median wars, BC 492 to the Pelopponesian War, BC 341.' *VPG: Werke* 12, p. 323; *G. W. F. Hegel, The Philosophy of History*, trans. by J. Sibree (London: George Bell and Sons, 1956), p. 265.

2	*PR: Werke* 7, p. 26, *Hegel's Philosophy of Right*, trans. T. M. Knox (Oxford: Oxford University Press, 1967), p. 13. Knox's translation has been used here and elsewhere because its style and language have a grandeur that do justice to Hegel, and is justly famous itself.

3	Plato, *The Republic of Plato*, trans. F. M. Cornford (Oxford: Oxford University Press, 1941), book V 473, pp. 178–9.

4	Foster's work is famous and is undoubtedly insightful. He does not, however, sufficiently recognise the openness of Hegel and Plato. M. B. Foster, *The Political Philosophies of Plato and Hegel* (Oxford: Oxford University Press, 1935). Ware has sought to justify Hegel's conception of the history of political philosophy in a number of writings. He directly addresses Hegel's interpretation of Plato in R. Ware, 'Hegel's Interpretation of Plato', in J. Stanyer and G. Stoker (eds), *Contemporary Political Studies 1997*, vol. 1. Ware is right to highlight Hegel's conception of Plato as a theorist reacting to novel, disruptive conditions. What Ware and Hegel underplay, however, is the radicalism and innovative character of what Hegel is proposing.

5	M. Inwood, 'Hegel, Plato and Greek "Sittlichkeit" ', in Z. A. Pelczynski (ed.), *The State and Civil Society (Studies in Hegel's Political Philosophy* (Cambridge: Cambridge University Press, 1984), p. 54.

6	Hall has challenged Hegel's interpretation of Plato by maintaining that Plato recognises subjectivity. He observes that the *Republic* is explicitly concerned with justice in the individual. Attention to the words of Plato's dialogues certainly problematises interpretations of Plato and a case can be made for seeing the *Republic* as a rhetorical call for the individual pursuit of philosophical certainty. Hall, however, tends to underplay the political authoritarianism that is countenanced by Plato, e.g. in regard to education and art. R. Hall, 'Plato, Hegel and Subjectivism', *Polis,* vol. 13, nos 1–2 (1994).

7	E. Gellner, 'Hegel's Last Secrets: From Marx to Expressionism', *Encounter*, April 1976, p. 33.

8	R. Plant, *Hegel* (London: George Allen and Unwin, 1973), p. 192.

9	*PHG: Werke 3*, pp. 22–3; G. N. H. Hegel, *The Phenomenology of Mind*, trans. J. Baillie (London: George Allen and Unwin, 1971), p. 80.

10	See D. Forbes, 'Introduction' to G. W. F. Hegel, *Lectures on the Philosophy of World History. Introduction: Reason in History*, trans. by H. B. Nisbet (Cambridge: Cambridge University Press, 1975); D. O' Brien, *Hegel on Reason and History* (Chicago, Ill.: Chicago University Press, 1975).

11   *VPG: Werke 12*, p. 13, G. W. F. Hegel, *Lectures on the Philosophy of World History*, trans. H. B. Nisbet, op. cit., pp. 17–18.

12   S. Houlgate, *Freedom, Truth and History – An Introduction to Hegel's Political Philosophy* (London: Routledge, 1991).

13   *VGP: Werke 18*, p. 54; G. W. F. Hegel, *Lectures on the History of Philosophy*, trans. E. S. Haldane and F. H. Simpson, vol. 1 (London: Paul, French and Traubner, 1892), p. 37.

14   A reasonable discussion of Hegel's combination of absolutism and appreciation of historical change is to be found in Houlgate, *Freedom, Truth and History*, op. cit., ch. 1.

15   *VGP: Werke 18*, p. 63; Hegel, *Lectures on the History of Philosophy*, trans. Haldane and Simpson, op. cit., vol. 1, p. 44.

16   Ibid., pp. 62–3, and vol. 1, p. 42.

17   Ibid., pp. 62–3, and vol. 1, p. 43.

18   Ibid., p.63, and vol. 1, p. 44.

19   Ibid., pp. 58–9, and vol. 1, p. 41.

20   Z. A. Pelczynski, 'Political Community and Individual Freedom in Hegel's Philosophy of the State', in Z. A. Pelczynski (ed.), *The State and Civil Society (Studies In Hegel's Political Philosophy)* (Cambridge: Cambridge University Press, 1984), p. 57.

21   *VGP: Werke 19*, p. 132; Hegel, *Lectures on the History of Philosophy*, trans. Haldane and Sinpson, op. cit., vol. 2, p. 1.

22   *VGP: Werke 19*, p. 106; Hegel, *Lectures on the History of Philosophy*, trans. Haldane and Simpson, op. cit., vol. 2, p. 96.

23   *VPRHN: Philosophie des Rechts: Die Vorlesung von 1819/20*, p. 48 (my translation).

24   *VGP: Werke 19*, p. 119; Hegel, *Lectures on the History of Philosophy*, trans. Haldane and Simpson, op. cit., vol. 2, p. 109.

25   *VGP: Werke 19*, p. 129; Hegel, *Lectures on the History of Philosophy*, trans. Haldane and Simpson, op. cit., vol. 2, p. 114.

26   See Ware, 'Hegel's Interpretation of Plato', op. cit., and M. Hardimon, *Hegel's Social Philosophy – The Project of Reconciliation* (Cambridge: Cambridge University Press, 1994), ch. 2. Both Ware and Hardimon do not reckon with the force of Plato's revolutionary recommendations, for example sexual equality, educational transformation.

27   Hegel observes, 'The independence of the I within itself and its explicit existence was foreign to him [Plato]: man had not yet gone back within himself; man had not yet set himself forth as explicit.' *VGP: Werke 19*, p. 66; Hegel *Lectures on the History of Philosophy*, trans. Haldane and Simpson, op. cit., vol. 1, p. 48.

28   T. Irwin, *Plato's Ethics* (Oxford: Oxford University Press, 1995); G. Klosko, *The Development of Plato's Political Theory* (New York: Methuen, 1986).

29   Polus appears in the *Gorgias* and Thrasymachus in the *Republic*, in the opening book of which he argues 'This is what I mean; in all states alike "right" has the same meaning, namely what is for the interest of the party established in power, that is the strongest.' Plato, *The Republic of Plato*, Book 1, 338, p. 18.

30   J. Annas, *An Introduction to Plato's Republic* (Oxford: Oxford University Press, 1981.

31   In the *Statesman* the Stranger declares that a true statesman would act in the free, unrestricted manner of a ship's captain. Plato, *Statesman* (297A), trans. J. B. Skemp, in Hamilton and Cairns (eds), *The Collected Dialogues of Plato*, pp. 1066–7. In the *Laws*, the Athenian Stranger suggests that in an ideal state, sense experience would assume a shared, public character. Plato, *Laws*, Book V 739C, trans. A. E. Taylor, in Hamilton and Cairns, *The Collected Dialogues of Plato*, p. 1324.

32   *VGP: Werke 18*, p. 61; Hegel, *Lectures on the History of Philosophy*, trans. Haldane and Simpson, op. cit., vol. 2, p. 49.

33   J. Glenn Gray, *Hegel's Hellenic Ideal* (New York: King's Crown Press, 1941), p. 78.

34   After observing the logical difficulties associated with the theory of Forms, Parmenides concludes: 'Only a man with exceptional gifts will be able to see that a Form or essence just by itself, does exist in each case, and it will require someone still more remarkable to discover it and to instruct another who has thoroughly examined all these difficulties.' Plato, *Parmenides*, 135B, trans. F. M. Cornford, in Hamilton and Cairns, *The Collected Dialogues of Plato*, op. cit., p. 929. Timaeus declares that what he has to say is only probable and that the father and maker of this universe is past finding out. Plato, *Timaeus*, 28C, trans. B. Jowett, E. Hamilton and H. Cairns (eds) *The Collected Dialogues of Plato* (Princeton NJ: Princeton University Press, 1973) in Hamilton and Cairns, *The Collected Dialogues of Plato*, op. cit., p. 1162.

35   Plato, *The Republic of Plato*, book VI, 505, p. 215.

36   R. Robinson, *Plato's Earlier Dialectic* (Oxford: Clarendon Press, 1975), p. 202.

37   C. Taylor, *Hegel* (Cambridge: Cambridge University Press, 1975), p. 6.

38   R. Ware, ' "Sittlichkeit and Self-Consciousness", Hegel's Metaphilosophy and Historical Metamorphosis', *History of Political Thought*, vol. 17, no. 2 (1996).

39   L. Strauss, *The City and Man* (Chicago, Ill.: Rand McNally 1963), p. 62.

40   J. Findlay, 'Hegelianism and Platonism', in J. J. O'Malley, K. W. Algozin and F. G. Weiss (eds), *Hegel and the History of Philosophy* (The Hague: Martinus Nijhoff, 1974), p. 74.

41   Foster, *The Political Philosophies of Plato and Hegel*, op. cit.

42   See Ware, 'Hegel's Interpretation of Plato', op. cit.

43   T. E. Wartenberg, 'Hegel's Idealism: The Logic of Conceptuality', and M. Forster, 'Hegel's Dialectical Method', in F. C. Beiser (ed.), *The Cambridge Companion to Hegel* (Cambridge: Cambridge University Press, 1993).

4   HOBBES, HEGEL AND THE MODERN SELF

1   See L. Siep, 'Der Kampf um Anerkennung: Zu Hegels Auseinandersetzung mit Hobbes in den Jenaer Scriften', *Hegel Studien 9* (1974). See also A. Pepperzak, 'Hegel and Hobbes Revised', in A. Collins (ed.),

Hegel on the Modern World (Albany: State University of New York Press, 1995).

2 A. Buchwalter, 'Hegel, Hobbes, Kant and The Scientization of Practical Philosophy', in A. Collins (ed.), *Hegel on the World* (Albany: State University of New York Press, 1995), p.178.

3 See C. Taylor, *Sources of the Self – The Making of the Modern Identity* (Cambridge: Cambridge University Press, 1991), p. 533.

4 Natural Law for Locke, Paine and Wollstonecraft specifies a rational set of values conditioning the human will.

5 *VGP: Werke 20*; G. W. F. Hegel, *Lectures on the History of Philosophy*, vol. 3 (London: Kegan, Paul, Trench & Tryber, 1892).

6 J. Taminiaux, 'Hegel et Hobbes', in J.Taminiaux, *Philosophie et Politique* (Bruxelles: Editions de l'Universite Libre de Bruxelles, 1981).

7 Taylor, *Sources of the Self*, op. cit., p. x.

8 Ibid.

9 T. Hobbes, *Leviathan*, ed. R. Tuck (Cambridge: Cambridge University Press, 1991), p. 39. (All subsequent references to the *Leviathan* refer to this edition.)

10 N. Malcolm, 'Hobbes and Spinoza', in J. Burns (ed.), *Cambridge History of Political Thought 1450–1700* (Cambridge: Cambridge University Press, 1991), p. 533.

11 Hobbes, *Leviathan*, op. cit., p. 88.

12 S. Smith, *Hegel's Critique of Liberalism* (Chicago, Ill.: Chicago University Press, 1989), pp. 116–18.

13 Hobbes, *Leviathan*, op. cit., pp.131–4.

14 M. Goldie, 'The Reception of Hobbes', in Burns, *Cambridge History of Political Thought*, op. cit., p. 615.

15 Hobbes, *Leviathan*, op. cit., p. 39.

16 Ibid., pp. 48, 71.

17 Ibid., pp. 90–1.

18 S. State, *Thomas Hobbes and the Debate over Natural Law and Religion* (New York and London: Garland Publishing, 1991).

19 R. E. Flathman, *Thomas Hobbes, Scepticism, Individuality and Chastened Politics* (London: Sage, 1993).

20 See J. Findlay, 'Hegel's Use of Teleology', in W. Steinkraus (ed.), *New Studies in Hegel's Philosophy* (New York: Rinehart and Winston, 1971). See also T. Wartenberg, 'Hegel's Idealism: The Logic of Conceptuality', in F. Beiser, (ed.), *The Cambridge Companion to Hegel* (Cambridge: Cambridge University Press, 1993).

21 *PR: Werke 7*, § 260; G. W. F. Hegel, *Elements in the Philosophy of Right*, ed. A. Wood (Cambridge: Cambridge University Press, 1991).

22 *PhG: Werke 3*, pp. 545–75; G. W. F. Hegel, *The Phenomenology of Mind*, trans. J. Baillie (London and New York: George Allen and Unwin), pp.750–81.

23 *VPG: Werke 12*, p. 74; G. W. F. Hegel, *The Philosophy of History* (New York: Dover Press, 1956), p. 54.

24 Ibid., pp. 30, 20.

25 *PR: Werke 7*, § 139, *Hegel, Elements of the Philosophy of Right*, ed. A. Wood, op. cit.

26 Ibid., § 157.
27 Ibid., § 241–5.
28 *VGP: Werke 20*, p. 227; G. W. F. Hegel, *Lectures on the History of Philosophy*, op. cit., p. 317.
29 Ibid., pp. 227, 317.
30 See A. Finkenstein, *Theology and the Scientific Imagination from the Middle Ages to the Seventeenth Century* (Princeton, NJ: Princeton University Press, 1986); and David Gauthier, *Moral Dealings: Contract, Ethics and Reason* (Oxford: Clarendon Press, 1982).
31 Note Hobbes's comments in *Leviathan*, op. cit., pp. 458–74, and Hegel's observations *in PR: Werke 12*, pp. 520–40.
32 R. Kraynak, *History and Modernity in the Thought of Thomas Hobbes* (Ithaca, NY: Cornell University Press,1990), p. 6.
33 R. Tuck, *Hobbes* (Oxford: Oxford University Press, 1989), see esp. pp. 40–64.
34 Goldie, 'The Reception of Hobbes', op. cit., p. 615.
35 Flathman, *Thomas Hobbes*, op. cit., p. 116.
36 Ibid., p. 142.
37 Ibid., p. 177.
38 M. Oakeshott, 'Introduction to *Leviathan*', in M. Oakeshott, *Hobbes on Civil Association* (Oxford: Basil Blackwell, 1975).
39 H. Brod, *Hegel's Philosophy of Politics – Idealism,Identity and Modernity* (Boulder, San Francisco and Oxford: Westview Press, 1992), p. 6.
40 S. Houlgate, *Freedom, Truth and History – An Introduction to Hegel's Philosophy* (London and New York: Routledge, 1991), p. 37.
41 Pepperzak and Siep contrast the naturalism of Hobbes with the idealism of Hegel. See Pepperzak, 'Hegel and Hobbes Revised', op. cit., and Siep, 'Der Kampf um Annerkennung', op. cit.
42 *VGP: Werke 20*, p. 226; Hegel, *Lectures on the History of Philosophy*, op. cit., vol. 3, p. 316.
43 Riedel urges that Hobbes and Hegel share a conception of nature and natural law in which the natural is not seen as possessing intrinsic value. See M. Riedel, 'Nature and Freedom in Hegel's *"Philosophy of Right"* ', in Z. A. Pelczynski (ed.), *Hegel's Political Philosophy: Problems and Perspectives* (Cambridge: Cambridge University Press, 1971).
44 J. F. Lyotard, *The Postmodern Condition: A Report on Knowledge* (Manchester: Manchester University Press, 1984), p. 15.
45 Ibid.
46 R. Rorty, 'The Contingency of Language', in R. Rorty, *Contingency, Irony and Solidarity* (Cambridge: Cambridge University Press, 1989), p. 22.
47 Ibid., p. 8.
48 Ibid., p. 22.
49 N. K. O'Sullivan, 'Political Integration, the Limited State and the Philosophy of Postmodernism', *Political Studies*, vol. XL1 (1993), pp. 21–42; J. Gray, 'The Politics of Cultural Diversity', *The Salisbury Review*, vol. 7 (1988), p. 38.
50 O'Sullivan, 'Political Integration', op. cit., p. 37.

51   Lyotard, *The Postmodern Condition*, op. cit., p. 15.
52   See O'Sullivan, 'Political Integration', op. cit., pp. 36–7.
53   A. Giddens, *Modernity and Self-Identity* (Oxford: Polity Press, 1991), pp. 70–109.
54   F. Dallmayr, *G. W. F. Hegel, Modernity and Politics* (London: Sage, 1993), p. 8.
55   Ibid., p. 10.
56   J. Habermas, *The Philosophical Discourse of Modernity* (Oxford: Oxford University Press, 1987).

5   STIRNER'S CRITIQUE OF HEGEL: *GEIST* AND THE EGOISTIC EXORCIST

1   J. Toews, 'Transformations of Hegelianism', in F. Beiser (ed.), *The Cambridge Companion to Hegel* (Cambridge: Cambridge University Press, 1993), p. 405.
2   M. Stirner, *The Ego and its Own* (Cambridge: Cambridge University Press, 1995), p. 5.
3   M. Stirner, 'Art and Religion', in L. Stepelevich (ed.), *The Young Hegelians* (Cambridge: Cambridge University Press, 1983), p. 333.
4   K. Ferguson, 'Saint Max Revisited: A Reconsideration of Max Stirner', *Idealistic Studies*, vol. XII, no. 3 (1982), p. 276.
5   D. McLellan, *The Young Hegelians and Karl Marx* (London: Macmillan, 1969), p. 126.
6   For a recent discussion of the project entertained in Hegel's *Phenomenology of Spirit*, see G. K. Browning (ed.), *Hegel's Phenomenology of Spirit: A Reappraisal* (Dordrecht and London: Kluwer Academic Publishers, 1997).
7   L. S. Stepelevich, 'Max Stirner as Hegelian', *Journal of the History of Ideas*, vol. 46 (1985).
8   T. Pinkard, *Hegel's Phenomenology* (Cambridge: Cambridge University Press, 1994), ch.3.
9   Stirner, *The Ego and its Own*, op. cit., p. 13.
10   Ibid., p. 154.
11   D. Leopold, 'Introduction' to Stirner, *The Ego and its Own*, op. cit., p. xxvi.
12   Ibid., pp. 68–9.
13   W. J. Brazill, *The Young Hegelians* (New Haven, CT: Yale University Press, 1970), p. 69.
14   Stirner, *The Ego and its Own*, p. 166.
15   Ibid., p. 175.
16   Toews,'Transformations of Hegelianism', op. cit., p. 404.
17   Stirner, *The Ego and its Own*, op. cit., p. 163.
18   M. Stirner, 'Stirner's Critics', *Philosophical Forum*, vol. 8 (1978), p. 78.
19   Stirner, *The Ego and its Own*, op. cit., p. 162.
20   L. Feuerbach, '*The Essence of Christianity* in relation to *The Ego and its Own*', *Philosophical Forum*, vol. 8 (1978), p. 88.

21   *PhG: Werke 3*, pp. 145–55; G. W. F. Hegel, *The Phenomenology of Mind*,
      trans. J. Baillie (London: George Allen and Unwin, 1971), pp. 228–40.

6   *THE GERMAN IDEOLOGY*, STIRNER AND HEGEL: THE
    THEORY OF HISTORY AND THE HISTORY OF THEORY

1   K. Marx and F. Engels, *The German Ideology* (Moscow: Progress Pub-
     lishers, 1976). The complete edition of this text is cited throughout this
     chapter.
2   T. Carver, 'Reading Marx: Life and Works', in T. Carver (ed.), *The
     Cambridge Companion to Marx* (Cambridge: Cambridge University
     Press, 1991), p. 17.
3   See the informative comments in D. McLellan, *Karl Marx: His Life and
     Thought* (London: Macmillan, 1973), pp. 152–5.
4   The first English-language version of the opening section was published
     in *The Marxist*, no. 3 (July 1926). *The Labour Monthly*, vol. 15, no. 3
     (March 1933) included an excerpt from the opening section. *The Ger-
     man Ideology Part One*, with an introduction by C. J. Arthur (London:
     Lawrence and Wishart, 1973), has been extremely influential in focusing
     critical attention on the opening section of *The German Ideology*.
5   Arthur sketches the significance of the place of Stirner in Marx's intel-
     lectual development in C. J. Arthur, *The Dialectics of Labour* (Oxford:
     Basil Blackwell, 1986), pp. 121–5. Kolakowski draws attention to the
     impact of Stirner's thought on Marx's conception of the individual in L.
     Kolakowski, *Main Currents of Marxism*, vol. 1 (Oxford: Oxford University
     Press, 1978), pp. 161–73. See also Thomas's comments on the significance
     of the Stirner – Marx relationship, which reinforce the line of argument in
     this chapter. P. Thomas, *Karl Marx and the Anarchists* (London: Routledge
     Kegan and Paul, 1985), pp. 125–75. See also the brief but suggestive
     comments on Stirner's impact on Marx in L. Stepelevich, 'Max Stirner as
     Hegelian', *Journal of the History of Ideas*, vol. 46 (1985).
6   D. McLellan, *The Young Hegelians and Karl Marx* (London: Macmillan,
     1969), pp. 129–37.
7   K. Marx, *Preface to a Contribution to a Critique of Political Economy*, in
     K. Marx and F. Engels, *Selected Works* (Moscow: Progress Publishers,
     1970), p. 182.
8   See S. Avineri, *Social and Political Thought of Karl Marx* (Cambridge:
     Cambridge University Press, 1968), where the discussion of *The German
     Ideology* concentrates overwhelmingly on the opening section – Stirner
     receives a single, inconsequential citation. Likewise in L. Althusser, *For
     Marx*, trans. B. Brewster (Harmondsworth: Penguin, 1969), there is
     merely a single, insignificant reference to Stirner. Somewhat surpris-
     ingly, given Althusser's conception of an epistemological break occur-
     ring within *The German Ideology*, there is very little discussion of this text
     at all, but what there is suggests that the putatively important 'break' is
     located in its opening section.

9   McLellan, *Karl Marx*, op. cit., p. 144.

10 Ibid., p. 159.

11 Marx and Engels, *The German Ideology*, op. cit., p. 42.

12 See R. Miller, *Analyzing Marx: Morality, Power and History* (Princeton: Princeton, NJ: University Press, 1984), p. 178. Miller highlights the general discrepancy between generalised, epigrammatic statements of Marx on the historical process and his actual detailed accounts of history.

13 Marx and Engels, *The German Ideology*, op. cit., p. 29.

14 Hegel is paradigmatic in this regard for Marx and Engels, though they show more respect for his historical sense than that of his successors. Ibid., pp. 189–90.

15 M. Stirner, *The Ego and Its Own*, ed. D. Leopold (Cambridge: Cambridge University Press, 1995).

16 Marx and Engels, *The German Ideology*, op. cit., p. 142.

17 Ibid., p. 158.

18 For a critique of the alleged teleology of Bruno Bauer and the True Socialists, see ibid., pp. 110, 493–513.

19 Ibid., p. 53.

20 Ibid., p. 43.

21 Ibid., p. 90.

22 Ibid., p. 74.

23 C. J. Arthur, 'Marx, Engels, *The German Ideology*', in G. Veysey (ed.), *Philosophers Ancient and Modern* (Cambridge: Cambridge University Press, 1986), p. 166.

24 Marx and Engels, *The German Ideology*, op. cit., p. 53.

25 Ibid., p. 53.

26 Arthur plausibly suggests a reference to Fourier in *The Dialectics of Labour*, op. cit., p. 36. McLellan suggests a parody of Stirner in *The Young Hegelians and Karl Marx*, op. cit., p. 132. For a well-informed survey and interpretation of the image in question, see T. Carver, 'Communism for Critical Critics? *The German Ideology* and the Problem of Technology', *History of Political Thought*, vol. IX, no. 1 (Spring 1988). Carver himself sees the image as representing a humorous end-up of Fourier. He draws upon Hiromatsu's edition of *The German Ideology*, which identifies Marx's own amendments to Engels's draft, to highlight Marx's concern to insert a reference to 'the critical critic', which, along with similar insertions in adjacent passages, he takes as evidence of Marx's satirical intent. See K. Marx and F. Engels, *Die Deutsche Ideologie*, ed. W. Hiromatsu (Tokyo: Iwanami Shoten, 1974).

27 Thomas rules out a parody of Stirner on the ground that Marx's comments on the division of labour are serious. I don't see why parody cannot be used to promote a serious argument. Thomas, *Karl Marx and the Anarchists*, op. cit., pp. 140–5.

28 Kolokowski, *Main Currents of Marxism*, op. cit., p. 163.

29 Marx and Engels, *The German Ideology*, op. cit., pp. 280, 53.

30 Ibid., p. 281.

31 N. Geras, *Marx and Human Nature: Refutation of a Legend* (London: New Left Books, 1983), p. 72.

32 Marx and Engels, *The German Ideology*, op. cit., pp. 280–1.

33   M. Stirner, 'Stirner's Critics', *The Philosophical Forum*, vol. VIII, nos 2–4 (1978), p. 73.
34   K. Marx, *Economic and Philosophical Manuscripts*, in K. Marx, *Early Writings* (London: Penguin, 1975), p. 327.
35   Ibid., pp. 328–9.
36   P. Kain, *Marx and Ethics* (Oxford: Oxford University Press, 1988), p. 88.
37   *PR: Werke 7*, see esp. §7. G. W. F. Hegel, *Hegel's Philosophy of Right*, trans. T. M. Knox (Oxford: Oxford University Press, 1971).
38   For instance the bad infinite is held to constitute an impasse warranting a transition to a richer conceptual formulation at the stages of quantity, quality and essence. See *WL: Werke 5*, esp., pp. 270–6; G. W. F. Hegel, *Hegel's Science of Logic* (London: George, Allen and Unwin, 1969), pp. 150–6. The notion of infinity in Hegel and Marx is taken up in the succeeding chapter of this book. See also my article, 'Marx's Doctoral Dissertation: The Development of an Hegelian Thesis', which is to be published in a book on Hegel and Marx edited by A. Burns and I. Fraser.
39   *PR: Werke 7*, §30.
40   Despite Arthur's words to the contrary in *The Dialectics of Labour*, p. 125, Hegel's *Philosophy of History* does in fact receive considered attention in *The German Ideology*. In comparison with Stirner, Hegel's historical approach is found to be energetic, involving much closer reference to empirical events. Note the following positive comments in Marx and Engels, *The German Ideology*, op. cit., pp. 189, 251, 345.
41   Marx and Engels consider seven of Hegel's works/lecture series in *The German Ideology*.
42   Note the following references, L. Kolakowski, *Main Currents of Marxism*, op. cit., p. 167; D. McLellan, *The Young Hegelians and Karl Marx*, op. cit., p. 126.
43   Marx and Engels, *The German Ideology*, op. cit., p. 295.
44   *EG: Werke 9*, §381 esp. R; *Hegel's Philosophy of Mind*, trans. W. Wallace (Oxford: Oxford University Press, 1971).
45   Marx and Engels, *The German Ideology*, op. cit., p. 109.
46   Ibid., p. 109.
47   Ibid., p. 109.
48   Ibid., p. 65.
49   Ibid., p. 66.
50   Ibid., pp. 489, 493.
51   Ibid., pp. 208–11.
52   Ibid., p. 43.
53   Cowling has advanced this thesis economically and clearly. For Cowling, the concept of human nature in *The German Ideology* does not commit Marx to a general moral theory in which the overcoming of alienation plays a central role. This chapter suggests that the 'Hegelian' normative conception of the individual to which Marx and Engels subscribe in *The German Ideology* implies a general moral theory embracing the overcoming of alienation. M. Cowling, 'The Case for Two Marxes Restated', in M. Cowling and L. Wilde (eds), *Approaches to Marx* (Milton Keynes: Open University Press, 1989), esp. pp. 16–17.

54 See A. Callinicos's comments in his 'Introduction: Analytical Marxism', in A. Callinicos, *Marxist Theory* (Oxford: Oxford University Press, 1989), pp. 3–5.

55 K. Marx, Thesis XI, *Theses on Feuerbach* in D. McLellan, *Karl Marx: Selected Writings* (Oxford: Oxford University Press, 1977), p. 158. This viewpoint is echoed in *The German Ideology* but this 'rejection' of philosophy is problematic given the significance of the normative dimension in that work, which is discussed in this article.

56 K. Marx, *Economic and Philosophical Manuscripts*, op. cit., pp. 356–7, 359.

57 Note that Althusser characterises this enterprise of settling accounts as simply constituting a break with Feuerbach. Althusser, *For Marx*, op. cit., p. 45.

7 GOOD AND BAD INFINITES IN HEGEL AND MARX

1   Most commentaries on the *Grundrisse* recognise its links with Hegel's *Logic* but do not pick up on its links with other works by Hegel.

2   *WL: Werke 5*, p. 152; G. W. F. Hegel, *Hegel's Science of Logic* (London: George Allen and Unwin, 1976), p. 139.

3   Ibid., pp. 164, 149.

4   C. Taylor, *Hegel* (Cambridge: Cambridge University Press, 1973); M. Rosen, *Hegel's Dialectic and Its Criticism* (Cambridge: Cambridge University Press, 1982).

5   See the excellent commentary in A. White, *Absolute Knowledge: Hegel and the Problem of Metaphysics* (Athens: Ohio University Press, 1983).

6   *Ph.G: Werke 3*, p. 23; G. W. F. Hegel, *The Phenomenology of Mind* (London: George Allen & Unwin, 1971), p. 81

7   Ibid., pp. 380, 547.

8   Ibid., pp. 429, 594.

9   Ibid., pp. 417, 580.

10 *PR: Werke 7*, § 5; G. W. F. Hegel, *Hegel's Philosophy of Right*, trans. T. M. Knox (Oxford: Oxford University Press, 1967).

11 K. Marx, *Grundrisse* (Harmondsworth: Penguin, 1974), p. 102.

12 See for instance the Introduction by Nicholas to the Penguin translation, ibid.

13 F. Uchida, *Marx's Grundrisse and Hegel's Logic* (London: Routledge, 1988).

14 See T. Smith, *Dialectical Social Theory and its Critics* (New York: State University of New York Press, 1993), pp. 36–138.

15. B. Ollman, *Dialectical Investigations* (London: Routledge, 1993), p. 11.

16 Marx, *Grundrisse*, op. cit., p. 490.

17 Ibid., p. 164.

18 Ibid., p. 101.

19 See the articles by C. J. Arthur and T. Smith in F. Mosley (ed.), *Marx's Method in Capital* (New Jersey: Humanities Press, 1993). See also C. Arthur, 'Negation of the Negation in Marx's *Capital*', *Studies in*

Marxism, vol. 2 (1995), and T. Smith, *The Logic of Marx's Capital* (New York: State University of New York, 1990).

20 Marx, *Grundrisse*, op. cit., p. 102.
21 Ibid., p. 80.
22 Uchida, *Marx's Grundrisse and Hegel's Logic*, op. cit.
23 Smith, *Dialectical Social Theory*, op. cit., p.55.
24 Uchida, *Marx's Grundrisse and Hegel's Logic*, op. cit., pp. 65–143.
25 Ibid., in particular pp. 84–8.
26 Ibid., pp. 28–9.
27 Marx, *Grundrisse*, op. cit., p. 186.
28 Ibid., p. 197.
29 Ibid., p. 216.
30 Ibid., p. 261.
31 Ibid., p. 301.
32 Ibid., p. 501. C. J. Arthur in *Dialectics of Labour: Marx and His Relation to Hegel* (Oxford: Blackwell, 1986) is generally right to underplay the importance of the master–servant figure for Marx's thought, but it does feature in the *Grundrisse*.
33 Marx, *Grundrisse*, op. cit., p. 270.
34 *PR: Werke 7*, § 191Z; Hegel, *Hegel's Philosophy of Right*, op. cit.
35 See S.Meikle, 'Was Marx an Economist?', in P. Dunleavy and J. Stanyer (eds), *Contemporary Political Studies*, vol. 2 (P. S. A. Exeter, 1994).
36 K. Marx, 'Economic & Philosophical Manuscripts', *Early Writings* (Harmondsworth: Penguin, 1975), p. 350.
37 Ibid., p. 382.
38 See my article, 'Marx's Doctoral Dissertation: The Development of an Hegelian Thesis', in a forthcoming book on Hegel and Marx edited by A. Burns and I. Fraser.
39 See Chapter 6 above.
40 Smith, *Dialectical Social Theory and Its Critics*, op. cit., pp. 84–6.
41 J. Elster, *An Introduction to Karl Marx* (Cambridge: Cambridge University Press, 1986), p. 106.
42 Smith, *Dialectical Social Theory and Its Critics*, op. cit. p. 99.

8 NEW LEVIATHANS FOR OLD: COLLINGWOOD'S HOBBES AND THE SPIRIT OF HEGEL

1 R. G. Collingwood, *The New Leviathan*, ed. D. Boucher (Oxford: Clarendon Press, 1992), p. lix.
2 *EG: Werke 9*, § 381; G. W. F. Hegel, *Hegel's Philosophy of Mind*, trans. W. Wallace and A. V. Miller (Oxford: Oxford University Press, 1975).
3 See K. Popper, *The Poverty of Historicism* (London: Routledge, 1972), and T. M. Knox, 'Editor's Preface', *The Idea of History* (Oxford: Oxford University Press, 1976).
4 *VGP: Werke 18*, p. 59; G. W. F. Hegel, *Lectures on the History of Philosophy*, vol. 1, trans. E. Haldane (London: Paul, Trench and Trubner, 1896), p. 37.

5   See D. Boucher, *The Social and Political Thought of R. G. Collingwood* (Cambridge: Cambridge University Press, 1989), p. 71; R. G. Collingwood, *The Idea of History*, ed. J. van der Dussen (Oxford and New York: Oxford University Press, 1994), p. 121.

6   Collingwood, *The New Leviathan*, op. cit., p. lx.

7   R. G. Collingwood, 'Progress as Created by Historical Thinking', in R. G. Collingwood, *The Idea of History*, ed. J. van der Dussen (Oxford and New York: Oxford University Press, 1994).

8   Ibid.

9   R. G. Collingwood, 'Lectures on Moral Philosophy for Michaelmas Term 1921', Bodleian Library Collingwood Papers, Dep. 4, 5.

10   Ibid. See also my article, 'The Night in Which All Cows are Black: Ethical Absolutism in Plato and Hegel', *History of Political Thought*, vol. XII, no. 3 (1991), in which I argue how Hegel maintains an absolutist position in ethics that differs from Plato's by including subjectivism.

11   Collingwood, *The New Leviathan*, op. cit. pp. 272–9.

12   See P. Nicholson, 'Collingwood's *New Leviathan*: Then and Now', *Collingwood Studies*, vol. 1 (1994); A. Vincent, 'Review Article: Social Contract in Perspective', *Collingwood Studies*, vol. 11 (1995), *Perspectives*.

13   Nicholson, 'Collingwood's *New Leviathan*', op. cit., p. 166.

14   Ibid., pp. 166–70.

15   Ibid., p. 172.

16   See D. Boucher, 'Editor's Introduction' to Collingwood, *The New Leviathan*, op. cit., pp. l–lvi, for a discussion of the impact of war on the assessment of Hegel.

17   R. G. Collingwood, *The Idea of History* (Oxford and New York: Oxford University Press, 1994).

18   See G. K. Browning, 'The Nature of Nature in Collingwood and Hegel', *Collingwood Studies*, vol. 4 (1997).

19   See for instance, R. G. Collingwood, 'Notes on Hegel's *Logic*, September 19, 1920', Bodleian Library, Collingwood Papers, Dep.16/2.

20   *PhG: Werke 3*; G. W. F. Hegel, *Hegel's Phenomenology of Mind* (London: George Allen & Unwin, 1971), trans. by J. B. Balhe.

21   Ibid., p. 24, 82.

22   See Chapter 4.

23   T. Hobbes, *Leviathan*, ed. R. Tuck (Cambridge: Cambridge University Press, 1991), p. 88.

24   S. Smith, *Hegel's Critique of Liberalism* (Chicago, Ill.: University of Chicago Press, 1989), pp. 116–18.

25   Collingwood, *The New Leviathan*, op. cit., p. 62.

26   *PhG: Werke 3*, pp. 82–93; Hegel, *Hegel's Phenomenology of Mind*, op. cit., pp. 150–60.

27   Collingwood, *The Idea of History*, op. cit., pp. 282–302.

28   W. J. van der Dussen, *History as a Science: The Philosophy of R. G. Collingwood* (The Hague: Martinus Nijhoff, 1981), p. 327.

29   Collingwood, *The New Leviathan*, op. cit., pp. 118–24.

30   *PhG: Werke 3*, pp. 464–95, Hegel, *Hegel's Phenomenology of Mind*, op. cit., pp. 663–84.

31 R. G. Collingwood, 'Method and Metaphysics', Bodleian Library Collingwood Papers, Dep. 19/3, p. 21.
32 R. G. Collingwood, 'Observations on Language', Bodleian Library Collingwood Papers, 16/3, p. 1.
33 Collingwood, *The New Leviathan*, op. cit., p. 148.
34 B. Haddock, 'Hegel's Critique of the Theory of Social Contract', in D. Boucher and P. Kelly (eds), *The Social Contract From Hobbes to Rawls* (London: Routledge, 1994).
35 R. G. Collingwood, 'Lectures on Moral Philosophy for Michaelmas Term 1921', Bodleian Library Collingwood Papers, Dep. 4, p. 83.
36 Collingwood, *The New Leviathan*, op. cit., p. 168.
37 For Hegel on the historicity of politics, see *VPG: Werke 12*; G. W. F. Hegel, *The Philosophy of History*, trans. J. Sibree (New York: Dover Press, 1956).
38 Collingwood, *The New Leviathan*, op. cit., p. 160.
39 Ibid. Although *The New Leviathan* sees politics and civilisation as developing historically, there is no single line of teleological development.
40 Ibid. pp. 261–7.
41 Ibid.
42 Collingwood, *The New Leviathan*, op. cit., pp. 119–24.
43 Ibid., p. 272.
44 Ibid., p. 278.

9 LYOTARD'S HEGEL AND THE DIALECTIC OF MODERNITY

1. Jean-François Lyotard, *Phenomenology*, trans. by B. Beakley (Albany: State University of New York Press, 1991).
2. Jean-François Lyotard, 'Apostil on narratives' in Jean-Francois Lyotard, *The Postmodern Explained to Children* (London: Power Institute of Fine Arts, 1992), p. 29.
3. Jean-Francois Lyotard, *The Postmodern Condition: A Report on Knowledge* (Minneapolis, MA: The University of Minnesota Press, 1984), p. 15.
4. Ibid., p. 26.
5. Ibid., p. 56.
6. F. Jameson, Foreword, in ibid., p. xx.
7. Jean-Francois Lyotard, 'Rewriting Modernity', *The Inhuman* (Oxford: Polity Press, 1988), p. 25.
8. Jean-Francois Lyotard, 'Answering the Question: What is Postmodernism', in *The Postmodern Condition* op. cit., p. 125.
9. Jean-Francois Lyotard, 'Analysing Speculative Discourse as Language Game', in *The Lyotard Reader* (Oxford: Blackwell, 1989), pp. 267–74.
10. Ibid., p. 274.
11. Jean-Francois Lyotard, 'Discussions, or Phrasing "After Auschwitz"', in ibid., p. 354.
12. Ibid., p. 386.
13. Jean-Francois Lyotard, *The Differend: Phrases in Dispute* (Minneapolis, MA: University of Minnesota Press, 1988), p. 121.

14. Ibid., p. 54.
15. Ibid., p. 181.
16. Ibid., p. 130.
17. *PR: Werke 7*, § 3R; G. W. F. Hegel, *Hegel's Philosophy of Right*, trans. T. Knox (Oxford: Oxford University Press, 1967), p. 21.
18. *PR: Werke 3*, 159; G. W. F. Hegel, *The Phenomenology of Mind* (London: George Allen & Unwin, 1971), p. 105.
19. *PR:Werke7,*§142–358;Hegel,*Hegel'sPhilosophyofRight*,op.cit.,pp.151–82.
20. F. Dallmayr, *G. W. F. Hegel: Modernity and Politics* (London and New-bury Park, CA: Sage, 1993), p. 156.
21. H. Haber, *Beyond Postmodern Politics – Lyotard, Rorty and Foucault* (London: Routledge, 1994), p. 54.
22. Lyotard, *The Differend*, op. cit., p. 174.
23. M. Drolet, 'The Wild and the Sublime: Lyotard's Post-Modern Politics', *Political Studies*, vol. 42, no. 2, p. 302.
24. B. Readings, Foreword, in *Jean-Francois Lyotard: Political Writings* (London: UCL Press, 1993), p. xx.
25. Jean-Francois Lyotard, 'A Svelte Appendix to the Postmodern Question', in ibid., p. 76.
26. See S. Benhabib, *Situating The Self: Gender, Community and Postmodernism in Contemporary Ethics* (Cambridge: Polity Press, 1992), pp. 200–30.
27. Jean-Francois Lyotard (with Jean-Loup Thebaud), *Just Gaming* (Manchester: Manchester University Press, 1984), p. 121.

10 RAWLS AND HEGEL: THE REASONABLE AND THE RATIONAL IN THEORY AND PRACTICE

1. See the critical articles T. Nagel, 'Rawls on Justice', and M. Fisk, 'History and Reason in Rawls' Moral Theory', in N. Daniels (ed.), *Reading Rawls* (Stanford, CA: Stanford University Press, 1989).
2. See M. Sandel, *Liberalism and the Limits of Justice* (Cambridge: Cambridge University Press, 1982), and the following key works by A. Macintyre: *After Virtue* (London: Duckworth, 1981); *Whose Justice? Which Rationality?* (Notre Dame, Ind.: University of Notre Dame Press, 1989).
3. See B. Haddock, 'Hegel's Critique of the Theory of Social Contract', in D. Boucher and P. Kelly (eds), *The Social Contract From Hobbes To Rawls* (London and New York: Routledge, 1994).
4. A. Gutmann, 'Communitarian Critics of Liberalism', in S. Avineri and A. de-Shalit (eds), *Communitarianism and Individualism* (Oxford: Oxford University Press, 1992), pp. 120–1.
5. See S. Schwarzenbach, 'Rawls, Hegel and Communitarianism', *Political Theory*, vol. 19, no. 4 (Nov. 1991); P. Benson, 'Rawls, Hegel and Personhood', *Political Theory*, vol. 22, no. 3 (Aug. 1992); A. Schwarzenbach, 'A Rejoinder to Peter Benson', *Political Theory*, vol. 22, no. 3 (August 1922).
6. See J. Rawls, *Political Liberalism* (New York and Chicester: Columbia University Press, 1996, paperback edition), esp. pp. xxvi, 285–8. See also

C. Kukathas and P. Pettit, *Rawls – A Theory of Justice and its Critics* (Cambridge: Polity Press, 1990), esp. pp. 144–8.

7. Soon after publication of *A Theory of Justice* Barry counterposed Rawls to the deep (unfathomable) Hegel. B. Barry, *The Liberal Theory of Justice: A Critical Examination of the Principal Doctrines in a Theory of Justice by John Rawls* (Oxford: Clarendon Press, 1973), p. 4.

8. For a plausible account of affinities between the constructivist standpoints of Rawls and Hegel, see Benson, 'Rawls, Hegel and Personhood', op. cit.

9. J. Rawls, 'Reply to Habermas', in *Political Liberalism*, op. cit., p. 395. 'Reply to Habermas' first appeared in *The Journal of Philosophy*, vol. 92, no. 3 (March 1995).

10. J. Rawls, *A Theory of Justice* (Oxford: Oxford University Press, 1971), pp. 17–40.

11. Rawls, *Political Liberalism*, op. cit., pp. 286–7.

12. Ibid., p. xxvi.

13. Ibid., p. xxxiv.

14. S. Mulhall and A. Swift, *Liberals and Communitarians* (Oxford: Blackwell, 1996), pp. 231–40. R. Bellamy and D. Castiglione, 'Constitutionalism and Democracy – Political Theory and the American Constitution', *British Journal of Political Science*, vol. 27 (1997), p. 598.

15. S. Caney, 'Anti-perfectionism and Rawlsian Liberalism', *Political Studies*, vol. 43, no. 2, June 1995.

16. Rawls, *Political Liberalism*, op. cit., pp. 35–6.

17. R. Bellamy and D. Castiglione, 'Constitutionalism and Democracy – Political Theory and the American Constitution', *British Journal of Political Science*, vol. 27 (1997), p. 604.

18. *VPG: Werke 12*; G. W. F. Hegel, *The Philosophy of History* (New York: Dover Press, 1956).

19. *PR: Werke 7*, § 3R; G. W. F. Hegel, *Elements of the Philosophy of Right*, ed. A. Wood (Cambridge: Cambridge University Press, 1991).

20. Benson, 'Rawls, Hegel and Personhood', op. cit., p. 498.

21. *PR: Werke 7*, § 4; Hegel, *Elements of the Philosophy of Right*, op. cit.

22. Rawls, *Political Liberalism*, op. cit., p. 19.

23. *PR: Werke 7*, § 34–70; Hegel, *Elements of the Philosophy of Right*, op. cit.

24. Ibid., § 71–81.

25. Rawls, *Political Liberalism*, op. cit., pp. xxxix–lxii.

26. Ibid., p. lxii.

27. J. Rawls, 'The Law of Peoples', in S. Shute and S. Hurley (eds), *On Human Rights: The Oxford Amnesty Lectures, 1993* (New York: Harper-Collins, 1993), pp. 69–70.

11   CONCLUSION: POLITICS, PHILOSOPHY AND CRITIQUE

1. For a more comprehensive account of the divergencies between Plato and Hegel, see G. K. Browning, *Plato and Hegel: Two Modes of Philosophising about Politics* (New York and London: Garland, 1991).

2. *VGP: Werke 18*; G. W. F. Hegel, *Lectures on the History of Philosophy*, vol. 1, trans. E. Haldane (New York: Humanities Press, 1968), Introduction.

3   B. Williams, 'The Truth in Relativism', in *Moral Luck: Philosophical Papers 1973–1980* (Cambridge: Cambridge University Press, 1981).

4   Ibid.

5   See the chapters in this volume on Plato and Hegel, and G. K. Browning, 'The Night in Which All Cows are Black: Ethical Absolutism in Plato and Hegel', *History of Political Thought*, vol. XII (Autumn 1991).

6   For the creativity inherent in human activity in, for example, jazz and poetry, see P. Winch, *The Idea of A Social Science* (London: Routledge and Kegan Paul, 1958).

7   Note the Hegelian influence on the perceptive treatments of Hobbes in M. Oakeshott, *Hobbes on Civil Association* (Oxford: Basil Blackwell, 1975); note also Hegel's inpact on R. G. Collingwood in *The New Leviathan* (Oxford: Oxford University Press, 1992).

8   For a plausible expression of a theistic reading of Hobbes, see S. State, *Thomas Hobbes and the Debate Over Natural Law and Religion* (New York and London: Garland, 1991).

9   A. Macintyre, *After Virtue* (London: Duckworth, 1985), p. 270.

10 Macintyre's disavowal of an uncontroversial object of ethical enquiry is neatly expressed in an early work: A. Macintyre, *A Short History of Ethics* (London: Routledge, Kegan and Paul, 1966), p. 269.

11 'Endism' in Hegel is taken up in Fukayama's reading of the collapse of communism in Eastern Europe. F. Fukuyama, *The End of History and The Last Man* (London: Hamish Hamilton, 1992).

12 A balanced view of Hegel's reading of history is presented in F. Beiser, 'Hegel's Historicism', in F. Beiser (ed.), *The Cambridge Companion to Hegel* (Cambridge and New York: Cambridge University Press, 1993).

13 Plant signals a possible accommodation between Rawls and Hegel in the final chapter of his book *Modern Political Thought*, which reviews how modern political thought justifies and criticises the provision of foundations for political life. He is sympathetic to the idea of reflective equilibrium and inclines towards a form of left Hegelianism. R. Plant, *Modern Political Thought* (Oxford: Basil Blackwell, 1991), pp. 320–75.

14 For a revisionary reading of Hegel that opts to cast aside Hegel's metaphysical claims for an interpretive reading of social practices, see M. Tunick, *Hegel's Political Philosophy – Interpreting the Practice of Legal Punishment* (Princeton, NJ: Princeton University Press, 1992).

15 The specific connections between dominant Western social practices and abstract Rawlsian assumptions about individuals is made neatly in D. Ivison, 'Postcolonialism and Political Theory', in A. Vincent (ed.), *Political Thought: Tradition and Diversity* (Cambridge: Cambridge University Press, 1997).

16 H. Brod, *Hegel's Philosophy of Politics – Idealism, Identity and Modernity* (Boulder, San Francisco and Oxford: Westview Press, 1992), pp. 62–6.

17 *PR: Werke* 7, §298–320; G. W. F. Hegel, *Elements of the Philosophy of Right* (Cambridge: Cambridge University Press, 1991).

18 See for instance, C. Bryant and E. Mokrzki (eds), *The New Great Transformation? Change and Continuity in East-Central Europe* (London: Routledge, 1994).

19 K. Marx, *Economic and Philosophical Manuscripts* in *Early Writings* (Harmondsworth: Penguin, 1975), pp. 379–400.
20 For a postmodern account of the processes of commodification, see D. Harvey, *The Condition of Postmodernity: An Inquiry into the Condition of Cultural Change* (Oxford: Blackwell, 1989).
21 J. Gray, *Enlightenment's Wake – politics and culture at the close of the modern age* (London and New York: Routledge, 1995), p. 4.
22 For a hard-hitting and convincing critique of the supposed priority of the right over the good see R. Beiner, *What's the Matter with Liberalism?* (Berkeley and London: University of California Press, 1992).

ABBREVIATIONS OF WORKS BY HEGEL

Recognised English translations of Hegel are cited along with the German original. Works are either cited by section number (§), which is common to German and English works, or by page number. Where page numbers are cited, the first number cited refers to the German pagination. In works cited by section, remarks are denoted by an 'R' and additions by a 'Z'.

Werke	*Hegel: Werke Theorie Werkausgaube* (Frankfurt: Suhrkamp Verlag, 1970). Cited by volume number.
EG	*Enzyklopadie der philosophishcen Wissenschaften, vol. 3* (1817, rev. 1827, 1830), *Werke 9*. Cited by section number.
EL	*Enzyklopadie der philosophischen Wissenschaften, vol. 1* (1871, rev. 1827, 1830), *Werke 8*. Cited by section number.
PhG	*Phänomenologies des Geistes* (1807) *Werke 3*. Cited by page number.
PR	*Grundlinelien der Philosophie des Rechts oder Naturrecht und Staatwissenschaft im Grundrisse (1821)*, *Werke 7*. Cited by section number. Preface cited by page number.
VGP	*Vorlesungen über der Geschichte der Philosophie*, 3 vols, *Werke 18–20*. Cited by volume and page number.
VPG	*Vorlesungen über die Philosophie der Geschichte. Werke 12*. Cited by page number.
VPRG	*Vorlesungen über Rechtsphilosophie*, ed. K. H. Ilting. Notes and transcriptions from Hegel's lectures of 1818–19 (transcription by C. G. Homeyer), 1821–2, 1822–3 (transcription by H. G. Hotho). Transcription of the 1824–5 lectures by K. G. von Griesham; 1831 transcription by D. F. Strauss (Stuttgart: Fromman Verlag, 1974). Cited by volume and page number.
VPRHN	*Philosophie des Rechts: Die Vorlesung von 1819/20*, ed. Dieter Henrich (Frankfurt: Shurkamp Verlag, 1983). Cited by page number.
VPRW	*Die Philosophie des Rechts: Die Mirtschriften Wannenman (Heidelberg 1817/18) und Homeyer (Berlin 1818/19)* ed. K.-H. Ilting. Transcriptions of the 1817–18 lectures by P. Wannenmann and of the 1818–19 lectures by C. G. Homeyer (Stuttgart: Klett-Cotta Verlag, 1983). Cited by page number.
WL	*Wissenschaft der Logik (1812–16), Werke 5–6*. Cited by volume and page number.

Index